"*Full Darkness* is extraordinary! In and through his profound analysis of the ways the sanctioning of war pervades American history and contemporary public life, Powers articulates a socio-cultural and theological understanding of original sin and the violence that lies within us—realities that so distort our human relationships that our very nature is profoundly damaged. Drawing on his own and others' experiences in war, he provides scores of vivid narratives and careful analyses of the multiple ways in which religiously and culturally sanctioned violence corrodes the very fabric of our humanity. *Full Darkness* is essential reading, certainly for theologians and ethicists, but perhaps more importantly for our nation's political and military leaders, for thoughtful citizens and religious leaders, and for healers and care-givers who seek by God's grace and mercy to help bind the wounds from which, because of our blind capacity for destructive violence, we all suffer."

Craig Dykstra
Duke Divinity School

"It is rare indeed to find a theological work that so powerfully combines analytical rigor with pastoral depth as this volume does. *Full Darkness* is a book about many things, from nationalism and violence to sin and guilt. But it is at bottom a profound reflection on the redemptive power of the gospel—and the ways in which we all too often thwart it."

Ian A. McFarland
Cambridge University

"In this important work of theology and personal reflection, Brian Powers restores the power of 'sin' to name our collective participation in evil, while simultaneously reclaiming what sin reveals about divine grace, forgiveness, and honest hope. In doing so, he illuminates the experiences of modern military veterans through the light of ancient theologians, such as Augustine, who also knew war and evil."

Rita Nakashima Brock
Volunteers of America

"Brian Powers here shines new light on the darkness of broken humanity. From his personal experience with the dehumanizing violence of wars in Iraq and Afghanistan, Powers offers a bracing defense of the Augustinian doctrine of original sin as uniquely able to describe the real distorting effects of war on the human psyche. All of us who live in this world plagued by human violence and unending war, and all who care about the redemption of real, wounded human beings, need this book."

Martha Moore-Keish
Columbia Theological Seminary

"Brian Powers speaks with a sincerity and clarity that demand our attention. He posits unequivocally that war-making has profound theological significance and that the human costs of such misadventures of power and violence must be wrestled with in our time. If the work of Christian theology is to be relevant to the needs of God's people, we must refuse to deny, minimize, or avoid the ramifications of organized violence in our world, because to do otherwise is to render the gospel incomprehensible."

Zachary Moon
author of *Coming Home*

FULL DARKNESS

Original Sin, Moral Injury, and Wartime Violence

Brian S. Powers

William B. Eerdmans Publishing Company
Grand Rapids, Michigan

Wm. B. Eerdmans Publishing Co.
4035 Park East Court SE, Grand Rapids, Michigan 49546
www.eerdmans.com

Published 2019
Printed in the United States of America

28 27 26 25 24 23 22 21 20 19 1 2 3 4 5 6 7 8 9 10

ISBN 978-0-8028-7651-5

Library of Congress Cataloging-in-Publication Data

Names: Powers, Brian S., 1977- author.
Title: Full darkness : original sin, moral injury, and wartime violence / Brian S. Powers.
Description: Grand Rapids : Eerdmans Publishing Co., 2019. | Includes bibliographical references and index.
Identifiers: LCCN 2018025303 | ISBN 9780802876515 (pbk. : alk. paper)
Subjects: LCSH: Sin, Original. | Fall of man. | Sin—Christianity. | Violence—Religious aspects—Christianity.
Classification: LCC BT720 .P69 2019 | DDC 233/.14—dc23
LC record available at https://lccn.loc.gov/2018025303

To my sisters and brothers

who are weary and heavy laden from the horrors of conflict,

in the hope that you will one day find peace for your souls

CONTENTS

Foreword BY JOHN SWINTON ix
Preface xi
Acknowledgments xv
Introduction 1

CHAPTER 1
Original Sin and the Trauma of Violence 13

CHAPTER 2
External Forces and the Contemporary Military Experience 39

CHAPTER 3
The Dichotomous American Experience of Violence 57

CHAPTER 4
Privation of Goodness and the Injured Soul 92

CHAPTER 5
The Enslavement of Agency and Betrayal of Identity 114

CHAPTER 6
Sin as Poisoned Memory and Hopeless Future 144

Bibliography 179
Index 183

FOREWORD

Violence is an ever-present physical and psychological reality that continues to inflict deep wounds on the world. It is a stark fact that more human beings have killed other human beings over the past hundred years than at any other period in history. It seems that the more we "progress," the more violent we become. At one level violence and technology are inextricably intertwined. The better we get at developing technologies, the better we are at orchestrating violence. However, we don't need sophisticated technology to engage in horrendous acts of violence. Machetes, fists, and knives will do the job just as well.

Violence is a spiritual matter. Those who experience violence know and understand the ways in which violence can empty your soul. It can strip the universe of its goodness and close down our certainty that God is in control. Violence makes trust tentative; it forces love to be distant. Lamenting violence can certainly end in praise: "but I trust in your unfailing love." But more often it simply ends in a deep sense of abandonment that resonates with the aching cry of the crucified Jesus: "My God, my God, why have you forsaken me?" Violence gives body to the psalmist's resignation that "darkness is my only companion."

For those whom society designates to engage in violence in order to prevent violence, the stakes are high. Even if one is trained, shaped, and formed to engage in violence, and even if that violence is assumed to be for the greater good, there is a price to be paid. Frightening rates of depression, anxiety, alcoholism, addiction, and suicide among veterans whip our heads round to face the devastating power of violence and force us to recognize the ways in which violence, even in the name of a greater good, distorts the love of the gospel.

Violence not only damages others; it destroys the self. Some things cannot be unseen. The memory of violence is a present and active force that can crush the self. Violence is the enemy of love for God, self, and others; it is the destroyer of peace, the dissonant voice that ends any possibility of harmony.

In this book Brian Powers reveals violence for what it is—a mode of sin and evil—but seeks to explore how the sting of violence can be drawn through the healing power of the gospel and the redeeming grace of God. By reflecting carefully, theologically, and compassionately on the nature and effect of violence he carefully draws out the ways in which the trauma experienced by veterans, properly framed, can provide deep insights into the nature of violence, the shape of humanness, and the way the language of sin in general and original sin in particular can be reclaimed to place violence in a different perspective within God's good creation. Sin and violence form a tight alliance that is so powerful that there is nothing that we can do about it . . . other than to cast ourselves upon God's active grace. Only when we begin by looking at and recognizing the power of grace can we truly begin to disempower violence. The language of original sin can provide a mode of speech that describes the violence of our world in ways that other concepts and other modes of language simply cannot. If we can talk more faithfully about violence, perhaps we can change the dominant ideology that perpetuates cycles of violence that threaten to destroy all of us.

Powers's work is deep, contemplative, illuminating, and above all else transformative. It digs into the issue of violence in a way that respects the experiences of veterans and others while at the same time offering deep and vital challenges to our thinking. Perhaps there is no more important task in our present times than to learn how to think faithfully about violence. This book gives us some tools for what will inevitably be a very difficult journey.

John Swinton

PREFACE

In my last unit in the Air Force, I had the privilege of serving as the commander of a small detachment of Special Operations Weather Team (SOWT) airmen at Fort Bragg, North Carolina. This unit, when fully manned, consisted of about twenty-two airmen, and during my time there its members were deployed piecemeal with elite American units in Afghanistan, Iraq, and other locations in support of the Global War on Terror. Fortuitously, throughout all of its deployments, this group's fine airmen suffered no combat fatalities; yet at the time of this writing, two former members of this small unit have taken their own lives and a third lost his life back home in the US after heroically confronting a troubled airman (and Iraq war veteran) who entered his training unit's headquarters and began shooting.

Since I was both a member of this close-knit group and a veteran of those conflicts in Afghanistan and Iraq myself, this work is one of enormous personal import. It is, at heart, a humble attempt to hold together Christian faith and the realities of wartime violence and its many tendrils. I grew up in the Presbyterian Church, and in my early life the faith I had known since childhood provided me with an identity and a solid life orientation based on the idea that the God who had forgiven me had a providential purpose for both my life and for the world. Yet after returning from my deployments and separating from the Air Force, I had deep struggles in understanding my own faith amid the violence that I had witnessed, the violence in which I'd participated, and the violence that seems to continue to claim lives long after the battles are over. I found, and still find, myself haunted by instances of civilian suffering and death and the particularly insidious consequences—both seen and unseen—of wartime violence. Doubting the "goodness" of the military endeavors amidst the suffering of so many, I came to question how a world that my faith attested was created and sustained by God could have such violence at its heart.

Veterans, of course, seek healing in a variety of ways. I sought to interrogate my own faith in seminary. In studying theology, I became captivated by the power of theological language to explore and express the broken and violent realities of our world as well as how faith could speak softly—yet confidently—of real, tangible, and transformative hope in their midst. I became particularly moved by the work of Jürgen Moltmann, a German theologian whose writings were influenced profoundly by his own experiences of extreme violence in World War II. I wrestled with the theologies of Karl Barth, Rowan Williams, Paul Tillich, and James Cone, as well as the writings of Hannah Arendt and René Girard. I found myself exploring how the Christian concepts of atonement, crucifixion, resurrection, and eschatology could help me articulate faith in a way that first and foremost looked unflinchingly at the violence of the world. Rabbi Irving Greenberg is famous for his dictum: "No statement, theological or otherwise, should be made that would not be credible in the presence of burning children." My own corollary to this is that the same hesitance should be made about any statement uttered in the presence of all who suffer from wartime violence—veterans, civilians, husbands, wives, daughters, sons, fathers, and mothers. This work is my best attempt to humbly make a statement of faith that acknowledges this reality.

In Augustine and his contemporary interpreters Alistair McFadyen, Charles Matthews, and my advisor, Ian A. McFarland, I find a complex and deeply compelling understanding of the fundamental distortions that reverberate through the human experience that speaks to veteran trauma and the insidious tendrils of wartime violence. After years of interrogating Augustine and these interpreters through the lens of the work of psychologists studying human behavior and the morality of conflict, I have arrived at a theological examination of several aspects of conflict that is faithful to my own experience of the world and in which I hope others may find meaning. The present project is my argument against the comfortable and simplistic understandings of morality that died to me in the deserts of Iraq and the mountains of Afghanistan. It is an argument that demands to be heard amidst totalizing and polarizing discussions about what is "right" and what is "wrong" in terms of national identity and American military endeavors. It is my hope that it speaks also to our broader conversations about how we come to understand something as "good" and fundamentally questions our capacity to come to absolute or total moral judgments.

As a person whose faith has been deepened exponentially through this journey, I have attempted in this project to illuminate and recapture the term "sin" in terms that are sufficient to convey the full significance and power of the "wrongness" at the heart of wartime violence. One of my seminary professors memorably cautioned our class to ensure that our theological formulations were complex enough to "bear the weight of the gospel." This work is my attempt to create an understanding of sin that bears both the weight of the gospel and the weight of the world.

BRIAN POWERS
Advent 2018

ACKNOWLEDGMENTS

With the exception of God's good creation, nothing springs from the mind of a book's author that is independent of the care and influence of those around him or her. I would like to acknowledge many people with deepest gratitude at the outset. First and foremost, I want to thank my loving and courageous wife, Jennifer, for her tireless support, love, encouragement, and—perhaps most of all—grace. The footprints not only of my life but of our journey together can be traced through these pages, and I'm forever grateful that I'm able to walk it with such a giving and caring partner and mother. I'm also grateful to my children, Dylan, Lucas, and Caroline, for their patience, their enlivening silliness, and their seemingly infinite capacity to love me at my worst. I am grateful to my mother, Barbara Powers, whose wonderful commitment to regularly care for our kids, even at their worst, allowed me the time and mental freedom to complete this project.

This project took place with the intellectual and very often pragmatic and life-giving advice of wonderful mentors and faculty members. I am grateful to Ian McFarland for his mentorship, guidance, support, encouragement and (often disquietingly) timely feedback on my work; to Wendy Farley for her guidance and warm encouragement in navigating the rigors of the program, particularly while raising small children; to Ellen Marshall for inspiring me to enter the doctoral program and for her graceful mentorship and friendship through various projects and teaching endeavors. I'm thankful to Joy McDougall, whose seminar kindled the fire of the idea around which this project developed, for her confidence in my abilities and help in developing my own teaching style. I'm thankful for the opportunity to have worked with Thee Smith,

Liz Bounds, Luke Timothy Johnson, Pam Hall, and Edward Queen. I am grateful to have had the opportunity to develop my ideas under the influence of such brilliant scholars. I have also had the privilege to have wonderful friends and mentors in Martha Moore-Keish and Mark Douglas; I am profoundly grateful for their encouragement and care.

I am also deeply indebted to my brilliant peers in the GDR at Emory University. I am grateful for the many conversations in the magical place more commonly known as the graduate student lounge in Callaway Hall. Those conversations both launched my critical thinking and provided great relief from daily stresses. I'm especially thankful for the friendship of Devin White, whose collegial yet critical advice saved me from academic paralysis more than once and inspired in me more than a few new ways of looking at things. I'm thankful for many ongoing conversations with Corbin Boekhaus, Adam Mathes, Chris Holmes, Jonathan Potter, David Carr, Kyle Tau, Tony Alonso, Jay Thomas, Meredith Doster, Ryan Kuratko, Winston Persaud, Michael Yandell, Becky Copeland, Ashley Graham, Layla Karst, Matthew Pierce, and so many others. Thank you for your friendship and inspiration, both inside the academic environment and outside it.

I'm deeply appreciative for the conversation with my peers in the Religion, Conflict, and Peacebuilding concentration—Joe Winnika-Lydon, Sarah MacDonald, Liz Whiting Pierce, Sarah Muwahidah, Georgette Ledgister, Adam Strater, and Sara Williams. It was a privilege to be around such brilliant, kind, and compassionate colleagues.

Finally, I'm quite grateful for the hard work of the many folks at Eerdmans that helped to bring this work into broader view—many thanks to Michael Thomson, Jenny Hoffman, and Reinder Van Til.

INTRODUCTION

Violence, argues René Girard, is a primary and preeminent force that dominates human nature, ritual, activity, and destiny.[1] Our societies are able to keep violence at bay only because we have developed complex mechanisms to control it. In the grand scope of human development, the primary function of religion, according to Girard, is to lend its profound symbol structure and mythos to these controlling mechanisms: creating and naming the critical distinction between "holy, legal, legitimate violence," which is done reluctantly in order to stave off outbreaks of "unjust, illegal [acts] and illegitimate violence."[2] Yet these delineations that mark off good violence from bad violence are ultimately illusory, Girard argues further, for violence, like a wild conflagration, will feed "on the very objects intended to smother its flames."[3] The problem is that the mechanisms designed to control violence, particularly as they are infused with religious symbolism, ironically enshrine it in human eyes as a sacred force, a powerful and primal thing that is external to humanity—something that continually threatens us from without. The mechanisms and religiously sanctioned forms of violence blind us to the violence that is within us, the distortions and violent tendencies that are passed from generation to generation.

1. René Girard, *Violence and the Sacred*, trans. Patrick Gregory (Baltimore: Johns Hopkins University Press, 1977), 31.

2. Girard, *Violence and the Sacred*, 23.

3. Girard, *Violence and the Sacred*, 31. Girard argues quite simply and compellingly that when violent sacrifice is performed as a means to ward off outbreaks of uncontrollable violence, when it is done in order to "deceive" the violent impulse of vengeance into satisfaction, the only real victor is violence itself.

In the American cultural discourse about violence, it is perhaps accurate to say that, in the wake of the terrorist attacks that claimed nearly three thousand lives in New York and Washington, DC, on September 11, 2001, everything changed and nothing changed. The violence we experienced was, at least for this generation, new. For the first time since the attack on Pearl Harbor in 1941, violence caused by an outside entity occurred on American soil, and for the first time in nearly two centuries, it occurred on the American mainland. Our vulnerability to this kind of violence became apparent to most, and in the conversations and debates that followed, it was widely recognized that technological advances in transportation, infrastructure, and weaponry had come with new and unique dangers. The fear of attack based on these new vulnerabilities tilted the sacrosanct and delicate cultural balance between freedom and security heavily in the direction of increased security. Reluctantly—and sometimes not so reluctantly—we embraced greater forms of violence, "enhanced interrogation techniques," and new legal definitions of combatants that allowed us greater freedom to act violently in response to the violence that threatened us. We embraced once more what John Tirman calls the "frontier myth," a deeply embedded cultural narrative of national strength and American exceptionalism that tacitly underwrites military ventures as culturally and religiously necessary in furthering the great American enterprise.[4] While salient discussion about the nature of conflict, the risks of violence, and the moral difficulties of torture have slowly emerged in the public consciousness, there remains a powerful religious and ideological undercurrent in our cultural imagination that uncritically accepts American military violence as categorically "good" in support of the American enterprise and exhibits an astounding blindness to its destructive effects.[5]

Standing in stark contrast to the frontier myth and its uncritical acceptance of US military action is what US Army psychologist Dave Grossman calls the "bitter harvest" of our participation in violence: the

4. John Tirman, *The Deaths of Others: The Fate of Civilians in America's Wars* (New York: Oxford University Press, 2011), 13.

5. I am referring primarily to the countless civilian deaths that Tirman chronicles in *The Deaths of Others*. However, as recent history has shown, the second- and third-order effects of military actions are rarely predictable. Whereas the invasion of Iraq was bound to be initially destabilizing, it would be difficult if not impossible to predict that the instability would eventually give rise to the horrifically violent and genocidal Islamic State in Iraq and Syria (ISIS).

psychological trauma of our military members.[6] The conflict in Afghanistan has become the longest conflict in American history. The war in Iraq stands as the third longest, with only the Vietnam War between the two. These lengthy, "low intensity" wars together have produced a generation of increasingly traumatized veterans. Recent studies show that as many as 20 percent of veterans returning from Iraq and Afghanistan have post-traumatic stress disorder (PTSD) or suffer from significant depression. At the time of this writing, twenty-two American military veterans commit suicide every day. Whatever its root, there is something pathological about the violence of conflict that cannot be easily integrated into either the psyche of the veteran or the narrative of uncritical American exceptionalism. The trauma—the psychic inability to make sense of the experience—that these veterans hold within themselves shatters notions of sanitized and uncritically "good" conflict in which death is always administered only to those who "deserve" it, and "collateral damage" is reduced to zero through technology and "smart bombs." Veterans often experience firsthand a force of violence that, as Girard argues, continually threatens to "overflow its confines and flood the surrounding area,"[7] invading and infecting those who contact it. Their trauma provides a window into the true heart of violence and its capacity to annihilate our ability to make meaning of our lives and to have hope for the future. It refuses to permit the powerful forces of American exceptionalism, the frontier myth, and cultural and ideological hegemony to pass unchallenged.

The deep disparity between the view that American military violence serves an uncritical "good," and the often traumatizing experience of those charged with applying it, reveals several significant concerns that resonate deeply with Girard's theory of violence—and that underlie this study. First, the disconnect between the "on-the-ground" reality of conflict and the public's understanding of it inhibits authentic reflection on our cultural, national, and religious values concerning violence and its merits and detriments. Tirman powerfully argues that the American cultural narrative provides a de facto justification for extreme "total war" strategies and anesthetizes the public to the real suffering of those involved. If we remain blind to our own capacity for destruc-

6. Dave Grossman, *On Killing: The Psychological Cost of Learning to Kill in War and Society* (New York: Back Bay Books, 1995), 89.

7. Girard, *Violence and the Sacred*, 10.

tive violence, how can we honestly discuss curtailing it or allowing the memory of it to influence our future decisions regarding the application of our inordinate military might? Second, the uncritical valorization of US military ventures and military veterans inhibits a primary avenue of recovery for veterans by significantly isolating them. Trauma theorists, from Sigmund Freud to Shoshana Felman and Dori Laub, have argued that one of the key aspects of trauma recovery involves the speaking and hearing of the testimony of the traumatized. Those veterans who experience significant moral ambiguity about their participation in conflict have difficulty exploring this ambiguity and witnessing about their experiences to a society that simply wants to lavish praise on their efforts and has seemingly little room for genuine reflection about American violence. Finally (and most critically for this study), the denial of the reality of the distorting power of violence in the world—and our own complicity in it—negates the redemptive power of the gospel by denying the severity of the condition from which Christ must redeem the world. It negates the power of the gospel to help the veteran, to envision that the world of violence is the world Christ entered, the world Christ took into himself on the cross, and the world that the risen Christ promises to redeem. To ignore or deny that is to render both cross and empty tomb incomprehensible.

Given these concerns, I intend to argue in this book that the experience of trauma in veterans provides a crucial perspective on the nature of violence, and that Christian theological anthropology, most notably the conception of original sin, is powerfully descriptive of the pathology of violence and its effects on us and the world, particularly as it refuses to locate sin and violence as either purely internal or external to human nature. I envision this project as the first of two interconnected parts. In the first part of the project (this book), I will explore the ways in which an Augustinian concept of original sin, particularly as envisioned by Alistair McFadyen in *Bound to Sin,* is salient to depict the power of violence in modern conflict and to describe how its destructive tendrils reach into many aspects of the combatants' lives. I argue here that the bound and compelled willing of the participant in conflict produces a unique stress that is bound up with an awareness of this bondage and the seeming hopelessness of escaping it. This stress and its suffocation of the soul can be viewed theologically as the suppression and distortion of the spirit of life: violence wounds one's ability to live in harmony with God, oneself, and others. It deeply affects one's ability to value life in creation and to express one's own life in loving community. I will argue further that this sequestered willing and suppressed spirit coalesce to produce two distinctive lasting wounds that are borne by many veterans: first, a memory laden with guilt, grief, horror, and sorrow that robs the present of positive meaning; second, a loss of hope, the inability to imagine a future that is unburdened and free. In the coda of this work, I will allude to the theme of the second part of this study (which will not be a part of this book): that resurrection and eschatology speak to the healing of memory and have the power to transform the present and infuse even the violent nature of the world with hope.

This book is primarily an exercise in public theology. In essence, I am arguing that the doctrine of original sin illuminates violence and human brokenness in a way that pierces through the dominant ideology in America regarding violence. The trauma of veterans "unmasks" the character of violence in a way that reveals deep insights about the fragile and imperiled human condition. In chapter 1, then, I seek to put the major concepts "on the table" and examine the doctrine of original sin as posited by Augustine and interpreted by Alistair McFadyen, highlighting its emphasis on the operation of the human will in the midst of powerfully distorting forces. The successive chapters are essentially reflections on the ways in which these concepts resonate with aspects of veteran trauma today. Thus, in chapter 2, I describe how the concepts articulated by Augustine and McFadyen illuminate the forces affecting military combatants. In chapter 3, I turn to the dichotomous views of violence present in American cultural discourse: the de facto cultural view of American exceptionalism and the traumatizing experience of veterans. Following this, in chapters 4 and 5, I use the insights of Augustine and McFadyen regarding human willing to analyze how the forces of modern combat damage the psyche of the veteran. In chapter 6, I make a synthetic argument for the power of theological language to describe violence and trauma, arguing that the theological category of guilt, particularly as described through the universality of sin, provides a uniquely descriptive concept of the pathological situation of human violence that begins to open avenues toward the possibility of healing and redemption.[8]

8. I am, of course, examining one facet of human violence—armed conflict—and certainly do not mean to imply that this analysis exhausts the larger category, merely that it suggests something about human violence, and that the theological claims that are applicable may be broader than the analysis itself.

Excising the Myth of Punishment

In setting forth an Augustinian model of original sin as descriptive of the human situation, I find it necessary to make a few preliminary remarks and qualifications. First and foremost, it should be noted that I do not intend to pursue a discussion of Augustine's theodicy and the theodical elements of his understanding of the Fall of humankind outside of these introductory remarks. Augustine, in order to simultaneously preserve the primordial goodness of creation and deny that the sin and evil that so characterize our world were inherent to it—and thus created by God—argues that original sin, as the congenital and inherited resistance to God's will, is the just punishment inflicted by God on humanity for Adam's willful disobedience. Suffering and sin are thus given their theodical meaning: humanity incurs condemnation before God because of this now-inborn resistance. Hence humanity has deserved this suffering, and no humans can rightly claim that they suffer unjustly as a result. As McFarland notes, many traditions that find great theological value in Augustine's concept of original sin nonetheless attempt to modify the doctrine in order to ameliorate or negate this notion that original sin is both the cause of and the explanation for human suffering.[9]

In keeping with many contemporary interpreters of Augustine, I find his continued use of the doctrine of the Fall for theodicy—as an explanation of suffering through the "myth of punishment"—deeply problematic. The notion that the extremely violent horrors the world has suffered throughout millennia of conflict—killing, rape, torture, brokenness—are deserved punishment for the sins of Adam fails to impress meaning upon these events to one who has witnessed and experienced them firsthand. The horror of a wedding celebration that is grotesquely transformed into death and misery by a predator drone, of a ten-year old boy stepping on a land mine, of girls disfigured with acid and even beheaded because they desired to go to school, and the debilitating lifelong trauma endured by so many touched by the violence of conflict—all these resist the notion of theodicy in the full force of their unyielding reality. Wendy Farley argues that "human history has been so badly stained by suffering that it cannot be endured. It has become

9. Ian A. McFarland, *In Adam's Fall: A Meditation on the Christian Doctrine of Original Sin* (Malden, MA: Wiley-Blackwell, 2010), 46.

literally meaningless."[10] Consequently, attempts to domesticate this meaningless suffering into an ideology or simple theodical worldview are "mocked by the destruction all around us."[11] I will argue that the very meaninglessness at the heart of suffering is what, in many ways, must command our attention: it should pierce through ideology and theory and give us an accurate barometer of the brokenness in which we find ourselves.

While the theodical dimensions in Augustine's concept of original sin are problematic, his understandings of psychology and human willing are profoundly descriptive of the human condition, particularly with regard to the force of violence. Like Alistair McFadyen, I will argue that the doctrine holds great explanatory power in describing human pathologies of violence and dehumanization. Specifically, I will argue and attempt to illustrate that sin, as a congenital and unavoidable force, given particularity here as violence, is so powerful, infectious, distorting, and ubiquitous that apart from God's active grace, humanity has no hope of redemption. Lost in violence, we are continually destroying ourselves, or, as Athanasius argued, "returning, through corruption, to non-existence again."[12] In other words, I maintain that there is a profound soteriological value in Augustine's concept of original sin: it demonstrates how profoundly broken humanity is and how helpless humanity is to save itself from the forces of sin and violence that are present both inside and outside our constructions of self.

Guilt, Innocence, and Blame

The key in separating the problematic *theodicy* of punishment from the powerfully descriptive *psychology* of original sin lies in the implication of universal guilt. For Augustine, original sin was not simply a corollary of the confession of Christ's status as universal Savior, but also the punishment for the sins of Adam. As such, for him there is a direct link between the universal guilt that humanity incurs through congenital sinfulness and blameworthiness. In other words, if we affirm that orig-

10. Wendy Farley, *Tragic Vision and Divine Compassion: A Contemporary Theodicy* (Louisville: Westminster John Knox, 1990), 11.

11. Farley, *Tragic Vision*, 11.

12. Athanasius, *On the Incarnation*, trans. and ed. by a religious of C.S.M.V. (Crestwood, NY: St. Vladimir's Seminary Press, 1996), 30.

inal sin tells us about the justified consequence of human rebellion against God, then we may affirm that, because we are guilty, we deserve punishment. On the other hand, the affirmation of hopelessness in sin apart from divine grace need not necessarily suggest such a connection. It can suggest a less juridical paradigm, a more basic linkage between universal guilt and alienation from God. If we affirm that original sin is the cause and explanation of human sinfulness—but not of humanity's experience of evil—then we may affirm that because we are guilty, we are alienated from the true source of life and are perishing, without concluding that human pain and suffering are deserved and divinely sanctioned punishment. As will become clear as the study progresses, I will affirm the connection between *universal guilt and alienation* while challenging the connection between *universal guilt and condemnation*, particularly at an individual level.

In the context of American society, we have been conditioned to understand guilt in a particularly penal sense, making it more difficult to understand how one may affirm guilt without correspondingly attributing blame. In our legal system, if one is not innocent, one is guilty, and if one is guilty, one is worthy of blame and moral condemnation.[13] In this study, I attempt to decouple these links on the grounds that the legal categories of "innocence" and "guilt" greatly distort our ability to adequately shape a moral vision that addresses the forces that shape our world and us. If individual, personal guilt is equated directly with individual and personal moral blameworthiness, then the ascription of guilt to oneself is something to be deeply feared and greatly avoided. As a result, in American society we have essentialized guilt and innocence into ontological categories to such an extent that we have become blind to our own complicities in pathologies of violence as a means of avoiding the intolerable burden of guilt-as-blameworthiness. In the context of military violence, our essentially "good" and "innocent" troops are valorized, and our "guilty" (and therefore blameworthy) enemies are demonized. We view our own soldiers with a particular kind of innocence as they use "legitimate and necessary" violence to keep "bad" violence away from the rest of us. Tirman says that we are particularly

13. A point driven into our cultural consciousness by the seemingly innumerable police and legal procedurals that have shown on television screens since the 1960s, in which courtroom dramas consistently end with the pronouncement of the verdict—guilty, not guilty (often made synonymous with "innocent"), or not guilty by reason of mental illness or defect.

apathetic about the consequences of our violence and have little empathy for those who are affected by it, for if their suffering were to truly affect us, it would upset our essentialized moral categories. Grossman argues that, as a society, we seem "unable to deal with moral pain or guilt," arguing that our inclination is to treat the moral ambiguity evinced through trauma as "a neurosis or a pathology."[14] Given the psychological damage that results from killing (guilt), our failure to attend to violence's own moral consequences ourselves is understandable, yet the result of this essentialization and avoidance is the degradation of moral language and the eventual loss of any meaningful moral category by which to name wrong actions themselves. Put a different way, if a victim must be declared "innocent" for a killing to be a moral transgression—whereas there is little moral dilemma in killing one who is "guilty"—have we not lost the moral language to describe the *act* of killing itself as inherently immoral and thus always needing forgiveness?

In other words, in the essentialization of our moral categories, I am concerned that, like Oscar Wilde's Dorian Gray, we have managed to separate our collective actions from their attendant moral consequences. Dorian was so enamored with his own youth, beauty, and vitality that he transferred his soul into an image of himself that bore the consequences of his natural aging along with his morally disfiguring hedonistic lifestyle in order that his physical body would not age nor bear traces of his "sins." Like Dorian, out of our love for our own perceived primordial innocence, moral goodness, and sacred mission to civilize the frontier, we have relegated the consequences of our collective violence to our military veterans in order that we may gaze and marvel at our own immaculate reflection in the mirror.[15] Treating the trauma of combat as a psychological disorder (PTSD), we ignore the moral component of the injury and what it suggests to us about our own violence, since veterans suffer the guilt of this burden. Veterans are sequestered in a bizarre moral space: they frequently deal with deep moral pain, yet society's uncritical valorization of them makes it difficult for them to witness to this ambiguity as it imposes an even greater expectation of moral heroism. Traumatized veterans thus often sink deeper into iso-

14. Grossman, *On Killing*, 96.

15. This is not to exclude others who have suffered from culturally conditioned violence, who certainly bear this same burden and relegation; I merely use it as a reference point for this particular study.

lation, cut off from the avenues of healing testimony by those who perhaps fear to hear, lest they be forced to face their own non-innocence.

In light of this situation, in chapters 4 and 5, I challenge many of the presuppositions that underlie the concept of individual guilt as linked to blame. Prior to doing so, however, I need to unpack a few of the implications of universal guilt. The concept of universal, existential guilt itself certainly suggests that true innocence is a category to which we do not have access. It holds that our guilt is existentially primordial: that is, we possess a congenital resistance to God's will and are thus always already guilty before God, even prior to committing any particular (sinful) acts. In theological terms, then, the resistance to understanding universal guilt as directly meriting blame and punishment has to be conditioned by our understanding of God's response to our guilt. If God is nothing but judgment and condemnation, then guilt unequivocally implies blame, desert, and punishment, and justice is nothing but the meting out of this deserved sentence. If God is present in Christ, however, there is the hope of mercy and of forgiveness, the chance that God will seek to redeem those who are guilty rather than judge them. In this case, justice does not necessarily equate guilt with condemnation, but with a sense of deep and urgent need for healing.

In merely rational terms, if guilt and innocence in individuals are acute, absolute, and essential—and are associated with blame and punishment—then the notion that we are congenitally guilty (even as infants) would rightly be met with repugnance. Yet, in developing notions of human willing and compelled agency, I argue that, in a society as deeply interconnected as ours, with virtually every member participating in both active and passive ways in the forces that shape it, guilt must be understood in a more communal and diffuse way. Critically, I am not claiming that there are not lesser and greater levels of accountability in violently pathological situations. Differing power dynamics create differing levels of responsibility and culpability for actions. But if we are to explore these levels, and are to trace the distorting and disfiguring forces that shape pathologies of violence, we must suspend the connection between individual guilt and blame at the outset. Otherwise, in our rush to judge one person guilty and another innocent, we miss the critical compulsions and forces that connect all of us.

Sin and Salvation

As with any exercise in public theology, a major component of my argument involves the recovery of theological language: here it is the rehabilitation of "sin-talk" in order to serve the purpose of illuminating and naming a societal ill. My contention is that our eyes have become blinded to *our own* capacity for and participation in great violence. With McFarland, I share a concern that the term "sin" itself, as it is used by both the church and society at large, has become relegated to the description of "issues of marginal moral significance," such as "smoking, dancing, playing cards," and other things that might be identified as "guilty pleasures," such as eating too much chocolate or indulging in a second glass of wine.[16] While even the cultural term retains some sense of sin as a mysterious force, if its primary usage is to name trifling indulgences, then the term itself holds little capacity to name what is truly evil. My argument is that a modified Augustinian concept of original sin allows us to again use the term to describe the condition from which violence arises within us and the force that numbs us to our own participation in it. Expressed in a more explicitly theological register, to name sin in these terms points to our situation of violence and apathy, one in which we are truly alienated from God as the source of life and love.

For Augustine, the immense rhetorical and conceptual weight of describing the human condition in these terms did not lie simply in naming the hopelessness of humanity, but rather in the testimony to the power of divine grace. Girard, despite his somewhat pessimistic view of violence as a force that "will not be denied," also understands that the crucifixion marked the end of sacrifice as a means of violence-avoidance, and that the Gospels, in narrating the death of Christ from the perspective of the truly innocent victim, refuse to allow us to view violence as a force that invades human nature, culture, and society from without. Similarly, it is my intention not only to identify the power of human violence through the doctrine of original sin in order to cast the destructive state of humanity as ultimately tragic or hopeless, but to identify it as one of urgent and dire need. Therefore, in the second (projected) part of this study, I plan to retrieve the resurrection as a hope among the seemingly hopeless—a way that guilt can be borne in the light of the one who does not judge but forgives, a way that memory can

16. McFarland, *In Adam's Fall*, 5.

be borne and redeemed in the one who himself embodies the infinite in finite form, a way that human vulnerability is tolerable in light of the promised end. Therefore, I stand with Augustine in arguing that the power and beauty of true hope can be glimpsed only in recognition of the full darkness of human sin and violence.

CHAPTER 1

Original Sin and the Trauma of Violence

> Sin came into the world through one man, and death came through sin, and so death spread to all because all have sinned.
>
> —ROMANS 5:12

Perhaps the primary task of Christian theology is to continually translate its doctrines, concepts, and symbol systems into the linguistic and conceptual lingua franca of the contemporary world. What is at stake in this enterprise is the relevance of theology to speak to the problems that present themselves in ways that are both consistent with world history and challenging to society by their historical novelty. In light of the violent threats and conflicts that much of the world currently faces, the doctrine of sin can hold a great deal of explanatory power. Yet it is in dire need of fresh translation, because in its current colloquial usage it appears to have lost much of its capacity to speak to the largest threats to life in the modern world. Its meaning has been colonized by a consumer culture, and its primary usages seem to describe trivial indulgences (the "sinfulness" of giving in to the "temptation" to eat a piece of chocolate cake) or transgressions of a societal norm (often sexual, e.g., the "sinfulness" of those whose sexual practice does not conform to the standards of the community).[1] These definitions have a neutralizing effect on the term: they become unable to speak about the distorting forces that corrupt our desires, and unable to speak about sin's most destructive and violent outcomes.

1. This is not to suggest that these examples exhaust the totality of the cultural meaning of sin; it is merely to demonstrate that it is often sequestered in these ways.

The deeply problematic aspect of this for Christian theology is that the notion of sin is deeply intertwined with and informed by the most powerful doctrines and symbols of Christianity: atonement and salvation—cross and resurrection.[2] Our understanding of sin thus shapes how we view the event of the cross and salvation itself. If sin is understood in a relatively trifling sense, then the potent images of crucifixion and empty tomb also become pale and colorless. Is our eating of chocolate or our failure to adhere to societal norms what we need the death of Jesus of Nazareth on the cross to save us from? Conversely—and even more to the point—are these indulgences and failures to conform the problems of the world that are revealed in the torturous violence of the cross? If sin is perceived as merely a trifling indulgence, then in a world of hunger, conflict, terrorism, torture, dehumanization, rape, oppression, and subjugation, certainly the message of the gospel seems absurd, and the brutal death of Jesus even more puzzling. Much of the power of the gospel rests on its insight about the force at the heart of the description of the world as it is: Does the notion of "sin" truly have the power to name what is wrong, what is functionally broken and awry? The gospel poses an answer to this question at the cross: the damage and danger of sin is laid bare in, among other things, our brutal capacity for violence against each other. Sin, then, must be redeemed from its stultifying cultural accretions in order to both faithfully convey the horror of the crucifixion's testimony to sin's reality and to adequately describe the wrongness of the world in a compelling way.

The deep irony of sin's current inability as a term to describe the wrongness of the world is that our society seems open to new descriptions of this wrongness, as multiple threats to the stability of the world challenge governments and philosophical constructions to account for danger, violence, and radical evil. While it likely didn't take airliners careening into the World Trade Center towers and the Pentagon to convince anyone that the world isn't as it should be, it is safe to say that

2. It is not my intention to "take a side" in terms of which way this epistemology properly progresses, that is, whether sin is revealed primarily at the cross (Barth) or whether a full and true understanding of sin can be felt and understood prior to the revelation of Christ (e.g., Jonathan Edwards). My intention here is to note the profound connection between salvation, atonement, and sin in an effort to draw attention to the term "sin" as it is scripturally informed by the Hebrew Bible and New Testament, and as it is theologically informed by the crucifixion and revelation of Christ Jesus's resurrection and the offer of forgiveness to the perpetrators.

after 9/11, Americans have a heightened awareness of the "wrongness" of the world. Indeed, in a larger sense, after the violence that closed the twentieth century shattered the progressive optimism that opened it, this sense of "wrongness" has developed a particular acuteness in the West. The continued virulence and boldness of militant nationalism, xenophobia, and religious radicalism around the world have resulted in alarming displays of dehumanization and misery; the specter and threat of new and continued viral outbreaks bring out the worst of our own fears and demonstrate our own fragility; hunger, poverty, and economic disparity continually plague our world. Most critically, governments around the world seem powerless to right the proverbial ship, opting instead for solutions that seem to exacerbate the problem, and that often simply reinforce the notion that things are not as they should be. In Girard's terms, it would appear that the very institutions we have established to control and curtail violence have often fanned its flames instead. Perhaps a deeper and more "mythic" conception of violence and wrongness may help us understand both the world and ourselves powerfully and authentically.

A central aim of this book is to demonstrate that the concept of sin has the gravitas and force to describe the wrongness of the world in a compelling way: it is to argue, building on Alistair McFadyen's work in *Bound to Sin*, that the doctrine of sin itself holds descriptive and explanatory power in naming a pathological force in our world that lies behind its violence and wrongness. I argue here that the specific concept of original sin provides a conceptual vocabulary that holds together the power of violence, respects its almost mythic nature, and provides a moral framework that resonates with the forces encountered on the modern battlefield. I argue in later chapters that, as a means of public theology, sin can be understood to describe violence and its metastasizing effects in a profound way that directly challenges ideologies that conceive of violence as domesticable and controllable. I argue that, further, because of the explanatory power of this understanding of sin as seen through the lens of violence, it can be used to illuminate the psychological wounds suffered by those who have experienced trauma as a result of participation in conflict. Ultimately, it sheds light on the pervasive, infectious, and insidious nature of violence itself. In light of these larger aims, I describe in the first half of this chapter an essentially Augustinian concept of original sin, highlighting Augustine's understanding of the constraints of human willing; then I discuss how this idea can be traced through specific pathologies, drawing a conceptual vocabulary from McFadyen's contemporary translation of Augustine's doctrine in *Bound to Sin*. In the second half of the chapter, I argue that this conceptual vocabulary resonates deeply with the forces that govern the modern battlefield and act on the psyche of its combatants to affect the horizons of their willing.

Augustine and Sin, Originally

Prior to Augustine, the discussion of sin revolved around two confessional foci: first, the conviction that the world is not as it should be, that things have somehow gone deeply wrong; and second, that humanity is implicated in this wrongness. In addition, early reflections on sin were further bounded by several theological claims that came to serve as "relative absolutes" in theological reflection; theologians navigate these in differing ways. The first of these bounding claims is that the world, including humanity and nature, was "good" as created by God. As Irenaeus demonstrates, this may not mean that the world, or humanity, was perfect; but it means that the world was not created in a defective state by God, thus protecting God from the charge of explicitly authoring evil.[3] Irenaeus distinguishes sharply between what is created—good and rational—and what is uncreated and perfect. What is created is good and can ascend "towards the perfect," but this perfecting is a process of growth by which the good creation asymptotically approaches God.[4]

The second of these claims is that the world as it is now is burdened and broken in a state of sin—that is, not how it was meant to be. Athanasius expressed this distortion as an existential threat in terms of being and nonbeing, arguing that while the world was created from nothing—and given the gift of life and being—sin, violence, and death have so powerfully twisted the world that it now risks utterly perishing and returning to nonexistence. In terms of humanity, Gregory of Nyssa

3. Irenaeus, *Against Heresies*, in *Ante-Nicene Fathers*, vol. 1, ed. Alexander Roberts and James Donaldson (Peabody, MA: Hendrickson, 1994), 4.37–39. For Irenaeus, perfection entails the full development of the spiritual capacity for God. Humanity in its infancy in the Garden (and even now) was good, but unprepared for, "unaccustomed to, and unexercised in, perfect discipline."

4. Irenaeus, *Against Heresies* 4.37–39.

says that our nature, composed of both spirit and flesh, has developed a "bias towards evil."[5] Rather than adhere to our higher, spiritual nature, which exhibits the image of God, we are weighed down by our lower, fleshly nature and have become deeply corrupted by our baser desires and instincts. According to Gregory, the darkness of evil has interposed itself between the light of God and the world and eclipsed God's goodness such that evil's shadow hangs heavy upon the earth.[6]

Third, whatever the state of distortion of the world, one of the basic tenets of humanity is the power of self-determination, more commonly understood as free will. Irenaeus understood that autonomy was simply a fundamental ground of moral existence, arguing that creatures could either be morally free and sometimes sinful or irrational and determined by an outside force toward good. He argues that if any being is created with an evil nature, it cannot be held morally accountable for its evil deeds, because "for such were they created."[7] Since all people are of the same (primordially) good nature, he argues, and since they all have the free will to either cling to this good or to reject it, the condemnation of those who do ill is just. What is crucial is that all persons have the power to act as they will, either heeding the good counsel of prophets and wise and godly individuals, or abandoning such goodness and acting against it. Similary, Gregory of Nyssa argues that, without free will, there is no morality, for "virtue must be a voluntary thing," neither forced nor compelled.[8]

These boundaries color early theologians' discussions of the Fall—the primordial event by which the world has gone deeply wrong—in widely varying ways. For Irenaeus, for example, it was not possible for creatures to be rational and morally free but unable to commit sin. Hu-

5. Gregory of Nyssa, *On the Making of Man*, in *Nicene and Post-Nicene Fathers*, second series, vol. 5, ed. Philip Schaff and Henry Wace (Peabody, MA: Hendrickson, 2004), 5.22.4.

6. Gregory of Nyssa, *On the Making of Man* 5.21.3. Gregory here uses an evocative astronomical metaphor to describe human sinfulness that continues into an understanding of the resurrection. He argues that, like the darkness imposed upon the earth by a celestial body that is positioned directly between it and the sun, evil is finite and has "necessary limits." In due time, the conical shadow passes over the earth, and the light again shines upon it. The resurrection and eschatological return to the good is a necessary matter of course, as the goodness of God is limitless and infinite and perseveres over the darkness.

7. Irenaeus, *Against Heresies* 4.37.2.

8. Gregory of Nyssa, *On the Making of Man* 16.11.

manity as created by God was to develop from its created state (which was good, but not perfect) into perfection through a long progression of maturity. The sin of Adam was a failure of obedience: the rejection of the divine plan of development and a reaching for "godliness" while still in a state of moral immaturity; it was a denial of God's ability to perfect humanity and grant flesh incorruptibility.[9] Irenaeus views the Fall as a serious rupture in the divine plan, but also as an outworking of the infantile exercise of humanity's capacity to freely will. Origen, using a more classically Greek conceptual vocabulary, posits that the creation of intelligences (*noes*) preceded the creation of the material world and that these intelligences originally contemplated God in the full warmth of divine love. Each intelligence (save that of Christ) became "satiated" and, from the resulting sense of ennui, fell away from this original state of intimacy, cooling (*psychesthai*) into souls (*psychai*).[10] The degree to which each fell away from God is revealed by the materiality of their being. Accordingly, angels fell the least, demons the most, and humanity fell to a position somewhere between them. The goodness of God and the free will of the creature are preserved in the postlapsarian state: the will mediates the soul's continual position in the material world between spirit and flesh.

Augustine's innovation is to affirm the essential goodness of the prelapsarian creation, while carving out a particularly nuanced understanding of free will that deeply colors his understanding of the Fall and the broken condition of the world. For Augustine, Adam and Eve (but primarily Adam) possessed the ability to freely will: that is, to be human is to possess a created will and to act rationally in the world by exercising one's own volition. The issue in the Garden concerns the proper exercise of the free will that is granted to Adam, who is unique among all nonangelic creatures as a personal agent. Augustine argues that, if Adam had kept the commandments of God "with pious obedience," then he would have passed from his mortal form into something far greater, obtaining, "without suffering death, a blessed immortality without end."[11] However, along with his capacity to exercise the will

9. Irenaeus, *Against Heresies* 5.5.2.

10. Origen, *On First Principles*, in *Ante-Nicene Fathers*, vol. 4, ed. Alexander Roberts and James Donaldson (Peabody, MA: Hendrickson, 2004), 1.3.8.

11. Augustine, *The City of God Against the Pagans*, trans. and ed. R. W. Dyson (New York: Cambridge University Press, 1998), 12.22. Hereafter, citations of this work appear in parentheses within the text.

"properly" in faithfulness comes the necessary capacity that Adam may use his "free will proudly and disobediently," in which case he would be subject to death, and to live "as the beasts do," as a "slave of his own lust, destined to suffer eternal punishment after death" (12.22).

The true Fall, Augustine argues, takes place at the level of the will. He argues that the will follows desire: it inclines by its nature toward that which it perceives as good. In the Garden, Adam is presented with a close connection with God, who, as Augustine repeatedly says, "supremely is" the ultimate and true good, "by which is bestowed upon [the will] the light by which it can see and the fire by which it can love" (14.13). Consequently, the will's ability to see truly and to love purely comes from its orientation toward God, and its obedience to the divine command. What precedes Adam's physical *act* of disobedience is the true moment in which evil enters humanity: the turning of Adam's perception of the ultimate good, and thus of his will, from God, the source of all true goodness, to himself. This turning itself is, for Augustine, the beginning of an evil will and the way that what was created good and rationally free becomes corrupted by evil and falls away from the one who is the very ground of being. It is not, Augustine is careful to note, that the will has turned toward something that is itself evil, but that it turns to itself and therefore, instead of desiring the ultimate good, which is God, it desires what is inferior—its own gratification. The disobedient act of eating the forbidden fruit is the act of a will that is following a corrupted desire to satiate itself rather than the naturally ordered higher desire to remain in communion with God.

For Augustine, since all of humanity and human society were united and held together in the person of Adam, the consequences of the turning of his will are catastrophic—not only for Adam and Eve, but for all subsequent generations. The most severe consequence, of course, is the loss of the path from mortality to immortality. After failing to exercise his will with piety and obedience, Adam—and subsequently all of humanity—is subject to death, both the death of the physical body and the death of the soul via eternal condemnation. Yet the Fall entails a particular distortion of human nature itself that binds humanity in separating from God congenitally. First, there is a disintegration of the connection between one's volition, the will to do something, and one's ability to carry out what one wishes to do. Augustine exhibits this primarily as a loss of control over one's own body, and that rebellion parallels Adam and Eve's disobedience toward God

(13.14).[12] But there is also the notion within this formulation that a disconnect exists between willing (as agency) and desire itself. Even while the will follows desire, one of the consequences of original sin is the severing of the close connection between the two, most primally exhibited by Augustine as a loss of sexual control, wherein one often acts as one may not will to act. Second, and far more distorting, however, is the alienation of the will from what is truly good. Having turned inward to the lesser goods, our desires are disordered and, instead of being oriented toward what is the highest good, we are oriented toward and driven by pursuit of lesser goods. Without divine grace, we cannot reorient our disordered and confused desires, and our wills are bound in patterns of distorted willing. Augustine argues that, since in both a mythical and a "seminal" sense "we all were that one man who fell into sin," these effects and distortions are propagated to all of humanity congenitally; the broken nature is propagated because "nothing could be born of them which was not what they themselves had been" (13.3). We are all born into this sinful condition in which our wills are bound and our nature "vitiated" by sin; humanity's "corrupt root" thus brings forth an entire situation of sin, whose tendrils reach into all parts of human life.

The radicality of Augustine's understanding of the Fall revolves primarily around this notion that, as a result of Adam's sin—when divine grace is absent—the will is hopelessly alienated from the true good. According to Augustine, the power of the evil unleashed is so great that it corrupts every facet of human nature, such that we can no longer choose to act rightly: our desires are too bent in pursuit of the lesser goods that we perceive to be ultimate. This presents a significantly darkened picture of human nature and human willing when compared to earlier theologians' understandings of "free will." Augustine affirms the human capacity to will (volition), to act as personal agents, to choose between alternatives and to direct our own being, even in a postlapsarian state. What we cannot do, however, is reorient the desires and goods that drive our agential capacities in certain directions, as these desires drive and exert an almost totalizing "pull" upon our willing. Alienated

12. Notoriously, as McFarland notes in *In Adam's Fall*, 71, Augustine refers to this loss of control as a man's inability to control his erection; *The Grace of Christ and Original Sin* 2.47. But this same lack of sexual control is at least implied also in *City of God* 13.13, 13.14, 13.15, and 13.16.

from what is supremely good, our willing is sequestered in patterns that are ultimately pathogenic and infected with the corruption of sin.[13] We cannot, through the power of our own wills, escape these patterns, and thus our capacity to act as agents, while remaining, is always bound: our horizons are limited by our situations and conditions, and our choices are restricted within those horizons.

Augustine's significant departure from theologians such as Irenaeus, Origen, and Gregory regarding postlapsarian willing can best be understood in light of his lengthy controversy with Pelagius and his followers. Pelagius, a British ascetic, held that human willing was not damaged as a result of the Fall. He argued that an essential part of our humanity, even in its postlapsarian state, is "to be free to choose between competing possibilities."[14] For Pelagius, sin is propagated by way of imitation rather than congenital defect: born with the same capacity to freely will that Adam had, we imitate his sin.[15] Personal autonomy is a critical component of human nature as created by God, Pelagius argued. The God-given capacity to do evil is just as important as the capacity to do good, "because it makes the good part better by making it voluntary and independent, not bound by necessity but free to decide for itself."[16] The will, as the controlling aspect of human decisions, remains fundamentally free, a "pure organ of free choice."[17] It acts out of no internal compulsion or force but always maintains a neutral disposition. The will itself is the sole causal force of human agency, the only force that can operate on one's action of "willing." It is unmoved by habit, action, or other forces that impact the self, though Pelagius

13. This is not to say that all patterns of thought, willing, and behavior are equally harmful—only to say that none, absent divine grace, are truly good. There are greater and lesser degrees of harmful patterns, to which I will turn my attention in subsequent sections.

14. Alistair McFadyen, *Bound to Sin: Abuse, Holocaust, and the Christian Doctrine of Sin* (New York: Cambridge University Press, 2000), 168. While this is certainly how Augustine and his interpreters understood Pelagius, his precise understanding of willing remains somewhat obscure, since few of his writings are extant, and almost none of the surviving documents are lengthy.

15. This is the view Augustine vehemently argues against in *On the Merits and Forgiveness of Sins and the Baptism of Infants*, in *Nicene and Post-Nicene Fathers*, first series, vol. 5, ed. Philip Schaff (Peabody, MA: Hendrickson, 2004), 1.9, 1.10.

16. Pelagius, *To Demetrias*, in *The Letters of Pelagius and His Followers*, ed. and trans. B. R. Rees (Rochester, NY: Boydell, 1991), 3.2.

17. McFadyen, *Bound to Sin*, 168.

noted that the will can be "bent" in a certain direction, partially due to the long habit of doing ill.[18] It is in this way that Pelagius understood sin to occur and to be passed from generation to generation; humanity is used to patterns of behavior that it habitually imitates. Yet there is nothing that prevents us from willfully contravening those patterns, as Pelagius understood the will to be resistant to external factors as well. While he understood that external forces could influence willing to a degree, he held that because of the will's "transcendence of social and psychological conditioning factors," we always are capable of willing and acting independent of them.[19]

In the thought of Pelagius, then, sin must be narrowly defined as "only free acts of the will" in which we freely and individually choose sinful action—in other words, a specific bad act.[20] Only the free choices we have made when we could have chosen otherwise can be morally evaluated, because the will possesses no inherent inclination (sinful or good) but rather remains neutral in its capacity to "orient oneself in action through free choice."[21] The heart of the argument with Augustine, of course, concerns the very capacity to orient oneself toward the truly good. Pelagius argues that our most crucial capacity as human beings is our ability to choose the good. According to Pelagius, we all possess the inherent capability of not sinning through the free, neutral, and unmoved will. We are "inherently capable of willing and doing the good and so are culpable for all failure to do so."[22] Hence sin can only be primarily spoken of in terms of individual sinful acts in which humans reject the good, which is always available to be chosen.

Augustine contends that this view is deeply flawed because it ultimately grants power and responsibility to humanity for its own righteousness, losing sight of the Pauline understanding that all have sinned and fallen short of the glory of God. Despite his own somewhat pessimis-

18. Pelagius, *To Demetrias* 3.2, 8.3.

19. McFadyen, *Bound to Sin*, 168.

20. Augustine, *On Nature and Grace* 21, in *Nicene and Post-Nicene Fathers*, first series, vol. 5, ed. Philip Schaff (Peabody, MA: Hendrickson, 2004). In *The Wounded Heart of God: The Asian Concept of Han and the Christian Doctrine of Sin* (Nashville: Abingdon, 1993), Andrew Sung Park uses a similar definition of sin, but does so in order to distinguish between sin as willful, deliberate action and *han*, the suffering and condition from which sin often arises.

21. McFadyen, *Bound to Sin*, 171.

22. McFadyen, *Bound to Sin*, 171.

tic view of human willing, what is at sake for Augustine in this argument is grace. Augustine argues, in *On the Spirit and the Letter*, against the notion that we simply sin by habit or imitation; he argues implicitly that if this were so, the law would have a salvific effect: it points to what is bad and wrong, and we can become habituated to following it. Yet, even if we become perfect servants of the law, he argues, our desire to break the law intensifies when something becomes forbidden, because in those circumstances the object desired becomes "all the more pleasant."[23] The problem, he notes, is that the law may keep desires in check—it may constrain our sinful actions—but it cannot alter our desire to break the law, to covet. In terms of desire itself, the law does not inhibit it, but like a flowing stream, which "becomes more violent when it meets with any impediment, and when it has overcome the stoppage, falls in a greater bulk, and with increased impetuosity hurries forward in its downward course," the law only "augments the evil desire" for an object by making it forbidden.[24] Therefore, even if the law were to constrain us to make proper choices, we would still be sinful on account of our *desire* to break the law; however much we have been conditioned—or even have conditioned ourselves—to follow it, it simply convicts us of our base and sinful desires. In order to be truly free from sin, then, what is necessary is the reorientation of our desires toward what is good. In other words, we need to be able to genuinely desire to keep the law out of love, not simply out of a fear of the consequences.

For Augustine, the distortion of human willing and its pathogenic pattern occurs at the level of what we desire: that object of desire toward which our wills are oriented as a valued good. As Rowan Williams notes in interpreting Augustine on this point, the corruption of the will is disastrous because of humanity's pursuit of "false or destructive goals" and of "illusory goods."[25] In Augustine's example in *On the Spirit and the Letter*, the desire to break the law, even if it is compulsory to follow it, can be understood to be buttressed at some level by the belief that there is some personal benefit (pleasure, wealth, safety) in breaking it. Ultimately, this is an illusory good: it appears as good only as a result of our inability to perceive and cling to what is truly good. Williams

23. Augustine, *On the Spirit and the Letter* 6, in *Nicene and Post-Nicene Fathers*, first series, vol. 5.

24. Augustine, *On the Spirit and the Letter* 6.

25. Rowan Williams, "Insubstantial Evil," in *Augustine and His Critics*, ed. Robert Dodaro and George Lawless (New York: Routledge, 2000), 111.

notes that it is a misreading of the world, a confusion of what is false and impermanent with what is true and permanent. As a force that acts on human nature by deeply distorting it, sin disfigures and confuses human understanding of what is good and thus sequesters the will's proper orientation through a desire for the object that proves to be a false good.[26] In practical terms, Williams argues, what this means is that the distorting force of sin, when combined with the powers of the human intellect and imagination, has the immense capacity to shape human willing through the creation of false and illusory goods. The malleability of human willing, then, turns not primarily on its ability to be compelled to act in opposition to what it views as good, but through the corruption of the good toward which the will is oriented. The control of the good to which we are oriented is beyond us, according to Augustine. We cannot control what we want.[27]

For Augustine, then, the reorientation of our desires toward what is truly good can be accomplished only by divine action. Since all humans congenitally possess concupiscence (disordered desire), all find themselves in need of grace. Even infants, Augustine argues, in their very helplessness, in the "darkness of their rational intellect," which contrasts with the rational free will of Adam (who was created in adult form), demonstrate the distortedness of human nature, even if they have not committed actuated sin.[28] They, too, are in need of God's grace.

26. What makes a good false is not that it is something inherently nefarious (indeed, for Augustine, nothing created is inherently nefarious; evil can exist only as the corruption of something inherently good), but that it is a good that is not God and thus not truly good.

27. Augustine, *On the Spirit and the Letter* 60. Augustine argues here that God brings about our reorientation by "acting on the incentives of our perceptions, to will and believe, either externally by evangelical exhortations . . . or internally, where no man has in his own control what shall enter into his thoughts, although it appertains to his own will to consent or to dissent." God works to reorient what we desire back to Godself, the source of true goodness, and God "sheds love abroad in our hearts." We consent via our actions on our desire, but that desire itself is shaped by God. The converse, then, is also true in this case: since human nature is alienated from God because of Adam's sin, our desires are acted on by the myriad sinful forces that affect our desires.

28. Augustine, *On the Merits and Forgiveness* 1.66–69. Augustine's argument here, while seeming strange and almost inverted to modern readers, essentially holds that, if Adam, in his prelapsarian state as a rational, obedient creature possessing unconstrained free will, is the model of God's good creation (though, since he is able to sin, not perfect—not as humanity will be eschatologically, i.e., unable to sin), and if in

The primary problem in Pelagius's understanding of willing, then, is that he attributes to humans the ability to turn toward and choose the good themselves. For Augustine, the result of this is a severely ascetic moralism, in which we are not only responsible for our sinful condition (which Augustine affirms) but also possess the means of turning from it. Therefore, we must always be anxious as to whether we are making proper choices, because the possibility of our very righteousness rests on our own capacity to will to choose the good. For Augustine, our very orientation toward and desire for the good is corrupted by sin. Consequently, we no longer have the capacity to choose what is good or act well—apart from divine grace.

In summary, Augustine presents a view of postlapsarian human willing that is sufficiently different from that of earlier theologians—that is, in describing the human will as bound—and he offers a distinct qualification to the notion of "free will" that holds significant power to articulate expressions of violence and trauma in our world today. Augustine would affirm that "free will" means volition, the capacity to choose; but since our willing is done in service of our disoriented desires, it is bound in patterns that we cannot escape by ourselves. Since we congenitally inherit the state of alienation from God that Augustine names as "rebellion against God," we are guilty before God. We act out of this condition, and thus we are responsible for our own bad actions; but due to the broken nature we inherit, there is a sense that we also "cannot help it." Augustine, then, qualifies the "free will" concept that exerted such a force on early discussions of sin in the thought of Irenaeus, Origen, and Gregory, and he affirms absolutely the goodness of God and the complicity of humanity in our own broken state. What emerges in Augustine's anti-Pelagian writings is another concept crucial to the discussion: the totality of God's grace in salvation.[29] For Augustine, the moralism that results from a Pelagian view misses something crucial about our human nature: the universality of our participation in sin. The Pelagian view makes the efficacy of God's grace dependent on human willing, which Augustine finds untenable. For Augustine, God's

---

remaining so, he would have been able to propagate more humans through means other than sexual reproduction, then infants in their helplessness and irrationality must mark out an effect of the distortion of human nature and thus the inheritance of sin and guilt.

29. By this I mean the totality of God's grace for those whom God saves. Augustine is obviously not a universalist.

grace comes to those who are totally alienated from the capacity to choose the good, those who are completely unable to earn that grace for themselves.

This capacity becomes a key in differentiating the Augustinian from the Pelagian understanding of sin itself. For Pelagius, the human capacity to will rightly endures after the Fall, and sin is thus made up of particular "bad acts." Augustine doesn't dispute that actualized actions are indeed sins; but due to his doctrine of the bondage of the will, he is able to affirm a broader understanding of sin itself, in which "original sin" connotes the initial sin of Adam as well as the condition in which all subsequent humanity finds itself. Augustine's conception of sin thus reflects the power of sin as a more diffuse force that affects and forms—but is not limited to—willed actualizations. This congenital corruption connotes a radical break with the original divine plan for ultimate human immortality, and its corrupting effects present the power of sin as a force that distorts human willing both from within and from without. This presents a significantly more complex moral system than that of Pelagius: it simultaneously recognizes sin and wrong as things we do and the conditions and forces from which those "bad acts" spring. In other words, there is more in play than simply our own "bad acts."

McFadyen: Compulsion and Sequestration

Augustine's complex view of sin and human willing provides a framework for a deeper examination of the most acute examples of violence and wrongness we encounter. More recently, in *Bound to Sin*, Alistair McFadyen reinterprets this Augustinian view of original sin in a modern context in order to test its ability to hold "descriptive power" in two undeniably pathogenic sets of human behavior: the Nazi killings of Jews during the Holocaust and the sexual abuse of children. He argues that many contemporary constructions of morality place considerable faith in the autonomy of the individual (as in Pelagius's view): that each person is his or her own efficient cause. Within this construction of morality, there are two possibilities: we are either entirely responsible for our own behavior or are forced in such a way that we "had no choice" but to act in a certain way—and thus are not responsible for our own behavior. McFadyen argues that the moral universe is considerably more complex, and he seeks to recover a language of sin that simultaneously holds people accountable before God for their actions and identifies the inherited, universal sinful condition from which those actions spring. In testing the ability of original sin to provide a compelling and descriptive morality, McFadyen uses the case studies of the Holocaust and child abuse to demonstrate how outside forces can deeply distort the lives, willed actions, and desires of those caught up in these "limit" situations. Interacting with psychological and sociological findings, McFadyen recasts original sin in ways that resonate deeply with many of the forces acting upon us in our modern world.

What emerges from his effort is a revised conceptual vocabulary that speaks about the effects of our alienation from God in terms of the obfuscation and confusion of what is real and what is right. What he develops is particularly salient to this study, as he articulates the capacity of this alienation to cordon off our willing within the particular bounds and the very limited orbits whose gravitational force constricts our options. Building on Augustine, McFadyen introduces a particular way of speaking of the force that desire holds over human willing, arguing that desire "compels" the will.[30] If our willing is simply the modality by which we exercise our own personal agency—even in situations in which we would wish to do otherwise—then, as the sum of our desires, goals, and interests, the core trajectory of our lives and characters is distorted and redirected through pathological situations.

Furthermore, as they are particularly salient to a discussion of modern conflict, it is worth highlighting the major corollaries that McFadyen focuses on from Augustine's concept of original sin that help to frame his interpretation of the doctrine and demonstrate its contrast to the ways we often construct modern morality.

First, he holds that sin is an outcome that arose from the condition of free will, but it was not an *inevitable* outcome. This describes how Augustine holds together prelapsarian free will while simultaneously

30. McFadyen uses the term "compulsion" to describe how the will is influenced by what we desire. Augustine would argue that the will follows desire, and McFadyen articulates this same idea by arguing that desire compels the will to act in certain ways. It is essentially semantic, but it merits clarification, since McFadyen is not arguing that one's will is compelled away from what one desires, but that one's desires are distorted by external forces and also that our desires can be preyed upon and twisted in ways extremely toxic and harmful to both ourselves and others. This section owes to McFadyen's detailed descriptions of the four corollaries of sin (*Bound to Sin*, 16–18), as he relates these four corollaries as "contingent, radical, communicable, and universal."

affirming the goodness of creation as created by God. Things could have been other than they are: the notion of the contingency of sin takes seriously the possibility that Adam, as Augustine declared, could have remained in communion with God and passed into immortality and perfection without suffering death. Human nature and human willing are not sinful by virtue of existing as such; rather, human nature as we inherit it from Adam is distorted. Our nature—and particularly our bound will—is not what it was meant to be or what it could have been, nor is it now what it initially was as God created it.

Second, sin's effects on humanity and human life are "radical."[31] The effects of sin poison humanity at its deepest levels and corrupt not simply our actions on occasion or in episodic fashion, but constitute and define the very situation of human willing and action. Our willing takes place within the bounds of an agency that is alienated from that good toward which our desires should be, but are not, oriented. The break here from true goodness is profound: the reality of sin continues as a disruption of the very aspects of humanity that ground our being. Its power is so pervasive and ubiquitous that it affects our internal compositions as well as our relationships with each other in deeply distorting ways, infecting our cultures and societies at a formative level and contaminating the most basic ways we interact in the world. In essence, sin's hold on humanity is so radical that we cannot act in the world apart from its distorting effects. It conditions every aspect of our lives, individually and together.

Third, sin is communicated to us before we establish our personhood. It is congenital: we inherit it in our very nature as human beings. Given the power of the conditioning force of relationality that follows from sin's radicality, the fact that we pre-personally inherit the sinful condition affirms the Augustinian notion that, while sin does deeply distort our relationships and social constructions, we do not come to be sinful through social conditioning. It is something that is infectious and distorting and is passed to us as if it were a flawed aspect of our DNA. As a congenital corruption, our very constructions of self and individuality are distorted in the formative stages by sin. As such, sin is inescapable: it is a part of who we are as individual agents as well as communal society. Through this inheritance, we also incur guilt as a result of the alienation from the source of true goodness.

31. McFadyen, *Bound to Sin*, 17.

Finally, since all human beings find themselves in this radical condition, which is inherited congenitally, it naturally follows that sin is "universally extensive."[32] The ubiquity of sin, both as an internal and external force, means that all human agency is marred by sin, by the inescapable condition from which we act, both collectively and individually. All humans, by virtue of being human, inherit through Adam the congenital sinful condition and distorted human nature. Augustine understands this as a sense of universal guilt: all are alienated, by virtue of being human and thus inheriting a nature that is in opposition to God and thus guilty of the sinful condition they bear. Sin's universality is thus a result of our personal decisions and actions that graft us as individuals into the corporate reality of sin.

What McFadyen draws out in a more modern conceptual parlance is the complex and multifaceted interaction between the corporate reality of sin and our individual participation in it.[33] Against Pelagius, Augustine maintained that the will is not a separate, self-motivated, and independent entity, but rather an integrated part of the willing agent, thus affected by the focus, desires, goals, and ambitions of that agent in a certain disposition. The particular disposition of this willing agent constitutes the person's life trajectory, which is the orientation and direction of the person's desire and affections. By virtue of being so integrated within and not separated from the internal mechanisms of the willing agent, the will is oriented toward what the agent values as the good. It is not neutral and apart from—but deeply embedded in and guided by—our desire toward what we determine to be good. In short, the will is always compelled toward the valued good and also affected and further embedded by the internal desire and pursuit of this good.

In addition, rather than a set of neutral individual choices, willing is more properly understood as the active personal pursuit of the valued

32. McFadyen, *Bound to Sin*, 17.

33. This section draws on the ideas McFadyen coalesces in his section on "compelled willing" in *Bound to Sin* (180–90), particularly his articulation of the idea of internalization of sinful influences as "the addition of personal energy" to a sinful dynamic (182). He also helpfully articulates the contrasts of the scenario of the "hostage situation" as compelled willing (in which one's willing is active), where one is given a choice to kill others or witness the death of one's family against a situation of forced willing (in which one's willing is inactive), where one's own fingers are curled around a trigger by a more powerful hand that then physically forces one's finger to pull the trigger.

good, whether constricted by circumstance or outside entity or otherwise unconstrained. The key for Augustine is that our willing is voluntary and operative, even if our choices are constrained. Not only can external forces (in the case of grace and faith, the activity of the Spirit) then affect and compel our will and orient our desires, but the very addition of our "personal energy" to these desires grants the corporate sinful dynamic more corruptive power. Thus our habitual actions and continued application of personal energy further embed and cement the will in the orientation of the desire we have pursued. As the will can be acted on for good or ill, it is, in other words, quite vulnerable to the shaping effects of outside forces.

These external forces deeply distort and disorient our individual personal life trajectories. Although such distortions may originate from outside us, we internalize and intensify them in our own lives. Sin is a radical distortion in the patterns of relationality from which we form our lives; it is not reducible to individual acts, but is instead a dynamic network of relations and interactions. These distortions have tendrils that constitute "fields of force," which affect a network of victims, perpetrators, and bystanders, all of whom are connected and enmeshed in the sinful condition.[34] In this way, the will of each of these actors in any given situation can be said to be bound in the midst of larger sinful dynamics and pathologies.

This understanding of compulsion is a crucial innovation because it expresses the claim that, though our choices appear to be (and in a real sense truly are) constricted, our actions remain voluntary. The sense that we retain our own capacity to commit our personal energies in an orientation that can be twisted is the key for the effort to hold together both an accountability for our individual sins and yet an acknowledgment that we inherit the sinful condition from which we commit sins. Augustine's category of sin enables us to draw out the nuances of these relationships because it is broad enough to name not simply sinful acts but also the sinful conditions and compulsions that constrain our choices. We commit and participate in sin because we commit active personal energy in willing; but this willful action does

34. McFadyen, *Bound to Sin*, 147. This is not to argue that all actors occupy the same space in terms of accountability and/or responsibility, but to note that these "fields of force" bind them all and that their relationality and agency are distorted in differing ways.

not exhaust the definition of sin. Rather, Augustine understands the term in a significantly broader and more pervasive way as that which is against God. Therefore, circumstances themselves can be sinful and defined as situations in which we are compelled to sin. We actively will and sin through our active commitment of personal energy, but both the situation and our action are sinful and reflect a will bound in a sinful orientation through the constraint of choices imposed by the situation. Sin, then, can be understood as both the force that conditions those situations and the actions, distortions, and effects that arise from them.

Despite the power of these forces to disorient our life trajectories, we also internalize these distortions and bear responsibility for them. Since the will is active in the context of a concretely lived life and not external to it or separated from it, Augustine argues that the external forces can penetrate the will and cause distortions within it. Sin's force field describes the powerful and dynamic complement of external and internal energies that twist and distort the internal orientation and intentionality of all those caught within it. Even then the actions that we originate in our own commitment of personal energy spring from and can be traced back to our own distorted and compelled intention. Though a distortion may originate from outside of us, through our willing we internalize and intensify the distortion in our own lives. Due to our extensive participation in and internalization of these dynamics in our own lives, Augustine does not discuss them as external to us. In sin, then, we are accountable for our own actions, though they are bound and compelled by forces that did not originate within ourselves.

From this conception of sin and willing, McFadyen distills four points of congruence with the pathologies of the Holocaust and child abuse. These points of congruence run counter to Pelagian, moralistic notions of sin and provide a richer and more nuanced definition in keeping with the traditional concept of original sin. If the most basic way to understand an Augustinian interpretation of sin is in terms of a force with a powerful ability to disorient people in their willing away from an inclination toward an objective good (God) and into the more subjective realm of partial and illusory "goods," then these points of congruence illustrate how this disorientation occurs in pathological situations. They provide the outlines of a framework for answering the question, "Does an understanding of sin have the ability to show us a fuller reality?"[35]

35. McFadyen develops these ideas in this section in *Bound to Sin* (esp. 194–99),

The first point of congruence is that sin is operative not as individual, atomistic acts but as a dynamic network of numerous relationships and interactions. This network of relationships is "suprapersonal," occurring within the sphere of the individual self; but the self is enmeshed in and participates in a larger framework of actions and relations that shape the condition of sin. In unavoidably acting in the world, our willing is compelled by these fields of force and sustains and propagates this sinful condition. To act in relation to others is to act according to the dynamics of those relationships, all of which are conditioned by these fields of force.

Second, the pathological dynamic invades and disfigures the desires, directions, and very lives of everyone involved in the pathology, whether one is a victim, a direct perpetrator, or one who simply observes any given situation. This distortion takes place for the different actors in different ways, depending on the nature of the influence. But whether through active commission, victimization, or even seemingly passive observation, we participate in the sinful condition and actively bring its disorienting effects into our own lives by doing so. This underscores one of the key aspects of the radicality of sin: even if we are largely the victims of particular violations or "bad acts," because our willing is always active, there are ways in which we are bound in the dynamic by which sin is internalized and distorting. Whether perpetrator, victim, or bystander, we all become bound in the distortions that result from our participation in the larger dynamics, and that intensify the effects—which we can almost never envision or predict—in ourselves and others.

Third, the pathological dynamic in which we are all bound confuses our understanding of what is real (particularly in terms of the possibilities and choices we have in our agency), of what is "true and false, valuable and pathogenic, good and bad, right and wrong," and—most importantly—why it is so.[36] In other words, sin obfuscates what is truly good and valuable amidst the multitude of false claims to goodness and value. Since our willing follows a pursuit of what we desire, it is that very desire that can be so misdirected and confused. One of the most insid-

particularly noting that Augustine conceives of sin "primarily in dynamic terms—more as energy than substance," as the disorienting of our willing. He also develops the term "supra-personal" (195) in order to describe the situation of sinfulness in a way that accounts for both individual participation and the distorting force of the larger societal dynamic.

36. McFadyen, *Bound to Sin*, 195.

ious effects of the pathological dynamic is that it isolates individuals from the very criteria by which they could judge whether something was right or wrong. It is the sequestration of our capacities to reason as well as our ability to morally evaluate. Alienated from what is truly good and valuable, we have access to no "Archimedian point" from which we can evaluate our actions, that is, an impartial place that is not enmeshed in the very dynamic we are attempting to evaluate. As a result, what should be sharp and important differences between moral orientations become blurred and relativized within a sea of competing values.

Fourth—and closely related to the third—the pathological dynamic erects a barrier to a sense of meaning and value that transcends the sinful condition and situation in which we find ourselves. The realities we experience often appear to constrict our choices in totality, with the powerfully binding effect of cutting off notions of good and evil that would allow us to get a firmer grasp on the realities of our situation. In other words, a more profound effect occurs than the relativization of values in an intense or extreme situation. The effect of sin in pathological situations is to block access to the sources of psychological and moral escape: it sequesters the moral compass in such a way that we cannot find a "true North" toward which to orient ourselves.

Case Studies in Sequestered Willing: Nazi Killing and Child Abuse

These four congruencies help to connect McFadyen's theological argument and its Augustinian roots to his conception of willing as it takes place in concrete pathological situations.

McFadyen first examines the willing of the victims, perpetrators, and bystanders of the Holocaust, a pathology that affected an immense network of complex relationships (an entire nation and arguably the majority of the Western world).[37] His argument about the bound will in

37. I should note that I am reading these criteria back into an earlier section of *Bound to Sin*. However, it is clear that the framework of willing and its relationship to a working definition of sin as applicable to the pathologies discussed is built on (or reflects) these factors. (McFadyen's discussion of the ways "willing," "loyalty," and "responsibility" play in the Nazi killing units can be found on 119, 120.) His excellent and disturbing discussion of the power of "confusion," "consent," and "secrecy" in situations of child abuse can be found on 120–26. This section will highlight these aspects of his argument as grounding vocabulary for later discussion.

the setting of the Holocaust hinges on two of these four congruences: the concept of restricted choice and confused notions of reality. What he describes in an earlier section of *Bound to Sin* as "the binding of reason" beneath a "totalitarian ideology" is, in effect, the constriction of the choices and life-intentionalities of those whose concrete lives are lived under the Nazi regime.[38] The imposition of a new reality defined by the utopian vision of a racially pure Europe and a powerful German Reich encompassed all the German citizens in its breadth and distortion. This newly imposed sense of reality and its totalitarian reason thus boiled down all sense of rational, moral choice to one: either accept or reject this reality. In this setting, the acceptance or rejection of reality presents itself as one of responsibility. In the dynamic of the Holocaust, a major assumption for the "cogs" and "killers" is that this distorted reality forms the effective working bounds of their capacity to will: the cogs and killers (those at the bottom of the chain of command) have no power to choose to dispute the overall ends (the ideologies and strategies behind the Nazi policies); instead, they must commit their energies to the means available in pursuit of those unchosen goals. There are specific forces acting to bind the willing of those in the killing units. The "killers" effectively operate as a subset of the "cog," albeit one charged with a heinous task. The will of those within these units is bound by the same forces as those operative for the "cogs."

The killers are separated from a greater framework of meaning and responsibility through the rigid structure and military discipline inherent in the chain of command. The frontline killers are not the ones who have made the decision to kill; this means that frontline soldiers are separated from a sense of responsibility. From the killers' perspective, the responsibility for the killing lies with the decision-maker. They might have willed otherwise (decided not to kill) if the choice had been theirs to make. Their willing is thus trapped in a strange moral framework: their responsibility is not to determine whether they should kill or not, but to follow orders in the most effective and efficient way possible.

Through the structure and firm emphasis on obedience and discipline, their access to a transcendent notion of right and wrong is effectively blocked. The responsibility is to do what had to be done, to do one's share and one's duty both in the sense of the unit and the

38. McFadyen, *Bound to Sin*, 88. In the remainder of this chapter, page references in *Bound to Sin* will appear in parentheses in the text.

larger task of the nation. The sphere of choice and moral responsibility became one shaped primarily by loyalty to the unit. Crucially, this is not to suggest that ethical judgment and willing are absent or inactive here; instead, the horizons of willing and morality have been greatly restricted. In the absence of access to higher-level decisions about policy and orders, soldiers divert their moral energies toward the virtue of loyalty. Loyalty to the profoundly powerful network of interconnected relations and ideas—illustrated at their most concrete and penetrating form in military units—strongly limits individual choice and shapes willing in pursuit of group goods rather than individual goods.

Willing, then, is still active, but bound deeply by these powerful forces. Within this restricted horizon of choice, Augustine's notion of *voluntas* can be understood as "the addition of personal and subjective commitment to that which one experiences as being outside the realm of one's own free choice in the strict sense" (120). This is an almost identical parallel to the illustration of Augustine's notion of a will that appears to be compelled: a hostage situation in which a person and his family are held captive, the man is given a weapon and then is told that, if he fails to murder a third party, his own family will be killed. In the case of the Nazi killing units, the killers themselves may not have chosen to kill if given the choice; but in their perception, they did not have a choice that they could exercise with any degree of committed responsibility not to kill. Their personal energies of willing were applied to the task of killing, since it was not forced but compelled; therefore, the killers internalized and propagated this distorted dynamic, and it became more and more a part of them and their own identity.

This internalization was accomplished in a specific and critical way for the killing units, such that they intensified their loyalty and commitment to the pathological forces. The units' repeated participation in "mass murder" essentially rendered it "normal" in the eyes of the perpetrators and desensitized them to its horror. The killers were conditioned against any qualms or reservations about killing and its transcendent "wrongness" through repeated participation. Thus the practice of killing and its subsequent normalization in the perception of the killers effectively restricted access to any notions of morality outside the realm of loyalty and responsibility to the unit. Furthermore, any remaining "scruples" were overcome through a cultural conditioning of "machismo," in which such resistance to performing acts that seemed wrong was deemed weakness and reflected a lack of courage (160). The use of alcohol by those involved in the killing (orchestrated by those in higher positions) confused the combatants' notions of reality by way of the creation of an entirely different conception of what is valuable and right. Being a good man, a good soldier, or even a good German meant simply to do your job and your share: to obey orders.

While McFadyen's discussion of the Nazi killers revolves around sin's capacity to sequester willing in pathological patterns, his discussion of child abuse highlights sin's capacity to deeply distort the relationality of everyone involved and its ability to bind those involved in it in secrecy—effectively cutting them all off from larger frameworks of meaning. What is particularly remarkable in this analysis of the dynamics of abuse is the way it highlights the notion that, despite the clear power differential between the abuser and victim, the will of the victim is active and internalizes the distortion of the abuse. In effect, it powerfully demonstrates how our desires themselves, particularly in children, can be twisted, confused and disoriented by the abusive relational dynamic. These desires and the choices made in their pursuit have an isolating effect on the abuser and victim, who are together bound in the pattern of abuse. This distortion of normal relationality affects all those with whom either is in relationship. The tendrils of the distortion affect the entire web of relationships the pair have now and will have in the future.

Rather than a singular act of violation, childhood sexual abuse is presented in this analysis as the description of a distorted and distorting sense of relationality. McFadyen, who has extensive experience as a law enforcement officer in England, notes that in order for abuse to occur, the child has to be isolated from caring and nurturing relationships. Abusers either select a victim who is already separated from the network of supportive, loving, and healthy adult relationships or "prepare the ground" for the abuse by isolating their victims from these relationships. This takes place through "a great deal of adult cunning, foresight, ingenuity and planning, manipulating, and manoeuvring the adult relationships in their general situation" (62). Consequently, abuse comes when a child is in a situation that is already permeated by the distortions the abuser has created or has entered into. Most child abusers are not sexually attracted to children; rather, they appear to act out of a need to re-create an abusive power dynamic that they experienced when they were children; hence, abusers often have a history of being abused themselves. Abusers then re-create the same relational dynamics out of their own distorted sense of relationality that can be traced back to the way they internalized the distortions they experienced. By isolating the child, socially and psychologically, and then manipulating the child's sense of trust, the abusers do not simply commit acts of abuse; they set up a damaged and damaging relationship with destructive tendrils in the psyche of both child and abuser.

The child's active willing is an integral part of both continued isolation and secrecy as well as the child's internalization of abuse. It is critical that the children, particularly in recovery from abuse, do not simply see themselves as passive and impotent objects that have been acted on, but as agents who must survive the situations in which their agency has been manipulated. Within the scope of the abuse, however, the manipulation of children's active agency is also the powerfully damaging and distorting aspect that binds them to isolation and secrecy. This often occurs when the abusers offer rewards or inducements (intimacy and affection) as incentives for the abuse. Since the children desire these benefits, which may, in their own reasoning, outweigh the abuse they have to endure, they become confused and come to think of themselves as willing the acts of abuse and the abusive relationship itself. Hence, children often see themselves as responsible for the abuse, and they internally bear the shame and guilt of that responsibility.

This sense of shame and guilt binds the children further within the abusive relationship, and their active willing in light of it often poisons their future search for identity. The threat of discovery becomes the threat that their own participation in and willing of the abuse will be discovered and condemned, and they then actively exercise willing against the discovery of the abuse. The dynamic becomes totalizing within a vicious circle: children who actively will against discovery because of the perceived condemnation of their own role in the abuse then may struggle to differentiate between having willed to keep the abuse secret and having acted to consent to the abuse itself, feeling they have "causal responsibility" for the abuse itself (125). Isolated from a larger framework of social relationships and those who could potentially intervene, victims of abuse work actively to ensure that there is no intervention, that the abuse is not discovered. Furthermore, even while children's active willing is what eventually enables recovery through an identification as a "survivor" of the abuse, the child's future willing is done in the context of the construction of an identity that is based on the truth of the abusive situation itself. Thus, even after the abuse has ended, the abuse itself so often dominates survivors' sense of self that every act they take simply cements the inescapable grip of the abuse in their life, more deeply forming it within the psyche. In other words, the *victims* of abuse can rebrand themselves as *survivors* of abuse, but cannot be fully free of the distortions: the abuse becomes a primary factor in the survivors' future willing, and in many cases they cannot truly transcend it.

Another dynamic of abuse that is salient to this study is the power of habituation to embed willing and to increase desire in certain directions. In manipulating the consent of victims through benefits and rewards, the abuser may incrementally increase the abuse or the severity of it, habituating the victim's acquiescence to it slowly and in careful steps. This gradual habituation—and the child's perceived acceptance of it—confuses the line between what is normal and what is abusive, to the point that the child can no longer clearly distinguish the two, and more corrosively, becomes removed from any criteria from which she or he could do so. Even when children reach the point when they desire the abuse to end, they have been conditioned to accept the abuse, and they may experience the compulsion to acquiesce to it based on their acquiescence to previous actions that do not seem qualitatively different. In their own minds, victims become "trapped in the trajectory" of their own choices, and they lose the psychological foothold from which they could resist the abuse (124).

From the perspective of the abusers, habituation in rehearsing fantasies of abuse can greatly increase their desire for the event to become reality. For those abusers who are sexually attracted to children, the imagining of particular sexual gratifications while masturbating can greatly enhance their desire to make these fantasies a reality. The focus and intensity of the marriage of internal fantasy and physical pleasure brings the desire to the fore of the imagination, and the habitual repetition of the act also has the effect of objectifying the children and dulling internal moral qualms that would inhibit abusers from acting upon the desire. It normalizes the act in the minds of the abusers and gradually reconfigures their conception of what is ultimately permissible and possible, while gradually dehumanizing the child at the center of the fantasy. Through the power of repeated habituation, abusers may, in their own minds, see their own sexual behavior as outside the realm of their active control, and that behavior takes on a momentum that they are powerless to stop themselves. In this way, the power of habituation within the mind of abusers is parallel to the victims' experience of habituation to actively agreeing to increased abuse. In both cases the actions and willing of the persons involved embed their willing in ways that they may feel unable to control.

CHAPTER 2

External Forces and the Contemporary Military Experience

> Now the earth was corrupt in God's sight, and the earth was filled with violence. And God saw that the earth was corrupt; for all flesh had corrupted its ways upon the earth.
>
> —GENESIS 6:11–12

As McFadyen articulates the specific ways in which powerful forces act to constrict willing in these two pathological situations, his conceptual vocabulary provides a means to identify the ways in which willing is similarly restricted in other situations. The way he describes the functionality of original sin, as fields of force that distort our active willing, is particularly powerful in depicting many of the forces that shape the environment and landscape of the modern battlefield. The distorting power of violence, I am arguing, cannot be understood in terms of modern moral constructs that hold individuals completely responsible for their actions; but as violence and its corruption tend to infect those who encounter them, it is necessary to take a much broader view of responsibility in order to attempt to describe it. It is important to note that what I am arguing here is that original sin provides a way of envisioning and naming the distortions that bind our willing in patterns that are ultimately harmful and, in this case, reflect our particularly violent participation in a violent world. Even if conflict is "necessary," then, using the conceptual framework of original sin, we can distinguish between something we deem "necessary" and something we deem "good." I am arguing, in essence, that we cannot participate in the force of violence in a way that is not deeply distorting and corrosive to our very being. In later chapters I will describe the ways in which violence metastasizes through the psyche of the military veteran and permeates our culture, and how "sin" is a powerful way to name this metastatic force.

In this chapter I will lay out the ways in which the fields of force that McFadyen describes are present in particular ways in the training of members of the military, their experiences of military life, and the pressures of the combat environment. Many of the ways in which McFadyen describes the sequestration of the will within Nazi killing units are relevant simply because there are significant commonalities in the nature, structure, and mission of most militaries.[1] Yet his emphasis on the ways that relationality is deeply distorted in situations of child abuse and the ways both the abuser and the victim become bound in secrecy is also a helpful lens through which to view the power of sin in the extreme violence of the battlefield.

It is worth reiterating here that, in naming these forces and suggesting the ways in which the willing of combatants is distorted and internalized, I am not attempting to demonstrate their guilt or ascribe blame to a group that does not usually receive it. My intention is quite the opposite. Like McFadyen (and Augustine before him), I am arguing against an interpretation of morality that assigns complete responsibility to any one person for his or her "sinful" actions. In demonstrating the power of external forces to distort the willing of combatants, I intend to highlight the pervasiveness of the sinful dynamic and the way combatants are enmeshed within deeply violent (and thus sinful) conditions and situations that have existed long before they were born. Indeed, I will seek to make it apparent that the forces acting upon combatants, while particularly acute and meaningful to them in the particular situation of combat, have roots and tendrils that stretch into the deepest parts of our cultural history and collective memory. I intend to illuminate the awe-inspiring power of sin and violence, as the distortion and misapprehension of what we *should* desire, to deform and bind the way we make the most basic decisions.

1. I am not suggesting a moral equivalence between the American (or any other) military and that of the Nazis. Doing so would, of course, be repugnant and horrendously disrespectful to the many members of the US military who serve incomparably more honorable and less totalitarian ideals than did those who served the Nazi regime. As McFadyen notes, there is a huge difference in affirming the universality of sin (we all are formed by and participate in sin) and the universality of sins (all sins are equal). The former is a corollary of original sin, whereas the latter clearly is not.

The Pressure of Combat on the Psyche

In his seminal work *On Killing*, US Army psychologist Dave Grossman advances a compelling theory about the human psyche in combat situations that is helpful to our understanding of how the force of violence binds the willing of combatants. He argues that human beings have, as an evolutionary trait, an innate revulsion toward the killing of other human beings. It is likely that this particular revulsion developed to give our species a greater chance of "winning" the evolutionary contest for long-term survival: the species that indiscriminately kills its own members seems to be at a significant evolutionary disadvantage. Accordingly, we experience a great deal of stress in situations where we are expected to kill other human beings—and where we encounter human beings willing to kill us. In light of this, what happens on the battlefield can be seen, in some ways, as a battle for the psyche of the combatants. Powerful pressures act on them in myriad ways, and combatants find themselves enmeshed in powerful force fields that bind their thinking and willing.

It is crucial for us to understand the injunction against killing that Grossman describes in order to grasp the context within which it was initially demonstrated, as well as the military response to that discovery. The central claim is that "there is within most men an intense resistance to killing their fellow man."[2] Contrary to popular belief, the immediate threat to one's own life—as well as the lives of one's comrades—is insufficient to motivate a soldier to kill: it is apparent that many combatants die on the battlefield before they are able to motivate themselves to kill another. As evidence for this claim, Grossman cites an astonishing example from the Civil War. Historian F. A. Lord has observed that "after the Battle of Gettysburg, 27,574 muskets were recovered from the battlefield. Of these, nearly 90 percent (twenty-four thousand) were loaded. Twelve thousand . . . were found to be loaded more than once, and six thousand . . . had from three to ten rounds loaded in the barrel" (22). The significance of this lies in the value of a loaded weapon on a black-powder-era battlefield: during that time, "more than 95 percent of the time was spent in loading the weapon, and less than 5 percent in firing it." It logically follows that "if soldiers

2. Grossman, *On Killing*, 4. Hereafter, page references to this work appear in parentheses within the text.

were desperately attempting to kill as quickly and efficiently as they could, 95 percent should have been shot with an empty weapon in their hand." This would mean that, of the 27,574 muskets found on the battlefield, only 1,379 should have been loaded; instead, 24,000 were found loaded. Furthermore, the fact that a soldier desperate to kill the enemy would have picked up any loaded weapon he could find to fire makes the abundance of loaded weapons discarded on the battlefield even more surprising. Grossman then comes to the uncontroversial conclusion "that most of these discarded weapons . . . represent soldiers who had been unable or unwilling to fire their weapons . . . and then had been killed, wounded, or routed" (22). He thus deduces that most soldiers were not actively attempting to kill the enemy: the evidence provided by the loaded muskets strongly suggests that most of them were simply rehearsing the actions expected of them without performing the crucial task of actually firing their weapons. Grossman concludes further that the majority of men who had previously carried these discarded muskets apparently wished to have nothing at all to do with the act of killing: "[They] appear to have not even wanted to fire in the enemy's general direction" (22).

This finding is by no means unique to the Civil War, since it appears to be consistent with the actions of soldiers almost a century later. S. L. A. Marshall, World War II historian and US Army brigadier general, conducted a study that concluded that "of every hundred men along the line of fire during the period of an encounter, an average of only 15 or 20 'would take any part with their weapons.' This was consistently true 'whether the action was spread over a day, or two days or three' " (22). What is remarkable here is that, given the nature of World War II equipment and engagements, an "encounter" for a soldier in this era would typically consist of considerably more intense enemy fire than a Civil War soldier would have experienced. Yet, even in extreme danger, 80 to 85 percent of soldiers with loaded weapons in hand refused to fire their weapons in an effort to eliminate that threat. Grossman contends that, despite the intensity and repetitive drill that soldiers received in weapons training during that era, "quietly, at the moment of decision . . . these soldiers found themselves to be conscientious objectors who were unable to kill their fellow man" (25). While he is uninterested in discovering exactly how and why this resistance to killing exists, he concludes that it is demonstrably present in the psyche as a "result of a powerful combination of instinctive, rational, environmental, hereditary, cultural and social factors" (39). It is the soldier's confrontation with this resistance within himself that produces the greatest stress on the battlefield.

This stress is manifest in two ways in this psychological resistance to killing: by the soldier's own revulsion at the thought of having to kill another person; and by the soldier's dread of facing an enemy who is willing to kill him. The issue revolves around the capacity to deny human status to the enemy "other," arguing that not only does the soldier "resist killing and the obligation to kill, but he is equally horrified by the inescapable fact that someone hates him and denies his humanity enough to kill him" (79). In naming these two ways the psyche experiences combat stress, Grossman identifies a major tension in the life of the combatant: he or she has a psychological posture, based in evolution, against killing other human beings, and dreads facing a determined enemy; yet the performance of his or her duty requires that he or she is able to both face and kill the enemy if necessary. This tension, while profound for the combatant, is a major dilemma for societies, governments, militaries, and even individual units that are called on to engage in combat. Many of the forces that distort the willing of combatants in combat are either direct outgrowths of the "irrational hatred" of those who set the injunction aside, or significantly act upon the combatants' default desire to avoid killing.

Habituation and Training

As early as the Korean War and the Vietnam War, governments began to take notice of the "problem" presented by large groups of non-firers and began making efforts to combat it. Because of the need to field effective armies that would be able to accomplish military objectives, militaries need to condition their combatants in very particular ways in order to produce warriors who will kill the enemy and will overcome their dread of those willing to kill *them*. This conditioning begins almost immediately and takes place throughout the whole training process. As Grossman contends, none of this conditioning is done in an overt or explicit way; rather, it is often found in the subtle (and sometimes not so subtle, yet "unofficial") ways officers conduct training. My own experience as an Air Force officer resonates with Grossman's claim that, while no military member—trainer or trainee—could or would testify that this form of conditioning was occurring, "from the standpoint of a psychologist who is also a historian and a career soldier, it has become increasingly obvious to me that this is exactly what has been achieved" (253).[3]

In basic training, one of the first things recruits encounter is a drill instructor screaming commands at them, often invading the recruits' personal space while assuming a threatening and demanding posture. Most recruits will "enjoy" this close attention of their drill instructor for several weeks as they adapt to the military environment and learn their chain of command; learn how to properly march; how to wear their uniforms and fire their weapons; and how to work as a group. The presence of someone who is constantly yelling, threatening, and berating the recruits obviously creates, by design, a stressful environment and teaches the recruits how to achieve tasks within this situation of prolonged stress. Its purpose is also more subtle: it implicitly inoculates recruits against a paralyzed reaction to an enemy's disinterested hatred of them. Recruits are faced with enemy combatants who appear to have no regard for them as human beings, and they are taught to despise the "enemy" despite knowing nothing about the enemies' life, history, or character. In this way, the "hatred" spewing out of the drill instructor—even though a façade—desensitizes the recruits to the dread of facing someone who despises them. Those who go through this training have been forced to perform their tasks while facing the dread of the instructor's attention and contempt, and by the end of training they are likely to have developed some way of dealing with it.

The process of desensitization is even more crucial in preparing combatants to overcome their inherent psychological revulsion against killing. Since the revulsion appears to be an evolutionary development that helps safeguard the life of the species as a whole by discouraging killing other members of the species, the measures the military uses act essentially to "short-circuit" the revulsion to killing by temporarily convincing the soldier that what he or she is doing is something other than killing another human being. The first method is a systemic dehumanization of the enemy by repeatedly identifying them with some form of slur. While seemingly simple, this has the effect of subtly defining the enemy as something other than human. It is an ancient practice. Many primitive tribes use the word in their language that translates as "man"

3. This section (through p. 47) demonstrates and integrates the arguments Grossman makes in greater detail in *On Killing* (250–55).

for the tribe itself, implicitly confirming the idea that those who fall outside of the tribal boundaries also fall outside the bounds of humanity and thus are subject to be hunted as any common beast. In common military parlance, the use of slurs such as "Krauts" or "Japs" accomplishes the same psychological task in the negative sense: we place those identified by such slurs outside the normative tribe of human beings and into the category of the "expendable other." In contemporary America, military officials who would acknowledge a training benefit of such slurs or condone their use would, of course, be excoriated and likely disciplined. In my own experience, the use of the term "haji"[4] for both enemy and civilian in the wars in Iraq and Afghanistan was simply an accepted part of the military lexicon. In my view, it often implied a far lower level of civilization and higher level of savagery compared to ourselves and our allies, and implicitly and explicitly disparaged those to whom it was applied.

A second way the military conditions its members to kill is through realistic training simulations. In these scenarios, the trainee shoots human-looking targets and becomes conditioned to watch them fall. Since the publication of *On Killing* in 1995, technology has advanced considerably, and the training scenarios used by the military have become more and more realistic. As the trainee repeats this realistic training, firing at human targets becomes instinctual: the effect of the training essentially serves as a conditioned response in which the action of firing becomes almost involuntary in response to a threat. For the trainee, the reward comes in the form of immediate feedback: the target falls (or, in more advanced simulations, an image or even an actor portraying the enemy falls to the ground wounded), and the trainee is praised for achieving high scores in the simulation. In psychologically remapping the firing of a weapon as a reflexive action, the training essentially bypasses the human instinct against killing. Amid the many euphemisms for attacking and killing (e.g., "engaging" and "neutralizing" one's enemy in pursuit of one's "objective"), the fact that one is actually killing another human being is driven from the front of the psyche. The decision to do so is effectively conditioned, in contrast to being a matter for consideration in a normal decision-making process.

With respect to McFadyen's notion of the distorting power of sin in binding the will, certainly this particular form of conditioning dis-

4. This term appears to have been somewhat oddly borrowed from its proper usage to identify those Muslims who are on their pilgrimage to Mecca.

tinctly narrows the horizons of choice of the trainees. In doing so, if we recall McFadyen's points of congruence between the pathologies of the Holocaust and child abuse, this conditioning subtly erects a barrier to a larger sense of meaning that transcends the situation. It does so seemingly by distraction: the larger concerns and debates of policy fade away as the intensity of training in very focused areas increases. While it would be improper to argue that the combatant is completely programmed to act in a certain way, the training conditions the choice the combatant makes until it is almost involuntary. It could be argued that the Pavlovian understanding of this stretches the limits of Augustine's and McFadyen's critical insistence that the will is still active in the process. Yet it should be noted that the combatants are still acting and making choices, even in the repeated training scenario: they are assessing the threats and acting, firing on the closer targets first, making immediate tactical decisions about when to reload and (in more complex exercises) larger operational decisions involving their unit and its specialized members. Their choices simply take place within the strict confines of the scenario. Much of the repetition of military training involves making simple actions almost instinctual in order to save one's conscious decision-making for tactical and operational decisions. For example, US Army Airborne training is relatively straightforward, as one learns to hook up a static line to a cable attached to an aircraft which automatically deploys one's parachute as one leaps from the plane. Yet trainees spend three weeks in Airborne school practicing the commands and simple actions involved so that, by the time they perform the jump out of an aircraft in real time, the actions are familiar and almost reflexive. Similarly, in more combat-focused scenarios, as trainees repeatedly move through it, the Pavlovian conditioning mechanism removes the decision ("Should I fire at my enemy?") from their conscious decision-making. Their willing is applied not to this decision but, as McFadyen notes with regard to the Nazi killing units, to efficacy. The trainees apply themselves to the speed with which to carry out their mission and "neutralize" the enemy effectively along the way.

In one sense, this desensitization and conditioning is similar to the normalization of killing that McFadyen describes taking place in the Nazi killing units. However, what is happening here is in many ways considerably deeper and perhaps even more troubling as it appears to happen at an almost subliminal level. Even when a trainee has completed a live-fire training scenario numerous times, no actual killing has taken place; thus, it cannot be argued that a horrific action is being normalized. The conditioned response that the scenario-specific firing drill inculcates bears striking resemblance to an extremely conditioned habit: the trainee is habituated through continual repetition to act in a particular way. The force of the habit bends the will of the actor in a particular direction; the Pavlovian concept here functions simply as a scientific analogy for the habituation's effectiveness. As McFadyen argues, the child abuser's will is sometimes bent in patterns by habituated fantasy, and he notes that the repeated imagining of a particular scenario (often paired in the case of the abuser with an autoerotic sexual release) increases the desire for the actual event imagined to come to fruition. Military training scenarios, certainly made increasingly realistic in both virtual and physical training environments, are little different when paired with the euphoric reward of doing well and receiving praise from one's superiors and increased status among one's peers.[5] These scenarios inculcate a strong desire in many soldiers to "get into the fight" and to do in reality what they have been trained to do. For example, as a Special Operations Weather Team officer in Afghanistan, I had several of my younger airmen repeatedly request to be placed with Army Special Forces teams that were experiencing consistent encounters with insurgents because they wanted to "get into the fight." These requests and the desire to be involved in active combat actually became a significant problem and often prevented them from properly carrying out their primary mission, which was to embed with the Army teams and send back weather data from the front. In this case, the continual habituation of training reshaped and formed the very desire of the airmen and thus formed the paths in which they sought to exercise their agency.

Obedience and Denial: The Sequestration of Personal Energy

While conditioning and habituation are powerful psychological forces on the battlefield, perhaps the most obvious force acting on the willing

5. The Army now often sends units to training in bases in the southwestern United States to "war-game" scenarios in an environment that most resembles the Middle Eastern areas to which they will be deployed. Units permanently stationed at these bases play the opposition forces in complex exercises designed to accommodate the units to battlefield conditions, actions, sights, and sounds.

of a soldier in the military setting is the human desire to obey. Stanley Milgram demonstrated the potency of obedience as a force over human willing via his experiments in the early 1960s, and his study adds significantly to the vocabulary and understanding of restricted willing. He powerfully demonstrated, via his experiments, that a figure of seemingly credible authority possesses a remarkable ability to influence a person to take a particular action, even when that action appears to harm—and even kill—another person.[6] Reflecting on his experiments and the postexperiment interviews that he conducted with his subjects, Milgram noted that, in situations where one is responding to the orders of an authority one judges to be legitimate, many subjects see themselves, not as individuals who are responsible for their own individual actions, but simply as willing agents of the responsible authority. In other words, people understood the responsibility for their own actions to rest with the experimenter rather than themselves. For Milgram, the fact that his subjects exhibited such a remarkable capacity to transfer their sense of responsibility onto the one conducting the experiment was the most profound aspect of the study. In part, he argues, this is an inevitable consequence of the move to a differentiated society: that is, part of moving to any hierarchy involves individuals relegating control to higher-level components. The behavior of individuals functioning in a hierarchical society is "modified in its functioning"—the suppression of individual direction and the acceptance of higher authority—in order to achieve a higher overall survivability for the larger group as a whole (131).

6. Stanley Milgram, *Obedience to Authority: An Experimental View* (New York: HarperCollins, 1974). (Hereafter, page references to this work appear in parentheses within the text.) Milgram set up an experiment in which a white-lab-coated experimenter would tell test subjects to shock a person in another room with increasing levels of electricity by pushing levers on a machine in front of them (marked with increasing voltage levels from left to right). While the "victim" in another room was an actor, and no actual shocks were administered, the persons doing the shocking believed that they were administering real shocks. What was a startling surprise, even to Milgram himself, was that the majority of subjects continued to obey the commands of the experimenter even to the point at which that person appeared to be unconscious—or even dead. While many people exhibited obvious signs of stress during the experiment, particularly when the victim begged them to stop and screamed and shrieked in pain (which the subject could hear), the vast majority of subjects continued to shock the "victim" with increasingly higher voltages (even ones marked "XXX" at the end of the scale) when the experimenter urged them to continue.

This evolution within human nature can be understood as the move from autonomous individual to hierarchical citizen: the "agentic" shift. This shift into an agentic state is characterized by the relegation of moral authority to another, so that "a person is in an agentic state when he defines himself in a social situation in a manner that renders him open to regulation by a person of higher status" (134). There are three primary factors that impact the agentic shift: the antecedent conditions that essentially prepare the individual's mind to accept this shift; the consequences of it in terms of how the individual's behavior and thought processes are altered; and the binding factors that hold a person in this state. The antecedent conditions primarily involve creation of the criteria for the legitimacy of the authority in the cultural consciousness. There does not appear to be a high psychological standard for individuals to perceive an authority as legitimate. Milgram notes that in the particular experiments he ran, a man in a white lab coat who sounded as if he understood his task was enough to convey a binding air of meaningful authority. More overt and outward markers—such as distinctive dress, uniforms, badges, and insignia of rank—signify and bolster the perception of authority that conditions individuals to accept their shift into an agentic state. Another primary antecedent condition is the level to which individuals understand themselves to be a part of the system itself. The more integrated and embedded within the system one feels, the higher the degree of obedience. Finally, a powerful component of the antecedent conditioning is the presence of an ideology that justifies the system and its authority, and the precise level to which the surrounding culture provides "the overarching ideological justification" for the authority system itself (142).

Within a conditioned authority structure, individuals can be shifted into an agentic state through the commands of individuals occupying higher positions. Within this state, several consequences are of interest to this study. First, within a powerful authority structure, the entire set of an individual's actions is contextualized by the presence of and interaction with the experimenter, and the individual becomes absorbed in the effort of carrying out the tasks in order to perform well and please the authority. The authority structure itself takes on a level of moral order, and thus the individual would deem the failure to perform the tasks a moral error. By far the most severe consequence is the loss of responsibility, since for individuals to understand themselves as accountable for their own actions, they have to understand that those actions have been effectively produced by their own will. The move to the agentic state disconnects individuals from this personal ownership of the actions they are ordered to perform and, further, it disrupts the internal process by which they assess their own behavior. If one has no actions that stem from the self, one cannot evaluate them within the confines of one's own moral code.

Once in the agentic state, a set of binding psychological factors hold the individual there. One of the primary forces is habit. Accordingly, during his experiments Milgram found that once initial instructions are given to the subject and the subject follows them, "the experimenter does not command the subject to initiate a new act but simply to continue doing what he is doing" (142). This certainly supports McFadyen's concept of habituated and normalized willing, in which it is far easier psychologically to perform even tasks one might initially consider morally suspect once one is accustomed to performing them. Milgram notes—again similar to what McFadyen observes—that once the subject has performed some actions, ceasing to perform similar actions in the future is tantamount to admitting that the previous actions were "bad." So there is a force that is somewhat akin to moral inertia built around the ego that prevents the individual from breaking from the agentic state. As a corollary, there is a sense of breaking a contract and commitment that would come when resisting the commands. If an individual had agreed to participate in an experiment, he or she would feel a considerable obligation to continue with it—even when he or she desired at some level to stop participating.[7] To break this contract would be to reject the authority of the system, and given the ideological support it is accorded, to do so would involve a significant rupture in the societal fabric.

The structure of the military presents an ideal authority structure for instilling obedience in its members (per Milgram's concept), and thus it inculcates obedience in its members in exceptionally powerful

7. This is a particularly interesting claim for Milgram to make, since he faced a great deal of ethical criticism on this exact point: that his subjects had *not* consented to participate in this particular kind of study, that they were there to participate in a study on memory. But this very fact stands as another remarkable support for Milgram's arguments because, despite the fact that the subjects did not fully understand the experiment they were committing to, the vast majority felt that, because they had agreed to participate in some study taking place here, they had ceded almost complete authority to the experimenter, even when the study took them in directions they did not appear to want to go.

ways.[8] In the United States, the military is perhaps the legitimate authority *par excellence* in terms of its level of prestige in American society, the commitment of its members, the ideology that surrounds it, and its compartmentalization of responsibility. Its members swear allegiance directly to the Constitution, the founding document that establishes and enshrines the US government, and they enjoy an almost mythic status among the American public. Although the military falls under the control and jurisdiction of the executive branch of government, its ultimate allegiance does not lie there, but to the Constitution itself and the ideals of goodness and democracy that come with it. Wars and those Americans who fight them hold a hallowed place within American history, as Stanley Hauerwas argues: "War is America's central liturgical act necessary to renew our sense that we are a nation unlike other nations."[9] Consistently, military members top surveys of American views of which professions contribute most to society and hold the highest ethical standards.[10] In addition, members of the military commit to the authority structure in ways that bind them to the system of authority

8. An argument could be made that this statement is tautological. Milgram set out to understand the behavior of the Nazis during the Holocaust, and so it could be argued that he entered the study with a strong bias in the direction of connecting authority structure with military organization. But as a counterpoint, Milgram conducted his studies in a laboratory setting and went through a great deal of variations in order to isolate the element of authority in the presence of the experimenter. He was surprised to find the power of the urge to obey to be as strong as it was, even in the variations that were manipulated to convey the least air of authority (the study took place in a shabby building in a blighted neighborhood, the experimenter acted with less precision, etc.). In surveys of his colleagues in psychology before he began his experiments, he asked them to predict how many people would follow the experiment to its end. They predicted that one person in one thousand would do so. Milgram repeatedly found that almost 60 percent of the subjects obeyed. In other words, if the power that an authority figure commands in these situations that involve minimal accouterments of authority and minimal commitment to the experiment (for $5 pay), then it is not a stretch to see that, in a situation of far more pressing, established, and legitimate authority—in which the individual is far more formally and psychologically committed to an organization that is valorized by the public—the power of obedience as a force cannot possibly be overstated.

9. Stanley Hauerwas, *War and the American Difference: Theological Reflections on Violence and National Identity* (Grand Rapids: Baker Academic, 2011), 4.

10. Pew Research Center, "Public Esteem for Military Still High," July 11, 2013, http://www.pewforum.org/2013/07/11/public-esteem-for-military-still-high/; and Gallup Polling, "Honesty/Ethics in Professions," accessed August 5, 2015, http://www.gallup.com/poll/1654/honesty-ethics-professions.aspx.

in almost absolute terms. They volunteer for military service, pledging themselves to the military enterprise even at the cost of their very lives. Once in that system, they have a clear place that is reinforced by the accouterments of their uniform and those of the other members, particularly those higher in the chain of command. Insignias of rank reinforce the particular position one occupies, and decorations and achievements that enhance prestige are noted with varying ribbons, patches, and badges. Within the military chain of command, one knows exactly the level of tasks that one is responsible for, the people one is responsible for, and the people one is responsible to. The military's setting of the antecedent conditions for a shift into the agentic state is very powerful.

The conditioning and normalization that Grossman describes, both in initial training and throughout firing drills, can be described as ways in which the experience of repetition and habituation bind the individuals into the agentic state. The social position the military occupies and the degree to which its members are inherently valorized as sacrificial protectors of democracy raise the moral consequence of disobedience to almost insurmountable levels within the closed system of the military organization. To exercise one's own conscience in disobedience is to risk the derisive scorn and moral judgment of the vast majority of American society.[11] In the heat of direct conflict, additional forces buttress the psychological desire to obey, since disobedience may be linked to a betrayal of one's friends and responsibility for any damage done or lives lost in the skirmish with the enemy. Even for the combatants whose circumstances permit the contemplation of nonobedience, there are several intertwined psychological levels of au-

11. A primary case in point is the saga of US Army Sgt. Bowe Bergdahl, who is widely believed to have voluntarily walked away from his duty station in the Patika Province of Afghanistan in 2009. According to him, his intention was to draw attention to ethical and leadership failures within his unit. He was captured by the Al-Haqqani network and held for five years before he was released in a prisoner swap in which the United States released five captives from the Guantanamo Bay Detention facility to authorities in Qatar. The Obama administration faced a great deal of criticism over the exchange, largely due to the prevailing opinion that Bergdahl was a deserter—and it is certainly undeniable that military members faced risks and that resources were spent in attempts to recover him. The implicit undercurrent in the criticism that the Obama administration faced was that Berghdahl was thus not worth saving. President Trump voiced exactly this view during both the 2016 Presidential campaign and his time in office.

thority and commitment that act as prohibitive forces. In their minds, to disobey a singular order also requires them to break their own sacred oath to the Constitution, which requires them to obey the lawful orders of those appointed over them. It also involves the violation of the legal contract that they signed upon enlisting or at commissioning.[12] In other words, the forces that create the profound conditions for the agentic shift within the structure of the military also bind the individual to obedience in a powerful way as they condition the dire social, legal, and moral consequences of disobedience.

The immensely powerful psychological and structural manifestation described above effectively demonstrates the way an individual's willing and moral energy are sequestered within a closed orbit. Similar to the situation of the Nazi killing units—and perhaps simply endemic to military organization in general—Milgram's experiment demonstrated the removal of personal responsibility for acts as a problematic consequence of formal structural authority. In terms of McFadyen's vocabulary, the power of the force of obedience here is that it erects a barrier to a sense of meaning outside the situation. As Milgram argues, the loss of responsibility for one's own actions coincides with an inability for authentic self-reflection and moral self-critique and correction. If none of one's actions emanate from the self, then certainly the capacity to make meaning of one's actions outside the closed orbit of the situation is virtually nonexistent. But, of course, willing is not inactive. As Milgram himself points out, his subjects often experienced great stress as they performed the task; yet they continued to do so at the urging of the experimenter.

The force of obedience, so potent in the military structure, is made up of what is perhaps the most Augustinian feature of distorted willing—the sequestering of the will at a moral level. In McFadyen's terms, the dynamic present in pathological situations confuses our understanding of what is real and of what is right or wrong. The forces that

12. It is worth noting that the United States military deeply instills in its members the notion that one cannot obey a direct order that is unlawful or immoral. Yet in practice, if one chooses to refuse a direct order, that refusal is likely to result in a court-martial or other disciplinary proceeding during which the burden of demonstrating that the order in question is immoral or illegal falls on the individual. The default position, in other words, is that the one giving orders is doing so properly. The system, then, serves to further suppress moral dissent and reinforce obedience as the cost of disobedience remains high.

Milgram identifies that are so potent in the US military structure bind the individual members of the military to the psychological notion that to disobey is to incur judgment, guilt, and blame. What is perhaps most relevant about Milgram's arguments—in conversation with McFadyen's analysis of willing in the Nazi killing units—is that the suppression of dissent and sequestration of moral energy in the structures of rigid authority is not limited to governments or societies with a totalitarian grasp. Even in a culture that prides itself on the freedom of ideas and representative access to governing power, the force of obedience restricts the moral horizon of its military members to a profound degree.[13]

Although military training is designed to condition combatants to kill and to overcome hatred, the actual act of killing is deeply traumatizing.[14] Recall that the dehumanizing use of slurs and the Pavlovian conditioning that occur in precombat training have the effect of essentially short-circuiting the decision-making process, of tricking the mind into thinking that it is *not* killing another person. In other words, they produce a profound psychological denial and are the two frontline defense mechanisms for the human psyche in combat situations. But Grossman argues convincingly that when these denial defense mechanisms fail, the psychic damage can be devastating.[15] The trauma experienced by those who have killed at close range (particularly with stabbing weapons or even bare hands) and are confronted with the humanity of the enemy most directly are thus most likely to experience psychic injury, while those who have killed from a great distance (as a bomber pilot dropping ordnance from 10,000 feet) can more easily escape the psychological confrontation. Many soldiers are overwhelmed by guilt, and quite a few veterans have described the crushing (and sometimes very

13. In the next chapter I will explore several cases that demonstrate the inability of military members to resist the force of obedience in the killing of civilians in Vietnam, Korea, Afghanistan, and Iraq.

14. This section integrates the argument Grossman makes in *On Killing* (250–55) about denial defense mechanisms with his collection of statements of veterans (114–19) and the overall trajectory of his argument about trauma and the range of killing (97–114).

15. Grossman does distinguish between the trauma suffered by someone who has killed at extremely close range and the trauma of one who has killed at a great distance. The underlying cause, Grossman argues, is that the soldier who kills at close range has a far more difficult time denying the humanity of his enemy than the airman who drops a bomb and never has to witness its results. The level of trauma increases as the killing range decreases (107–37).

gradual) realization that the people they had killed were, in so many ways, "just like them."

Once the combatant has killed, the soldier's unit often functions as a post facto denial defense mechanism. In many ways, the level of psychic damage soldiers experience is determined not only by the distance they are able to achieve between themselves and their victims, but by the level of social support they receive from the group around them (the inside group) and society at large (the outside group). Part of the strength of a military unit is its ability to absolve the specific actions of the individual into the group: guilt and shame, rather than being experienced individually, are diffused into the group identity.[16] The close identification with the cause of the group insulates individuals from direct responsibility and the crushing individuated realization that they themselves have killed. In similar fashion, the support veterans receive from the civilian populace can mediate the traumatic experience. The generally positive reception that World War II veterans received likely had an ameliorating effect on their trauma, while the generally negative reception that Vietnam veterans received likely aggravated theirs.[17] The relationship here is complex, since it is not simply a "positive" reception by society that makes a difference, but a positive predisposition that allows veterans to explore their experiences in the context of those who care and value them enough to allow it.

Yet the return home is often a difficult experience for veterans, particularly as society at large and the specific groups of family and friends cannot replicate the support and absolution the veterans received from their unit. The denial-defense mechanism of the unit dynamic may continue to provide the psychological benefit of the diffused sense of guilt and shame, even though the unit's members may be physically scattered for some time, if the vet manages to stay close to the surviving members of the group as time passes. Yet the friends and family closest to the vet, mirroring forces and trends in society at large, will likely praise their loved one effusively and shower him or her with expressions of pride and gratitude. Unfortunately, this often creates a profound barrier to positive relationships, since their expressions of pride in and

16. Grossman, *On Killing*, 152. This sense of shame and its diffusion resonates with Milgram's understanding of differed responsibility through the military hierarchical structure.

17. A larger point that Grossman makes in *On Killing* (254–57).

valorization of the veteran's efforts often contrast starkly with the moral ambiguity and sense of guilt and shame experienced by the veteran who has killed. This contrast and psychological barrier make it significantly more difficult for veterans to explore their moral ambiguity with those around them and share their experiences and testimony in a healing way with others who may help them bear the moral burdens of guilt and shame. Many veterans thus sink into a difficult psychological isolation, deeply troubled by their own experiences but unwilling to upset the valorized image others hold of them, perhaps because the valorization from others is evidence that they do not understand the moral universe of combat and cannot possibly help.

The way the veterans' feelings of guilt and shame bind them to a unit in order to diffuse the sense of responsibility, while isolating them in secrecy from the larger society, bears a remarkable resemblance to McFadyen's analysis of the way an abused child becomes trapped into isolation and secrecy. The veteran cannot be fully absolved from the act of killing, since his will is, of course, active; but, as I have argued in earlier sections, the act itself is conditioned and the combatant's desire is distorted by profound forces that act on the psyche. Combatants' views of relationality in general are greatly deformed by the entire process that leads them to kill: the dehumanization and conditioning in training; the forces of hatred that further harden the perception of the "other"; and, once they have killed, their isolation from healthy relationships and paths to healing because of their own guilt and shame.

CHAPTER 3

The Dichotomous American Experience of Violence

> The LORD said to Cain, "Why are you angry, and why has your countenance fallen? If you do well, will you not be accepted? And if you do not do well, sin is lurking at the door; its desire is for you, but you must master it." Cain said to his brother Abel, "Let us go out to the field." And when they were in the field, Cain rose up against his brother Abel, and killed him.
>
> —GENESIS 4:6–8

The first mention of "sin" in Genesis is intimately connected with its narrative of fledgling humanity's first act of explicit violence: Cain's murder of Abel. The story of the Fall one chapter earlier certainly describes the initial break from a unified and "righteous" existence with God; but in the primordial narrative it is violence that becomes the explicit problem that grows out of this condition of a broken relationship with the divine. God explicitly tells Noah, "I have determined to make an end of all flesh, for the earth is filled with violence because of them; now I am going to destroy them along with the earth" (Gen. 6:13). Sin and violence share an intimate linkage, but significantly, they are not synonymous: violence in the narrative is the primary and most problematic manifestation of the condition of sin. God regrets that humanity's thoughts are "evil continually," and ultimately he grieves that he created humanity on account of its "wickedness" (Gen. 6:5). From this evil, wicked (sinful) condition arises the problem that the world has become "filled with violence." What has gone wrong is most evident in violence that threatens to spiral out of control. For Cain's murder of Abel, his punishment includes a hard life of toil, but with the Lord's guarantee that he will not be harmed, and that a sevenfold vengeance will befall his attacker. Four generations later, people are using the Lord's promise to Cain to commit violence with seeming impunity: Lamech boasts of his murder of an unnamed "young man" on the basis that he enjoys a similar yet tenfold greater divine guarantee from harm. It is because of this increasingly violent wrongness that God vows to "wipe the slate clean" and begin again with Noah and his family.

Far removed from the primordial narrative in Genesis and its direct linkage between sin and violence, the meaning of violence in our own American context is contested in the public sphere.[1] Where there is a multiplicity of differing positions on—and experiences of—violence in our culture, I will argue here that there are two primary *experiences* of military violence that are radically divergent and form a sharp epistemological dichotomy. First, in the national narrative that is ubiquitous in American politics, culture, and conceptual vocabulary, violence is a force that has been harnessed and yoked in the service of the American enterprise. If this is so, one could easily argue that the forces of obedience and conditioning that I have described in the preceding chapter certainly bind the willing of combatants, but do so in the pursuit of a "greater good" that is truly a "good." The second experience of violence is the experience of those who actually engage in violence on behalf of the nation—that is, its combatants.[2] Their testimonies often exhibit a distinctly different experience that challenges any notion that violence is a domesticated force. The trauma experienced by many of those who have killed in combat, as well as those who experience in varying degrees the psychological torment of the combat environment, strongly testifies that violence is pathogenic and toxic, and has second- and third-order effects that cannot be predicted, let alone controlled. Trauma testifies that violence serves no particular good, but simply intensifies, distorts, and propagates the sinful condition.

1. This claim is, of course, linked only to the early narrative in Genesis. Clearly, Scripture—from Genesis to Revelation—contains myriad axiological positions on violence itself, ranging from explicit connection to sin (and thus condemnation) to reluctant acceptance to holy act.

2. Certainly, combatants themselves have widely differing experiences of violence and even wider ranges of reflections upon it. I do not intend to generalize all veterans or combatants under one particular view of their own actions—this would be highly offensive and, perhaps more critically, deeply disingenuous. Rather, it is my intention to demonstrate that the experience of a great many war veterans is distinctly different from that of the American populace.

Something that is pathological, by definition, is something that exhibits a wrongness, a malformation, an abnormality that is usually related to suffering. Throughout this study I argue that original sin provides a compelling framework within which to describe how, at its roots, the violence of combat is a potent pathological force that arises from a sinful condition and propagates that condition in a unique way. Trauma is an important indicator: it identifies something pathological that has gone profoundly wrong in the fabric of the human experience. While trauma is horrendous—markedly destructive and disfiguring, corrosive and meaning-killing—it is also, in this case, revealing: it unmasks violence as a double-edged sword, an unwieldy thing that damages victim, perpetrator, and bystander.

In light of the revelatory aspect of combat trauma, it is my argument that the contesting over the meaning of violence is not one between two truths, but between truth and falsehood. Whereas the veteran experiences violence in an immediate and firsthand way, the general populace experiences it, if at all, at a great physical and psychological distance. This distance and the comfort it provides (the average citizen does not have to engage in the extreme violence of combat or its distinctive dread, and thus avoids them) permit violence to be examined from without and allow its seductive and distorting character to be masked in political and religious ideologies and, most powerfully, in the ways those ideologies coalesce into nationalistic narratives.[3] The experience of trauma unmasks the national narrative as one that is based on a construction of goodness that is false and illusory. I will argue that an Augustinian conception of the perversion of desire is helpful in unmasking the falsehood of the national narrative of exemplary violence in service to the American enterprise.

American Exceptionalism and the Other

An underlying and tacit approval for violence in service to the American enterprise permeates the collective history and culture of American society. In the grand narrative of the United States, military violence is

3. It is not my intention here to minimize the threat of violence that many in our society face daily, but to highlight our loss of memory of the experience of this particular kind of extreme violence.

seen as a tool that can be, and indeed has often been, used in faithful service—both to America's defense and to its larger democratic and civilizing mission. This is not to say that the society is or has ever been univocal in support of military violence: in times of conflict, there have almost always been dissenting voices that opposed military action. Yet the dominant narrative in American culture has been, and continues to be, that America has been granted a unique position in the world, which is to protect and further democracy and the best aspects of civilization. Therefore, it has a moral duty, not only to protect itself and its interests as the bearer of the goods of history and civilization, but also the duty to combat uncivilized behavior as a matter of principle. Our country's history has a certain mythos woven into it that reflects these claims: its very founding is a narrative of an oppressed people throwing off the yoke of the tyrannical British monarch King George III in the conflict we recognize as the War of Independence (or Revolutionary War). The moral mettle of the United States as a whole to withstand the evils of slavery was tested and proven in the crucible of violence that was the Civil War. In World War II, the United States stood with the Allies against the horrendous evils of Nazi Germany and imperial Japan—and perhaps saved the world from totalitarian rule. A major thread of the narrative is that military violence has created a more secure and safe world and has protected the interests and security of the citizens of the United States of America.

The tacit approval of this narrative is perhaps best seen in the public's overwhelming support (at least at the onset of hostilities) for every American conflict in the twentieth century and beyond. As polling numbers indicate, initial support for each of the conflicts was extraordinarily high: for example, public support for World War II was initially around a breathtaking 97 percent of the populace.[4] The wars in Korea and Iraq both enjoyed an initial public approval rating of around 75 percent, and

4. David W. Moore, "Support for War on Terrorism Rivals Support for WWII," Gallup News Service, October 3, 2001, http://www.gallup.com/poll/4954/support-war-terrorism-rivals-support-wwii.aspx. Gallup did not begin extensive polling until the mid-1930s, so no specific data exists on the public's support of World War I, though it is noteworthy that during World War II, 62 percent of the public still viewed the first war favorably. Given the general pattern of waning support for a conflict and the obvious (by the 1940s) failure of the Treaty of Versailles to stabilize Europe at that conflict's close, it appears safe to conclude that the public's initial support of the war would be consonant with the general pattern evinced in later twentieth-century conflicts.

the post–9/11 war with Afghanistan achieved around 90 percent public support—approaching World War II levels in terms of initial approval. Even during the Vietnam War, which was well known for the strength and radicality of movement against it within the American public, initial public support hovered around 75 percent.[5] While support for every conflict since World War II has waned conspicuously as the conflict progressed in a fairly consistent pattern, it is safe to say that, no matter what causes the American public to sour on any particular conflict during its execution, it does not seem to have a significant impact on support for the next one.

While support for the conflicts tends to wane as time passes, support for the military institution in the public eye does not. As I noted in the preceding chapter, the US military and its members are almost always viewed as the most ethical professionals in society and are deeply admired within our culture. Veterans who have served in particular conflicts are valorized and deeply honored in numerous books and films, in the rhetoric of politicians, and at major sporting events. The experience of war for the vast majority of the American public is contained in these narratives and the publicly sanctioned experiences of swelling pride in the valor of our veterans.[6] They consume the films and stories, and they internalize the messages they contain. The language these narratives use conveys the sense that America is an exceptional place that is forced to use violence in order to achieve greater levels of civilization and general "good" in the world.

The continued support of military endeavors has attained a certain cultural inertia over the history of the United States. Stanley Hauerwas argues that, as the nation puts considerable stock in proving its cultural and moral mettle in war, each new conflict serves as a way to validate the former conflicts and the national narrative as a whole. Those who choose not to engage in the conflict—or who oppose it when politicians make an appeal to the mission of the United States and the grand democratic, civilizing enterprise—are perceived as dishonoring those who have previously fought and sacrificed, and that would seem to risk the collapse of the whole narrative. Based on this, the American system of

5. Moore, "Support for War on Terrorism." Although pinpointing "the beginning" of the Vietnam conflict is a murky endeavor, I am, for the sake of simplicity, referring to a 1965 Gallup poll taken in the immediate aftermath of the arrival in Vietnam of the majority of primary American combat forces of 184,000 troops.

6. Whose valor and bravery I am in no way questioning.

war and the sacrifice of its heroic combatants "is crucial for the renewal of the moral commitments that constitute our lives."[7] Those who fight in contemporary conflicts do so in part to honor the sacrifices of those who have fought in previous conflicts, and thus continue to give those conflicts meaning. Hauerwas compellingly argues that to break the course of events would be to undermine the narrative that powerfully undergirds our sense of morality, honor, and goodness. The greatest speeches from wartime presidents—Franklin D. Roosevelt, Abraham Lincoln, and George W. Bush—all heavily invoke the honor of the American enterprise through the memory of the cherished past and its brave citizen-soldiers. In reminding the present generation of the sacrifices of those who have gone before them, these leaders are reminding them of their duty to preserve the honor and tradition of their forefathers. The meaning of the enterprise—past, present, and future—rests on them, and it becomes a moral duty for them not to allow the past to fall into meaninglessness.

A crucial aspect of the cultural experience and consideration of violence is that it is used in response to political and existential *threat*. The violence of our military saves and safeguards the nation against the dangers posed by these threats, and this redemptive violence is often performed not only on behalf of the United States, but for the good of all peoples. The Native Americans and their "savagery" constituted a threat to the colonists and eventually to civilization at large. The Revolutionary War was fought on the basis of unjust political treatment of the colonists at the hands of the British—and the threat of this injustice continuing in perpetuity. The threat of the continued practice of slavery and the dissolution of the United States was met with the violence of the Civil War, which ended slavery and restored the union. The Nazi menace threatened the entire world, and the world was saved by the Allied victory. The threat of nuclear annihilation in the cold war was met by our own preparation to annihilate the Soviet Union—an interesting approach that was known as "Mutually Assured Destruction." And today, under the shadowy threat of Islamic terrorism, the War on Terror is justified in order to protect civilian lives and our very political system.

It is instructive that violence, in this narrative, is carried out in response to the threat that we deeply fear. Rowan Williams argues that the "contemporary fantasy world" of American cinema tells us a great deal

7. Hauerwas, *War and the American Difference*, xv.

about our own attitudes toward fear, violence, and the world outside ourselves. Films, particularly those we go to see in order to experience fear, can be the projections of our deeper views of violence and destruction. Williams argues that, on the basis of his analysis of movie trends, they convey the ubiquity and randomness of suffering and death.[8] In the most notable part of his argument, he makes the powerful claim that the popularity of certain cinematic tropes reveals that, against this unpredictable threat, we accept and are willing to commit a violent response without any reservations about the way we conduct it. This unreserved violence is necessitated because it is directed against those who threaten us absolutely and essentially, and thus are not moral beings whose behavior could be understood as rational and thus predicted and considered. Instead, Williams argues, it is revealing that we view that violence done in response to threat as essentially amoral, since it has nothing to do with choices and calculated decisions but is simply a necessity, even an animalistic and primal response. In these films, it is crucial that violence never originates within the protagonist (within ourselves), but comes from some nondescript and terrifying outside entity. In other words, the cinematic trends can be understood to reveal our deep-seated belief that violence resides initially in the "other," and since this other poses such a dreadful threat, we are ready to use whatever means are necessary to annihilate it.

This larger national narrative of necessary and redemptive violence is psychologically reinforced through both a subtle and powerful cultural justification *and* a physical and emotional distancing from wartime violence itself.[9] In *The Deaths of Others: The Fate of Civilians in America's Wars*, John Tirman argues compellingly that the factors mentioned by Williams and Hauerwas coalesce into a metanarrative that provides the tacit cultural justification for military violence. Tirman's explicit task is to find out why the American public shows a profound indifference to the high number of civilian casualties in US conflicts. He finds the apathy expressed "puzzling" in light of the "dominant cul-

8. Rowan Williams, *The Truce of God* (Grand Rapids: Eerdmans, 2005), 8. This paragraph contains summations of his argument from pp. 8–10 about the moral nature of our views of the violence we commit when confronted with what we view as existential threats.

9. In truth, a great many forces weave the narrative of American exceptionalism together. I will focus on the two most powerful factors that seem to inhibit critical reflection on this narrative.

tural influence" of Christian ethos and the ubiquity of "Jesus's teachings about compassion" in American society.[10] In answer to this, he argues that the "frontier myth," a deeply embedded cultural narrative of American strength and exceptionalism, holds psychological power to explain this overwhelming public apathy toward the deaths of millions of foreign civilians. At the heart of the frontier myth is the encounter between "civilized" and "civilizing" humanity and "savage" and "natural" humanity—those that come to constitute the ultimate *other*. A primary aspect of the power of the frontier myth is that it continually focuses our collective attention on the problem and threat posed by this "other," tacitly downplaying or denying any harmful effects from the destruction of the "other." The myth itself effectively imposes a dehumanizing definition of the "other," a definition—in word and in deed—containing the implicit assertion that the "other" is, in critical ways, *not like us*. Consequently, it not only prevents the public (who receive this communication within the framework of the larger frontier myth) from recognizing even a degree of humanity in the "savage," but it creates an emotional and even ontological distance that prevents the public from viewing their slaughter with any degree of sympathy. It is hence impossible to view their suffering as a window into the "civilized" human's own vulnerability.

The primary function of the myth in the American psyche, Tirman argues, is to provide a de facto justification for "total war" strategies that result (both intentionally and unintentionally) in large civilian casualties—the deaths of "others" (4).[11] The primordial fear of the demonic "others" who oppose civilization and threaten the very values that lie at the heart of the American enterprise is a trope evoked continually in American history by its leaders. It is evident in the first European settlers who found themselves in conflict with the Native Americans, who were always portrayed in colonial accounts of the "Indian wars" as responsible for a level of savagery that was foreign to the

10. John Tirman, *The Deaths of Others: The Fate of Civilians in America's Wars* (New York: Oxford University Press, 2011), 14. Hereafter, page references to this work appear in parentheses within the text and notes.

11. This section largely draws on Tirman's discussion of the concept of the "other" in American history (*The Deaths of Others*, 19–30). Tirman particularly highlights the "bestial" (23) status of the Narragansetts in the colonial accounts in a way that resonates with Grossman's notation about primitive tribes and their endogamous boundaries for humanity itself.

colonists. Yet these early conflicts resulted most often in the complete extermination of the Native American tribe at the hands of the Europeans—rarely the other way around (21).[12] The dehumanization of the Native American tribes is evident in both the language used to describe them and the treatment they received. In 1637, for example, Roger Williams described the Narragansetts, with whom the English were previously allied, as "barbarous men of blood who are as justly to be repelled and subdued as wolves that assault the sheep" following several incidents with the tribe (23). The accompanying action demonstrated the "bestial" status the colonists assigned to the Narragansett people. The English subsequently attacked the tribe and killed everyone they found in the community, regardless of age. The attitudes that are reflected in the colonial accounts of violence with Native Americans carry forward in American history as justifications for horrendous atrocities. Such attitudes, appealing to racial differences, ethno-nationalistic views, and religious identities, were common all the way through the North American wars of the nineteenth century. US militia committed brutal sexual assaults on Mexican women during the Spanish-American War, and during the "Civil" War, the Confederacy would, as a matter of policy, slaughter black soldiers whenever they encountered them, whether as active combatants or prisoners. This pattern persisted in the seventeenth, eighteenth, and nineteenth centuries as the United States expanded to the Pacific Ocean, continually "pacifying" the "savage" through conquest. The summarily malevolent and morally savage status accorded to the "Indian" was simply a given: it never saw scrutiny from colonial leaders. In other words, the "other" encountered in the wilderness bore absolutely no human relation to any recognizable version of "us."

With the closure of the American frontier at the turn of the twentieth century—by the time the memory of the continental wars had faded and the United States found itself involved in conflicts on a more global scale—a new "other" quickly rose to reinforce the frontier myth: the

12. This comment should be understood in terms of large-scale conflict with Native American groups. It is certainly true that in early conflicts, colonial villages and settlements were destroyed and their populations slaughtered. As Tirman argues, the "frontier myth" was forged in these "Indian wars," and colonial military tactics were influenced in significant ways. For an excellent discussion of the idea of the development of "savagery" in this context, see Jill Lepore's *The Name of War: King Philip's War and the Origins of American Identity* (New York: Vintage Books, 1998).

communist.[13] The "red scare" of the 1950s exhibited a new variety of "othering" than what had occurred previously in the development of the American mythology. First, the advent of nuclear weapons had raised the stakes of the conflict significantly, and the imminent threat of another war so quickly after the destruction wrought by World War II fed into the fear of the new communist "other." Though the phrase had no doubt been uttered thousands of times in order to justify conflicts throughout history, it could be said for the first time that in reality civilization itself was at stake: both the United States and the Soviet Union possessed the capability of annihilating the industrialized world in a nuclear holocaust. Second, since the United States and the communist "other" in the Soviet Union were a great geographical distance from each other, the hunt for the other was turned inward on American society. A great multitude of the populace believed that American policy was catastrophically impotent in light of the Soviet threat because of the intentional sabotage committed by communists within American society. The mysterious and insidious "other" now had to be rooted out of the American society like a malignant tumor. Catholic televangelist Bishop Sheen claimed that communism was "intrinsically evil"; the infamous Joe McCarthy deemed the communists living secretly in America to be "treacherous" (63).

The secret communist "others" looked like Americans, appeared to participate in American life and in the building of American society; but at the same time they were fundamentally *not like us.* All of the seeming affinities the secret "others" shared with us were merely a façade; the ideological difference presented the "other" with an identity fundamentally different from ours. This secret, evil identity was who they really were. The powerful ideology of the frontier myth and its unwavering American exceptionalism here provides an ability to understand any perceived affinity with an accused communist as false and traitorous to the uncritical goodness of the American enterprise. In essence, even if one's best friend were a secret communist, who would one day be exposed (accused) as such, the identity of the "other" had been so firmly established in the collective psyche that one was able to nullify

13. In this section I am drawing on Tirman's discussion of communism and McCarthyism and how the idea of the "other" in the frontier myth carries over into this era. Tirman notes how the stereotypical "communist" was portrayed in the same terms as Native Americans were in the frontier myth, both in terms of "savagery" (61), and even as a "heinous race" (63).

the relationship as "false" and thereby deny the "other's" humanity and similarity.

At the turn of the twenty-first century, of course, the enemy "other" became the Islamic terrorist. What Tirman's frontier myth continually provides in its ever-evolving state in American society through its conception of the enemy "other" is essentially a profound way to deny that the encounter with the "other" is an encounter with a fellow human being at all. The demonization inherent in the language about the "other" gives them a subhuman status and creates a great emotional distance between the faraway victim and Americans living their lives. It is exemplified in oft-repeated phrases about war that describe how the enemy "other" "only understands the language of violence" and "will hate us no matter what we do." Against such existential threats, there is but one answer: the absolute destruction of what seeks in its very essence to destroy us. When conflict has been culturally painted in these terms, the wars America fights are essential conflicts: our enemies are the enemies of civilization, order, and goodness. The violence that we use against them becomes not only necessary but perhaps even obligatory when moral values are cast in these terms. American military action is hence continually justified in the name of the singularly unique civilizing enterprise that benefits not only the United States, but the world at large.[14]

The cultural myth of American exceptionalism and redemptive violence that Tirman conceptually explores enjoys a sense of hegemony because of the physical distance of combat, both in our present-day reality and in our cultural memory. In *On Killing*, Grossman argues that the level of trauma associated with extreme violence—particularly killing—is inversely proportional to the distance from which the violence is done. The same principle applies to societal views of violence: our physical distance permits us to make meaning of it and to further distance ourselves from it psychologically. America's physical distance from battles is fairly obvious: the last time ground conflict took place on American soil was in 1865. Directly to the point, then, none of us wit-

14. It should be noted that the critique of this myth that follows is not predicated on the idea that its claim of existential threat to the United States is *always* incorrect or an exaggeration. Certainly, it is difficult to argue that the Nazis in World War II and the Soviet Union in the Cold War did not constitute real, existential threats to the US. Rather, as will become clear, a significant part of the problem is that the myth's pervasiveness reveals our ease in casting far lesser conflicts in these terms and can lead us to respond with extraordinary violence.

ness the reality of combat, suffering, and death in our own backyards. Moreover, the experiences of those who did is now lost to our collective cultural memory, since the very last of those citizens died over fifty years ago. While many veterans carry the weight of combat experience, the distant nature of those events allows the greater public to compartmentalize it: they can accept combat violence without imagining it spilling over into their homes, taking the lives of their sons and daughters. The loss of the personal and cultural memory of battlefield violence leaves little experiential weight to provide a counterbalance to the historical, social, and ideological forces that seek to define violence by way of a greater national narrative.

Combat Trauma and the Disintegration of the National Narrative

Soldiers, of course, experience violence, not at a physical or psychological distance, but as an imminent physical and psychological reality that defines their experience of the world in the combat zone. The violence they encounter resonates deeply in the psyche, and those who deal with it in the most acute ways—directly killing the enemy at close range—often experience immediate trauma, revulsion, and guilt. In light of the visceral reality of killing and the experienced reality of life in a combat zone, the carefully constructed, conditioned, and rationalized frameworks of meaning that are intended to carry the psychological heft of participation in conflict often collapse immediately. Those who participate in killing in a less direct way may experience a slower breakdown of the framework and experience a more diffuse moral ambiguity. Yet the sheer number of veterans who experience significant psychological injury suggests that few who experience the reality of killing and wartime violence walk away physically and psychologically "unscathed."[15]

15. This is not to say that there are no "positive" psychological phenomena that surround the military and the combat environment. Certainly, combatants often find themselves bonded together in a brotherhood that becomes a source of lifelong fulfillment. There can be a sense of accomplishment and achievement in attaining rank, certifications, and status. Yet, as is indicated by the number of cases of PTSD and the current rate of veteran suicide (22 per day in the US), it is apparent that these psychological benefits are counterbalanced by the traumatic damage experienced in combat.

Their proximity to violence means that combatants encounter it in a direct, immediate, and visceral way. The soldiers, sailors, airmen, and Marines that are the implements of American policy actively flip the switches, push the buttons, and pull the triggers that launch bombs, missiles, and bullets at the enemy. They witness the enemy buildings exploding and the bodies torn apart by bombs and bullets. They see the blood and carnage that results, and they hear the accompanying human reactions—screams of terror, pain, agony, and loss. In short, they witness the results of their own violent actions. Of course, those involved in intense combat also experience the impact of violence against themselves: the wounds and death that are the results of the enemy's improvised explosive devices (IEDs), bullets, and bombs. The extremely stressful nature of these experiences of death, pain, and fear in turn trigger profound physiological responses in the body. The endocrine system floods the body with adrenaline, and the combatant experiences what many of us do in stressful situations—increased heartrate, rapid breathing, a feeling of increased awareness and mental acuity, and so forth. Yet the extreme, life-or-death nature of these experiences triggers a more significant "fight or flight" response in which every bit of energy is made available toward the goal of survival. Grossman describes the severity of the process that often shuts down "nonessential activities such as digestion, bladder control, and sphincter control" and causes uncontrolled "stress diarrhea" and urination.[16] After the threat has passed, the body essentially experiences an adrenaline backlash: the "neglected demands" of the other bodily functions assert themselves, and the combatant feels an immense exhaustion and weariness.

While the human body is able to adapt to survive in this way, continuous and repeated cycles of exposure to this level of existential stress are debilitating to both the mind and body. It appears that human beings simply are not psychologically equipped to handle the stresses of battle for long periods of time. In a study of World War II soldiers, neurologists Roy Swank and Walter Marchand concluded that "after 60 days of continuous combat, 98 percent of all surviving soldiers become psychiatric casualties of one kind or another."[17] More recent studies have revealed that "excessive arousal" and periods of extreme adrenaline rushes and the subsequent system crashes can "promote physical

16. Grossman, *On Killing*, 70.
17. Grossman, *On Killing*, 43–44.

damage to certain neurons in the brain," with the result that the tissue of the brain can actually degenerate, affecting the mind's ability to make effective decisions in even mundane situations and its ability to properly process memories.[18] The survival mechanism of arousal in response to threat becomes literally toxic to the body. Grossman notes that, with increasing advances in technology, weaponry, and logistics, we have completely outpaced our physiological ability to handle the accompanying stress. Military historian Richard Gabriel similarly notes that "we have reached a point where almost everyone exposed to combat will, within a comparatively short period of time, be killed, wounded, or driven mad."[19] The psychological stress of conflict, despite the increase of distanced or "stand-off" weapons, continues to increase with the increased lethality of modern combat, as combatants are repeatedly exposed to situations of intense stress and arousal for longer periods of time.

In addition to the physiological-psychological stresses of contemporary warfare, the combatant experiences a psychological stress that manifests itself in moral terms. As I noted earlier, Grossman argues that within each human being there is a deep-seated psychological injunction against killing his or her fellow human beings, particularly at close range. When, as a result of careful conditioning and training processes, one overcomes the injunction and kills another person, one experiences significant psychological consequences almost immediately. While some combatants do experience the triumphant exuberance one would expect from the national narrative, numerous interviews with frontline soldiers in various conflicts attest to the immediate sense of guilt and regret that often accompanies the act of killing.[20] A British World War I veteran who had just killed his first enemy soldier testified,

18. William P. Nash, "Combat/Operational Stress Adaptations and Injuries," in *Combat Stress Injury: Theory, Research, and Management*, ed. Charles R. Figley and William P. Nash (New York: Routledge, 2007), 53. I will draw on Nash's larger points in this article in several places in this section.

19. Richard Gabriel, *No More Heroes: Madness and Psychiatry in War* (New York: Hill and Wang, 1987), 43–44.

20. Grossman, *On Killing*, 235. Grossman argues that, even in those soldiers that experience "the thrill of killing," the overwhelming majority of those who kill, particularly at close range, move to a response stage of remorse after the euphoria is gone and the war ends. Those who never move into a state of remorse after killing at close range he categorizes as the 2 percent who are immune to psychiatric casualty in combat because they are sociopathic and physically lack the capacity for empathy.

"When things quieted down I went and looked at a German I knew I had shot. I remember thinking that he looked old enough to have a family and I felt very sorry." A US Army Special Forces veteran describes an episode in Vietnam in which he encountered a young combatant:

> And I froze, 'cos it was a boy, I would say between the ages of twelve and fourteen. When he turned at me and looked, all of a sudden he turned his whole body and pointed his automatic weapon at me, I just opened up, fired the whole twenty rounds right at the kid, and he just laid there. I dropped my weapon and cried.[21]

The immediate sense of revulsion is often expressed viscerally and physiologically; numerous veterans articulate how they vomited just moments after killing an enemy. These reactions testify to the horror of the act of killing itself and to the difficulty that even highly trained military members often have in participating in it.

According to Grossman, much of combat conditioning comes from the training the combatant receives in short-circuiting the injunction against killing and temporarily obscuring the action of killing from the psyche. As I have noted above, militaries developed their dehumanizing and Pavlovian conditioning techniques as a result of studies that showed that, as late as World War II, as many as 80 to 85 percent of frontline combatants were refusing to fire their weapons at the enemy even when engaged in direct combat. As the military began to understand the "problem," and accordingly conceived of and implemented new conditioning techniques to increase the percentage of firers, the firing rate in Vietnam rose to about 95 percent—an effect that Grossman describes as the psychological equivalent of removing the safety from a weapon. Corresponding to this increased firing rate, Vietnam veterans have a spectacularly high rate of psychiatric casualties. Jonathan Shay, a psychiatrist working with veterans in Boston, notes that over 70 percent of Vietnam combat veterans have "experienced at least one of the cardinal symptoms" of PTSD at some point in their lives.[22]

21. Grossman, *On Killing*, 88.

22. Jonathan Shay, *Achilles in Vietnam: Combat Trauma and the Undoing of Character* (New York: Scribner's, 1994), 168. It is difficult to compare specific rates of PTSD since it is currently recognized in Vietnam veterans and "psychiatric casualties" as classified by the military prior to the official inclusion of PTSD in the DSM-III

While Grossman acknowledges a variety of factors that contribute to the rate of PTSD in Vietnam vets (the prevalence of child soldiers trained by the Viet Cong, the presence of psychotropic drugs in American units, and the lack of public support for the conflict), in the end the denial-defense mechanisms that were set up to rationalize the killing or protect the psyche of the combatant from the realization that he had killed systematically failed in this particular conflict. Despite the dehumanization of the enemy, when the combatant experienced killing with the intimacy that often occurred in the jungles of Vietnam, the realization that the enemy was "just like me" created significant psychological problems. With so many more combatants engaged in direct combat, it remains highly likely that the primary cause of this high rate of PTSD is that many more combatants were forced to struggle with the crushing guilt and shame of killing amidst the failure of the denial-defense mechanisms that are built into the military system.

Yet, as Grossman also notes, it is not simply the act of killing that is traumatizing, but the experience of violence in its many forms on the battlefield. Just being a witness to the direct effects of violence—the suffering of those, both enemy and compatriot, who have been grievously wounded; the reactions of civilians to the deaths of their loved ones; the very sight of bodies and body parts disfigured by bombs—proves to be deeply troubling to the psyche. As psychologist Edward Tick argues, the psyche has trouble handling the encounter with death, and so "we do our best to numb ourselves to the reality that they are human beings, whether or not we have been the agent of their deaths."[23] The

---

in 1980. Grossman presents figures that indicate that as many as 504,000 American men fighting in World War II suffered from psychiatric collapse and that the rate of this malady was such that, at one point during the war, the number of soldiers being discharged as psychiatric casualties exceeded the number of new recruits being drafted in. The huge number of American combatants in World War II (over 16 million), and the difficulty in discerning the percentage of those participating in direct combat, make arriving at a percentage to compare to Shay's statistic concerning Vietnam combat veterans an exercise in futility. Yet, nearly any rough comparison performed on the World War II numbers would seem to yield a psychiatric casualty rate well below Shay's figure of 70 percent for Vietnam veterans. Granted, this may be attributed to an increasing understanding of the ways PTSD presents itself, increased long-term oversight of veterans facing difficulty, and other societal changes. But almost all psychologists and psychiatrists note a marked increase in cases of psychiatric distress in Vietnam veterans compared to those of previous conflicts.

23. Edward Tick, *War and the Soul: Healing Our Nation's Veterans from Post-Trau-*

psyche has difficulty processing destruction and carnage on the scale it is often encountered in modern combat, where the lethality of weaponry and the very nature of "area weapons" that destroy everything within a certain sphere frequently produce unintended civilian casualties. The combatant is increasingly likely to witness the unintended victims of warfare and to struggle with the moral implications of his or her own worldview as a result. Iraqi veteran and US Navy psychiatrist William Nash describes this type of stress injury as a kind of damage to one's "core beliefs." All humans, out of necessity, have their own set of "core assumptions about the world and [their] place in it," which guide their interpretations of their own experiences and their decision-making.[24] All people have a basic need to be able to sleep at night knowing that they are secure, that they are not in imminent danger of death, and that there is a basic moral justice in the world. Both the sense of relative safety and the notion of moral order are violated and betrayed by the swift and sudden deaths of noncombatants; the combatant can experience an immediate and intense sense of vulnerability and strong notion of injustice, particularly when the side one is fighting for causes the damage.

In other words, experiences of conflict deeply upend any internal notion of moral "fairness." One of the most haunting and enduring memories I have of my time in Afghanistan with the US Army was when an eight-year-old Afghan boy immediately lost both legs—and subsequently died—after he stepped on a landmine while playing just outside the walls of Bagram Air Base. The mine had been placed there by the Soviet army nearly two decades before the boy was born; hence the cause of the conflict was entirely irrelevant to this child's life. In another incident—which I was not physically on the ground to witness, but which did occur during my time in Afghanistan—a funeral was targeted by the coalition forces and attacked with a Predator drone, resulting in significant noncombatant casualties. These incidents stayed with me, I believe, because of the haunting randomness of the violence and the deep sense that violence had disfigured the lives of many civilians, who had little to do with the conflict. Noting the unique way young combatants often have to deal with death, Nash argues that the experience of death as it encroaches on the lives of combatants, as

---

matic Stress Disorder (Wheaton, IL: Quest Books, 2005), 103. Hereafter, page references to this work appear in parentheses within the text.

24. Nash, "Combat/Operational Stress Adaptations and Injuries," 53.

they witness the deaths of relative innocents around them, is extremely difficult to process and can continue to poison any sense of moral order for some time to come.

Combatants processing this "death imprint" struggle to retain a sense of meaningful self and moral order against the forces that seek to redefine their sense of both self and morality. As I argued in the previous chapter, the willing of combatants is deeply impacted by the demands of authority, training, and obedience. Those who study PTSD note also that war at its most basic forces its combatants to think in stark terms about humanity and moral order. Tick notes that it "demands that we love some of our neighbors and destroy others. And it asks us to align ourselves—to love and hate thus—in the most uncompromising terms" (119). In light of this, Tick argues that war inverts many aspects of morality: rather than being viewed as a reprehensible crime, the killing of the enemy is a moral good. To those we are supposed to hate, kindness and compassion are weakness and, in the extreme, treachery and betrayal. The experience of violence rewires the morality of its combatants and, in doing so, creates great amounts of confusion, especially when one is asked to reenter a world where killing is considered "bad" and compassion and kindness are considered "good."

Perhaps the most insidious form of moral disquiet that occurs in combatants is the feeling of shame at suffering from forms of traumatic disorder at all—from not being "strong enough" to "deal with it" and move on with their lives. Nash notes that while civilians experience degrees of shame following traumatic experiences, the feeling of shame in veterans is perhaps unique. All members of today's military serve because they have volunteered; at present there are no conscripts or draftees. Therefore, when they experience difficulty in adapting to the moral environment of the battlefield, when they experience guilt as they perform their duty and kill the enemy, when they experience profound moral ambiguity and difficulty in their return to civilian life, they are often ashamed of their inability to simply overcome it. They volunteered with what they believed to be a full awareness of the risks and consequences involved, and they experience a profound sense of failure when they are unable to meet those challenges successfully in the combat zone or in transitioning back to civilian life.

In examining the profound ways that violence in conflict shatters elements of personal identity—and how combatants often describe their experiences in distinctly moral terms—several recent researchers have argued that PTSD should not be classified simply as a stress disorder. Shay began to use the term "moral injury" precisely to address the aspects of experienced violence that were distinct from physiological damage. It casts a much more direct focus on the experience of guilt and shame, and it attempts to encompass more holistically the aspects of personal morality and identity that are surely related to stress, though not exhaustively caused by an adverse reaction to that stress. In a similar way, Tick has argued that PTSD is often not a stress injury but an identity disorder. He argues that societal conditioning and military training build an identity for the combatant that breaks during the encounter with violence; yet neither the military nor society at large assists veterans in rebuilding or reforming their identity in positive or meaningful ways. As a result, veterans struggle mightily with the task that Nash argues accompanies their return: to "construct new belief systems that transcend the old and incorporate, somehow, the brutal realities of war without sacrificing everything that is positive about human existence" (54).

The Spread of Violence and the Collapse of Moral Frameworks

Veterans returning from conflicts experience a number of detrimental effects from their engagement with wartime violence. Some of these effects stem from particular physiological injuries sustained in the combat environment and others appear to result from the intense moral dilemmas in which veterans often find themselves. Both cases draw attention to the profound effect of intense violence in reshaping the way veterans process the events around them—both physiologically and psychologically—as well as work through their own needs and desires. While the effects are felt most profoundly by the veteran who suffers them directly, many of the behavioral issues that result directly from PTSD affect the families, colleagues, co-workers, and friends of the veteran. The violence of the combat zone is, in this indirect way, brought home and experienced by those who come to know it through its distortion in the life of the veteran. In his two studies, *Achilles in Vietnam* and *Odysseus in America*, Shay draws on those two titular mythic warriors as archetypes because they are complex and nuanced characters who have experienced deep and profound trauma but, perhaps more critically, because they both, in sometimes shocking ways, have brought the violence of war back to their homes with them. The difficulties veterans have in returning home often alienate them from loved ones, make relationships with friends difficult, and cause difficulties with employers—each effect further isolating those veterans and often intensifying their psychological struggles.

Like many civilians who suffer from PTSD, veterans are prone to experience the "return" of their most traumatic experiences, in which the unassimilated memory[25] of the event is brought to the fore in the mind.[26] Veterans, in their own minds, are reliving the experience as though it is happening in the present, with many of the corresponding physiological reactions: adrenaline surge, elevated heart rate, increased arousal, and intense sweating.[27] They also relive the emotions of the experience: fear, anxiety, stress, and even intense feelings of guilt and shame may come flooding back as the unassimilated memory overwhelms the nervous system. In veterans, the experience of intense hyperarousal, which often occurs in a particularly violent, "berserk" state in combat, can also be reexperienced via an "adrenaline storm."[28] The experience of these storms reflects a "permanent imprint" left on the physiology of the combatant, and when they occur, the veteran suffers from all the effects described above, along with an accompanying sense of overwhelming rage.

In the wake of repeated experiences of extreme violence and death, veterans often feel as though they have lost all agency. As Serene Jones notes in *Trauma and Grace*, this sense of a lack of agency is also common among many civilian trauma survivors, who "lose confidence that they

25. While there are varying theories that attempt to explain how "the return" is experienced so strongly in traumatized persons, most seem to hold that the brain's process of making and storing memories somehow fails in the face of extreme stress. Some argue that the experience of trauma floods the system with so much information that it essentially "floats about the mind" instead of being time-date stamped and filed as past experience. See Serene Jones, *Trauma and Grace: Theology in a Ruptured World* (Louisville: Westminster John Knox, 2009), 30.

26. I do not mean my observation about civilians with PTSD to in any way mark them out as "lesser sufferers" of the disorder, merely to mark the common ground of traumatic effect, from which I will discuss the particularities of the combat variety of PTSD.

27. Jonathan Shay, *Odysseus in America: Combat Trauma and the Trials of Homecoming* (New York: Scribner's, 2002), 24.

28. Shay, *Odysseus in America*, 24.

are effective actors in the world."[29] Jones says that this failure of agency is based in a feeling of extreme passivity during the traumatic event and a sense, based on this passivity, that their own agency is meaningless. Though combatants carry weapons, execute detailed missions, and witness and examine the results of their actions in combat, many of them experience significant feelings of passivity. They may see themselves as pawns in a larger scheme of violence during their own traumatic events. Shay argues that warfare is a form of "captivity" for those who participate in it: he notes, in resonance with McFadyen and Milgram, that the sense of responsibility and even agency is often located far from the frontline combatants who follow the orders of their tactical and operational commanders. Shay also argues that, in the face of their own government, veterans experience a feeling of "powerlessness," the result of which is that they are "liable to be eaten alive" and completely lose their meaningful identity in the bureaucracy that is "blind to how things interconnect."[30] They experience an objectification that threatens to become absolute. In this same vein, Tick argues that PTSD should not be classified as a stress disorder but as an "identity disorder," in which one's own sense of agency has become unmoored from meaningful activity.

Attempting to recapture some sense of effective action, many veterans become "mission-focused," fixated on a particular task or goal to the complete disregard of any other demands or responsibilities. Shay observes that many veterans work long hours—far in excess of the standard forty hours a week—yet have virtually no regard for the money they earn doing it. Instead, he argues, their workaholic tendencies come from the need to take on a "mission," in order to both recover a singular sense of motivation and block out everything else from their minds. Shay notes that this method of avoidance of unresolved traumatic events often becomes so important in veterans that what eventually triggers a "breakdown" for them is the imposition of an external event that prevents them "from keeping the workaholic schedule [they] had followed."[31] Shay intimates that the veteran who cannot find consistent work and the workaholic veteran share a mission-focused mentality: the latter is simply able, either by circumstance or effort, to

29. Jones, *Trauma and Grace*, 17.
30. Shay, *Odysseus in America*, 47.
31. Shay, *Odysseus in America*, 58.

translate her military mentality to her employment, while the former cannot find a job that affords him the same singular focus to which he has become accustomed. Family life for these veterans suffers greatly, of course, as they spend nearly all of their available time and energy at work, religiously avoiding other commitments.

Families often suffer the most from the violence that veterans bring home from war, both in terms of physical danger and broken relationships. Studies of veterans from the Vietnam War forward estimate that combat veterans account for 21 percent of all cases of domestic violence in the United States (though they make up a fraction of 1 percent of the population).[32] Given the training of the modern combatants, these incidents of domestic violence can be particularly dangerous when they are paired with severe cases of PTSD. In 2002, in perhaps the most tragic example, three Army Special Operations soldiers who had been stationed at Fort Bragg, North Carolina, returned from Afghanistan and killed their wives within a period of six weeks, prompting the Army to radically reexamine its family counseling program. Violence is so likely to spread in varying intensities from veterans to their spouses or partners that the phenomenon of "secondary traumatization" is being studied, with wives of combat veterans as "indirect victims of their husbands' traumatic experience."[33]

Observing the intense way that many returning veterans with PTSD appear to exhibit tendencies toward domestic violence, several researchers have argued that combat situations often inculcate a sense of misogyny. Noting Homer's trope of dangerous, wily, and seductive women in the *Odyssey*, Shay argues that many soldiers in Vietnam experienced sex for the first time with Vietnamese prostitutes. These encounters took place against a backdrop of mistrust. The suspicion that the prostitutes were Viet Cong agents who would harm the soldiers if they could was widespread, and the soldiers' experiences of intimacy were colored by this deep mistrust of their sexual partners. This inculcated a "visceral sense that women are dangerous," Shay argues, and it coincided with significant instances of violence toward the Vietnamese

32. Holly G. Prigerson, Paul K. Maciejewski, and Robert Rosenheck, "Population Attributable Fractions of Psychiatric Disorders and Behavioral Outcomes Associated with Combat Exposure among US Men," *American Journal of Public Health* 92, no. 1 (January 2002): 59.

33. Rachel Dekel and Zahava Solomon, "Secondary Traumatization among Wives of War Veterans with PTSD," in *Combat Stress Injury*, ed. Figley and Nash, 137.

prostitutes, crimes that for political reasons were almost never investigated by US or South Vietnamese authorities.[34] Sex, sought as welcome intimacy and connection amid the harsh and unforgiving combat environment, thus became mingled with the idea that sex partners cannot be trusted and that violence against them is often warranted (and never seems to have consequences).

Some contend that the experience of combat actually alters the combatants' relationships to love and sexuality. Tick argues that the experience of killing and sexual release can become tightly intertwined, noting that "innumerable descriptions of wartime killing sound like acts of love or sex."[35] The release of rounds from a rifle directed at an enemy was referred to as an "orgasmic discharge" in the intense stresses of life-and-death situations. Tick describes numerous veterans who were unable to be intimate with their partners without the sight of exposed flesh, which would trigger images of death and destruction. The Department of Veterans Affairs has actually created a specific program called Intimate Partner Violence (IPV) in the wake of repeated instances of sexual violence that would appear to be deeply consonant with Tick's conclusions. In a similar vein, Tick argues that the repeated exposure to death and dead bodies may instill a desperate need in the combatant to feel life and the "human touch" in a compulsive way. Returning veterans may thus end up deeply unsatisfied with the sexuality they express with their wives or partners, and thus attempt to fulfill their needs with other women or men. This often leads to deep feelings of betrayal, shame, guilt, anger, and resentment on the part of veterans' partners, leading to strained and broken familial relationships. Veterans, who are intimately aware of the hurt they have caused, and the myriad ways in which they now seem to be irreconcilably estranged from their loved ones, are often filled with shame at the brokenness they seem to cause among their family members and often sink into a physical and psychological isolation from others.

In the crucible of the physical, ethical, and psychological forces of combat, what becomes clear is that the moral framework that often supported the combatant prior to conflict tends to collapse under the weight of the actual wartime experience. In its simplest and most basic construction, the act of killing that combatants experience arouses

34. Shay, *Odysseus in America*, 70.
35. Tick, *War and the Soul*, 125.

moral conflict with the values instilled in the combatant in training. As Grossman points out, the combatants' training is meant to systematically dehumanize the enemy, to numb them to the fact that the enemy is a human being. The guilt and shame that frontline ground combatants experience appears to have a direct correlation with the realization that this framework is essentially false, since, on close inspection, the enemy appears to be "just like" them. Yet these experiences—as well as other encounters with the violence of modern combat—cause veterans not simply to reject this singular principle, but to reject their general moral ordering of right and wrong, good and evil. The expression "the first casualty of war is innocence" has become so prevalent that it is a cliché, and its clichéd status masks the truth it tells: that the loss of one's moral footing and the loss of a framework that gives actions meaning is deeply disorienting and damaging.[36]

The loss of innocence is particularly disorienting in a culture that so stringently identifies itself as innocent, and is thus devastating to a combatant's sense of identity and self. Tick argues that America "claims innocence and goodness as fundamental traits," so much so that we expect men and women to be able to train to be fierce warriors, to go off to war, and to "get the job done"—and then return without significant moral consequence.[37] The guilt, shame, and other degrees and variations of moral ambiguity that many combatants experience intensely in combat not only shatter the narrative of their own personal innocence, but also may shatter the notion of national innocence as well. Soldiers actually often discover the opposite of their own cultural belief: that they are perceived in the foreign land as the "bad guy," so much so that "those we are trying to save see us as the savage invaders, needing to be stopped by their own painful, heroic sacrifices."[38] What Nash describes as a category of "damage to core beliefs" about one's own innocence and the validity of one's cause could also be understood as

36. This expression was the tagline for the 1986 Oliver Stone film *Platoon*, which portrayed the horrors of combat within an American infantry platoon in the Vietnam War. It is an alteration of US Senator Hiram Johnson's 1917 quote that "the first casualty of war is the truth," which is itself a paraphrase of Aeschylus's fifth-century BCE quote: "In war, truth is the first casualty." In the context of the loss of the moral framework provided by the American exceptionalism narrative, both variations would seem to apply.

37. Tick, *War and the Soul*, 155.

38. Tick, *War and the Soul*, 160.

the destruction of one's very identity, since the psychological damage done in conflict "destroys one's ability to participate in the culture's mystique of goodness and its forward propulsion at war's end."[39] Shay, too, recognizes that those suffering from "complex PTSD" are suffering from a betrayal of what they understood to be true and right. For him, the damaging situations that occur in combat have the capacity to "undo character" and send it spiraling in various directions in search of an anchoring meaning.[40]

Tick evocatively draws on the Greek narrative of the affair of Ares and Aphrodite to illustrate the power of social constructions of morality and their relationship to the lived experience of violence. Aphrodite, he argues, represents to us "tenderness, beauty and feminine receptiveness," while Ares, on his own, is "sheer rage and rampage." Without a guiding narrative that would attempt to give it greater meaning, war is simply slaughter and death, but joined together in grander terms, it "gains grace, beauty, and nobility."[41] We go to war with the grand visions of honor and nobility in mind and make passionate cases to do so, and yet the true experience of conflict rarely matches these visions. Tick argues that the failure of this myth and the cultural expectation about conflict is deeply connected to veteran suffering. He argues: "PTSD is the expression of the anguish, dislocation and rage of the self as it attempts to cope with its loss of innocence, reformulate a new personal identity and cultural role, and awaken from massive denial."[42] In denying our own capacities for violence and placing "evil" far away from ourselves—in "other people and their systems"—we deny, Tick argues, that warfare is really Ares alone: it is death and slaughter.

Working with veterans today, several psychologists focus on ways to reform combatant identities with an emphasis on bearing witness to the truth about the violence of conflict. Both Shay and Tick decry the lack of rituals of purification and cleansing in our culture that recognize that veterans cannot simply reintegrate into society and that implicitly

39. Tick, *War and the Soul*, 157.

40. Shay marks a distinction between "simple PTSD" and "complex PTSD." Simple PTSD is what I've essentially noted as physiological damage, such as what happens to the central nervous system through repeated hyperarousal. Complex PTSD has a distinctive moral element to it—a betrayal of what Shay deems "Social Trust," which is the understanding that power will be used responsibly to do what is right.

41. Tick, *War and the Soul*, 121.

42. Tick, *War and the Soul*, 170.

and explicitly acknowledge the traumatizing nature of violence suffered. Shay describes the intentional creation of a veterans' group at the VA in which they can witness to their own trauma, be heard, supported, and essentially "reborn"—having been "cleansed" of war.[43] Tick works to develop what he terms an identity based on the attainment of a tribal elder-like "warrior status," which involves (among other things) the bearing of the truth of the nature of violence and conflict and the somewhat sacred duty to testify to this reality in the larger societal conversation.

Additionally, it can be said that society at large and its addiction to a false narrative must bear a great deal of the responsibility for PTSD and the conditions under which veterans suffer it. In order to cling to our own mythical foundations and cultural beliefs about innocence, we deny war's destructiveness and the corrupting nature of violence itself. For example, Tick argues that society turns a blind eye to the reality of war in a particular way, rejecting the notion that it "changes its participants forever" and treating veterans and their profound axiological suffering as something that can easily be "repaired."[44] Just as restoration of a veteran involves the restoration of moral fiber that is able to come to terms with the veteran's encounter with violence, PTSD and moral injury are problems of societal morality. In its "addiction to security," Tick argues, America has become unable to take responsibility for the violence of its wars and perhaps more critically for its "war-making tendencies." Taking responsibility, of course, entails that there is a shared burden of responsibility for the results of conflict, and this necessarily entails the renunciation of our mythic sense of innocence. The veteran is isolated in the absence of the communal, national responsibility and he or she becomes a scapegoat who "carries [the nation's] secret grief and guilt for all of us."[45]

Synthesis: Reframing Violence and Moral Order

The veterans' traumatic and damaging encounters with violence challenge the truth of America's narrative of exceptionalism in two major areas: its conception of our national innocence and goodness; and the

43. Shay, *Odysseus in America*, 169.
44. Tick, *War and the Soul*, 155.
45. Tick, *War and the Soul*, 237.

understanding that violence can be used cleanly in service to the larger good of the American enterprise. The distortions many veterans bear within themselves shatter the notion that we can both view ourselves as innocent and unquestionably good *and* use violence to maintain that innocence and goodness in the world. Their trauma questions the redemptive role that violence plays in the American narrative, and, perhaps more fundamentally and crucially, they call into question our sense of our own identity and our capacity for honest moral reflection. If we are a "good" and "innocent" people, then violence is not something that we find within ourselves; rather, it is something that invades from without, something that must be controlled and kept at bay. In Girardian terms, our views of violence and its necessity inform our social construction of "good" violence: that is, what is done in order to keep the external "evil" violence from spreading uncontrollably through the good and civilized world. But resonant with the experience of many veterans, Girard notes that this distinction is ultimately inconsequential: more violence is thus done in the name of ending violence, so that violence itself is ultimately the victor, since it cannot be mastered. The high number of civilian casualtics in Amcrican wars and the increasing number of morally traumatized veterans call into question our belief in our national innocence—and the "goodness" of our violence.

Let us explore how the doctrine of sin can inform our identity and moral order in a way that allows us to soberly analyze our own capacity for violence. One of the primary issues inhibiting this authentic understanding in our own society is our acceptance of tribal, or national, boundaries as an unequivocal and necessary "good." Augustine's discussion of "inordinate love" provides a framework within which we can understand national identity and security to be proper goods, but only when understood as penultimate goods in rightful competition and in balance with other goods. Furthermore, Augustine's presentation of the fall of the angels (which precedes that of Adam) as the dissolution of unified creaturely integrity provides valuable insight into the way tribalism and violence tear the common good of all humanity. This concept suggests that violence is a direct assault on the integrity of both collective and individual human nature. In this section I argue that Augustine's concept provides a pivotal framework from which we can construct a more authentic moral order that is attentive to the realities of violence and that provides a way to critique American exceptionalism and essentialized moral categories.

Augustine argues that a primary result of the Fall is humanity's alienation from what is truly good and its elevation of more temporal goods to an ultimate status. The world is composed of many things that are good in themselves—physical beauty, gold, even a sense of pride. He goes to great lengths to argue that these things are not evil in themselves; as a part of creation they are, by their nature, good.[46] Yet disconnected from the one who is truly good and who provides the framework within which these other goods can be adequately appreciated, the human will desires them to such an obsessive extent that the good order of humanity becomes damaged. Augustine argues, for example, that greed is "not the fault of gold, but of the man who loves gold perversely, and who therefore neglects righteousness, which ought to be held in incomparably higher esteem than gold."[47] The perversion of desires leads, as he notes in the case of greed, to the abandonment of other goods, and this disturbs and damages the order of the whole. Perverse love elevates one good to the detriment of all others and makes the lover himself evil, for even as he attains what he desires, he finds himself in a worse state than before, because he has deprived himself of something greater.

There is also a sense in Augustine's descriptions of good natures and perverse love that the common good of creation as a whole is damaged by the turn to the self as the ultimate good. In the discussion of the fall of the angels, he argues that those who fell, "delighting in their own power," fell from "that higher and blessed good which was common to them all and embraced a private good of their own."[48] The contrast of the "private" good of the fallen angels who look to themselves for fulfillment and the "common good" of those who cleave to God suggests the shattering of a whole into self-interest as a primary motif for sinfulness. The Fall, understood in this way as a turn to the self, fractures the very commonality of the community, and Augustine contrasts the "zeal for selfish ends" of the fallen angels with the "uniting

46. This is more or less the main thrust of book 12 of the *City of God*: demonstrating that it is the turning of the will to what is inferior, which is evil itself. He is concerned here to maintain the goodness of creation on its own merits and in its proper order and to argue that evil is insubstantial: it is not what is opposed to what is good, but what corrupts it. Almost akin to a virus, evil cannot exist for Augustine apart from what is, by its nature, good.

47. Augustine, *City of God* 12.8.

48. Augustine, *City of God* 12.1.

force of love" of those who remain blessed in communion with God.[49] For Augustine, blessedness is caused only by the unifying force of love in communion with the commonality of God, while those who have departed this communion for their own ends are miserable. Alienated from what satisfies them, the fallen exist in misery. In seeking for satisfaction from their own ends, in preferring "vanity to truth" and individuality over community, they become false. The individual angel cannot achieve satisfaction apart from the community of angels that cleave together to God. Thus sin here can be cast as the prideful quest for satisfaction, at the necessary expense of true community united in love for God and each other.

In Adam's turning to his own self for satisfaction, there is a loss of moral focus on community as a good and love as a unifying force. The Fall thus includes the fracturing of the idea that "the good of all persons is both unified and interdependent."[50] In seeking what Augustine identifies as selfish ends, we become quite dangerous to one another. A "wicked human," whose will is corrupted and turned toward its own ends, can be catastrophic, because, as the will seeks its fulfillment, it gives rise to "twisted and nightmarish desires" in an attempt to achieve a sense of order according to its own ends.[51] Fractured into selfish ends, but yearning for the satisfaction of some sense of order, human beings misapprehend the world with tragic results to others and the global community. Separated from the natural order of what is good in community—that the good of all people is unified and interdependent—the pursuit of private goods and personal ends disregards the needs and the good of others. In other words, the evil and sinfulness of perverse love can manifest itself in a way that elevates one community and its flourishing but abandons the flourishing of another. Yet this is a false and illusory good, since humanity's true and proper good is to be unified and interdependent.

Contesting the meaning of violence described in this chapter identifies the construction of a nationalistic moral order that cannot bear the weight of real experiences of violence, trauma, and guilt. A key question becomes: How can we understand goodness, guilt, and wrongness in a way that is faithful to the reality of our own violence in the world? In attempting to authentically describe violence, innocence,

49. Augustine, *City of God* 12.1.
50. Williams, "Insubstantial Evil," 89.
51. Williams, "Insubstantial Evil," 112.

and goodness, one of the primary strengths of the model of original sin is its sober view of human nature and the world's brokenness. It provides a way of ideologically resisting all claims to ultimate goodness and meaning that arise from human construction, not because such claims are inherently evil or negative but because they are a part of a broken world and cannot bear the weight of the label of absolute goodness. In other words, human civilization's need for something to cling to as an absolute has the capacity to be horrifically destructive and to usher in extreme violence and death in an effort to preserve the "good" that is deemed so valuable. Violence, then, can be understood to stem from this shattered and broken sense of goodness, from a need to protect our private selves physically, but also in order to protect and continually validate the "goodness" of our own private goods. The national narrative serves to shield our sense of vanity from the ugliness of the reality of wartime violence and destruction.

As a description of the situation in which humanity finds itself, original sin utterly rejects concepts of human innocence. This rejection is consonant with the way combatants seem to experience violence and its effects in a combat zone. Few who have participated in or experienced this violence would use the term "innocent" to describe it or anyone involved in it.[52] Combatants experience the world as intensely—often tragically—broken. They also experience varying forms of guilt in response to their participation in this brokenness. The model of original sin upholds this experience as a true experience of the world in which seemingly good intentions and desires perversely result in deadly, tragic, and traumatic results, since the base condition of the postlapsarian world is one of deep brokenness. Original sin affirms the experience of the combatant over against the notion of American exceptionalism, and it provides resources to critique this notion as a false perception of self and the larger world. In axiological terms, it affirms the guilt and moral anguish that so many veterans with PTSD experience as a true, valid, and appropriate moral response to participation in the brokenness of the world in such an acute way.[53] As Shay and Grossman

52. This appears to be understood at some level in our culture as well. When reporting deaths, even in training accidents stateside, the American media never reports young military men and women as "innocent" victims. Whereas nearly every report of deaths from either natural causes or even the 9/11 attacks describes the death toll in terms of "innocent lives lost."

53. I remind the reader that it does not follow in my line of reasoning that guilt

both note, American society has great difficulty tolerating any degree of moral pain or ambiguity.[54] Shay recounts that veterans returning from even the earliest American conflicts have met with stiff resistance to feelings of guilt or shame born of their war experience. He argues that this attitude stems from a "Platonic/Stoic/Puritan" interpretation of virtue that holds that since fighting for the nation (particularly *this* nation) was a virtuous thing, veterans should experience well-being when they return. When this was not the case, the clear implication was that the soldier's virtue was "defective."[55] In the eyes of society at large, it is the veteran—in his guilt—who misperceives the world and perhaps even reflects his inability to adhere to the truth of American values.

Yet Augustine's model of inordinate love poses a strong theological and ideological critique to the notion of American goodness and our own cultural desire to maintain it. Tick identifies what he terms America's "addiction to security," and Tirman argues that the effects of this addiction include a profound apathy toward the suffering of others in the wars that ostensibly provide this "security."[56] When we inordinately love security (which Abraham Maslow thought of as the second most crucial and basic human need, behind only the air, water, and food our bodies need to survive),[57] we become callous toward the needs of any others and reify our own private good regardless of its intrusion into the well-being of others external to it. Not only that, but as the notion that combatants' suffering reflects their own insufficient virtue suggests, we have a desire to protect this inordinate love of our own security by asserting it as a primal and moral good. Over time, its defense in axiological terms takes on a certain inertia. As Stanley Hauerwas argues, it appears that, as a nation, we need to engage in violence in order to renew "the moral commitments that constitute our lives."[58] In order to give meaning to the sacrifices of the past, we must make sacrifices in the present. We have fought so long under the auspices of the frontier myth that if we are willing to soberly acknowledge that our cause is not

---

necessarily deserves punishment, but rather it is an intense experience of human brokenness that profoundly identifies the need for redemption, not condemnation.

54. Grossman, *On Killing*, 96.

55. Shay, *Odysseus in America*, 154.

56. Tick, *War and the Soul*, 244.

57. A. H. Maslow, "A Theory of Human Motivation," *Psychological Review* 50, no. 4 (1943): 370–96.

58. Hauerwas, *War and the American Difference*, xv.

uncritically good, it would damage the legacy and tradition that our morality has been built on as a nation since its inception.

Yet, as Augustine's description of sin as "inordinate love" suggests, all attempts at defining a "good" must be understood as temporal and limited. We are capable of inordinately loving every principle and tradition that we cherish, and this distorts our intentions in a particularly deep way: in seeking to do well and perform nobly in the world, and in thinking that we are acting in such a way, we are increasingly blinding ourselves to the destructive effects of our inordinate love. This concept of distorted love helps describe American society's inordinate love for its own security and goodness, particularly as it acknowledges the effects of this quest for ultimate security: the apathy that Tirman says Americans have toward the civilian victims of their wars. It also provides a framework for understanding the axiological failure of constructions of morality against the experience of combat violence and its effects. In military training, a combatant's sense of what is good and right is intensely re-formed, such that performing one's duty well and eliminating the enemy (and thus, ultimately, the existential threat to America) constitute ultimate success and victory. Tick describes this as the ideal of a mythic warrior: that in participating in battle, one will achieve a profound degree of nobility by way of proving oneself courageous and brave in the face of threat and danger.

The trauma of veterans, Tick continues, results from the unfulfillment of this ideal for multiple reasons, but chief among them is the moral de-formation that occurs due to the combatant being asked to kill "without clearly just cause."[59] Shay bases his concept of complex PTSD on an experience of the betrayal of "what's right," arguing that there is a direct correlation between the unity and cohesiveness of the cultural understanding of "rightness" in the military's combat actions and PTSD.[60] Yet all of these constructions assume that they are able to

59. Tick, *War and the Soul*, 169.

60. This is what he describes as having a distinctive moral-psychological component rather than simply a physiological one. For Shay, the most cohesive societies, in which a shared sense of morality governs actions of citizens, soldiers, and those in ultimate positions of power would experience almost no cases of complex PTSD, since it is caused by a betrayal of social trust—a violation of the shared sense of moral goodness. Shay works primarily with veterans of the Vietnam War, and in this subset of combat veterans, the betrayal of social trust and society's dubious treatment of returning soldiers certainly lend credence to this assertion. In light of my own experi-

protect the psyche against trauma in the combat environment, specifically in the act of killing. Much of the experience of combatants chronicled by Grossman and others suggests otherwise: it suggests that, regardless of the construction of "good" or what's "right" or what's "just," the experience of slaughter, of the "death imprint," of the expectation to kill in support of the concept of what is good, is ultimately traumatic and creates stress within the psyche. Perhaps our human conceptions of "goodness" simply cannot bear the weight of the ultimacy that the act of killing presupposes. It may be, as Bonhoeffer suggests, that the only responsible decision among many terrible options is to use violence, but this does not mean that we can ever consider it "just" or "good." We must always understand it as the breaking of a rule or commandment, an action taken in a situation of sinfulness.[61]

The description of the angelic fall as the rejection of the common, unified good in favor of private goods provides a way of understanding the rise of violence as a result of the world's brokenness. The cultural belief that undergirds all of military training and drives many people to overcome its rigors—that the good of the nation is of surpassingly greater value than the lives of those torn apart in its conflicts—reflects the degree to which the tribal senses of good have become hardened. There is little wartime violence today that cannot be described in terms of the elevation of tribal goods over the welfare of one's enemies or the good of the enemy tribe. Shay's entire concept of moral injury and conflict rests on the notion that a strong sense of tribal identity and common value promotes psychological health when conflicts arise with other groups.[62] Tick's concept of the

---

ence in more recent conflicts, in which veterans were welcomed home as heroes who were not subject to criticism, I cannot affirm Shay's claim that the moral elements of PTSD arise solely on the basis of this breach of social trust. Given that Shay's latest work, *Odysseus in America*, was published in 2002, I am curious about how he would describe complex PTSD as it occurs in Afghan and Iraqi veterans.

61. Dietrich Bonhoeffer, *Ethics*, ed. Clifford J. Green, trans. Reinhard Krauss, Charles C. West, and Douglas W. Stott, vol. 6 of *Dietrich Bonhoeffer Works*, ed. Wayne Whitson Floyd Jr. (Minneapolis: Fortress, 2009), 221–27.

62. In the third and final section of *Odysseus in America*, entitled "Prevention," Shay advocates a model of military manpower that keeps personnel in a single unit through initial and advanced training and into combat. In this way, values and relationships develop that facilitate common ideals, communication, respect, and loyalty to the point that betrayals of social trust and communal values that are psychically destructive are rare.

mythic warrior ideal is also set in the context of crucial tribal values and goods, and its fulfillment depends on the experience of combat being "just" by tribal standards and providing a proving ground for cultural virtues. While there is little doubt that both visions are extremely helpful for veterans in many ways, Augustine's description of the angelic fall argues, implicitly, that the tribal goods can never be considered ultimate or universalized because they are a result of the shattering of what is truly good for all humanity (angelkind). It also suggests that violence done in service of a national ideal or religious cause or done in defense of cultural values must never be understood as an uncritical good; instead it should be understood as coming from a place of brokenness and fractured identity, which by its very nature is disconnected from a sense of truly unified good that is common to all humanity.

A strength of this model of original sin is that it allows for the construction of a moral framework complex enough to handle the guilt of combatants without absolutizing it. The moral trauma and guilt experienced by veterans are precisely what create the profound dissonance with the morality tacitly present in the underlying narrative of American exceptionalism, and they identify its falsehood. If the American enterprise is uncritically good, and a combatant serving it experiences guilt, then, just as Shay's Puritan articulates, it must be because the combatant's own virtue is deficient. In light of the radicality and prepersonal character of original sin, acting morally is not an exercise to determine the proper good to strive toward and to adhere to it with all one's ability; rather, it involves the recognition that our very sense of goodness is deeply malleable. It involves recognizing the "goods" of security and safety as valued but not absolute, as those whose pursuit can, if held too tightly, lead us into greater violence. As I argued in the preceding chapter, combatants face forces in training and in the combat environment that deeply affect their own willing by shaping the good toward which they act. The power of sin's distorting force acts on combatants, who are shaped by these outside entities, and the combatants internalize and propagate that distorting force. If in acting in accordance with this sense of good—based on an inordinate and extreme love of security—combatants who act to kill their enemies experience an intense sense of guilt as a result, then it cannot be said that the guilt for this rests *solely* with them. It is not a failure of the combatants' virtue, constitution, or ability to adhere to the path commended to them. Rather, the combatants' experience of radical brokenness serves to critique the very "goodness" of the good in whose pursuit they have acted. The distortion of the cultural addiction to and inordinate love of security bears responsibility for the situation that is ironically unmasked via veteran trauma: rather than build up and instill in the combatant a sense of virtue, it frequently results in profound guilt and moral anguish.

CHAPTER 4

Privation of Goodness and the Injured Soul

> Look, O LORD, and consider! To whom have you done this? Should women eat their offspring, the children they have borne? Should priest and prophet be killed in the sanctuary of the Lord? The young and old are lying on the ground in the streets; my young women and my young men have fallen by the sword; in the day of your anger you have killed them, slaughtering without mercy. You invited my enemies from all around as if for a day of festival; and on the day of the anger of the LORD no one escaped or survived; those whom I bore and reared my enemy has destroyed.
>
> —LAMENTATIONS 2:20–23

The encounter with death on a broad scale is deeply troubling to the psyche. Over the terrible course of human history, many human beings, like the residents of Jerusalem during the sixth-century BCE destruction of that city by the Babylonians, have witnessed and experienced death en masse and with disturbing physical and psychological proximity. Yet few in the world today experience death and destruction with the same degree of proximity and savagery as those who directly participate in or are affected by contemporary warfare. Modern technology and distance weaponry has made the experience of death more swift, sudden, and larger in scale. The encounter with this degree of death can be particularly toxic to one's ability to experience the positive aspects of human existence. US Navy psychiatrist William Nash argues that it is necessary for our psychological health to feel safe, to know that our "lives will not be snuffed out in the next few seconds."[1] Those who have experienced the violence of combat have experienced the real and immediate fear that their lives may, in fact, be ended in moments, and many have seen others mortally wounded around them, friend and enemy alike. The damage to this core belief, Nash argues, can be rehabilitated through the construction of new systems of meaning that take into account the experience of violence and synthesize it with the more beneficent aspects of human life. Even so, this "death imprint" may have a tendency to linger, leaving a lasting, poisoned memory of the vulnerability of human beings to the destructive force of violence.

I would argue that Augustine's understanding of the postlapsarian condition of humanity as being cut off from the life-giving grace of God is particularly resonant with this aspect of veteran trauma. I would argue that the veteran experiences humanity with an extreme vulnerability, not only in the physical way described by Nash as the "death imprint," but also in a profoundly psychological way that is resonant with trauma research. In the combat environment, the evolutionary features in the psyche that served to protect the health of the psyche—indeed, the survival of the whole person—have been stripped away. This can be understood as consistent with Augustine's notion of a damaged human nature: it is a distortion of life in which all "goods" one reaches for are tainted by death and violence. I argue that the accumulated effect of willing apart from the grace of God—the connection to life and goodness—moves us closer to what Augustine describes as nonexistence, and that the veteran experiences this in a damagingly acute way. In arguing this, I draw on the work of political theorist Hannah Arendt, which describes the encounter with "savage" humanity that has been stripped of civilization. I then draw on Dave Grossman's argument that the very nature of combat restricts our psychological "fight or flight" options for interspecies conflict into a particularly unforgiving set of choices. Finally, I will turn to Augustine to describe this experience as an acute manifestation of the world deprived of the connection with the life-sustaining fullness of God.

1. Nash, "Combat/Operational Stress Adaptations and Injuries," 53.

Arendt and Grossman: Vulnerability, Evolution, and Civilization

From very different fields, perspectives, and methodologies, Hannah Arendt and Dave Grossman both provide descriptions of the way we encounter human vulnerability. In a segment of her book *Origins of Totalitarianism*, Arendt argues that what are often considered "human rights" are not, in fact, inherent to human beings; but each right is granted or denied by a governmental power. In "stateless" peoples, those who had previously been granted these rights but no longer have access to them because of their loss of affiliation with a governmental polity, there will be a sense of suspicion, fear, and revulsion that is deeply interwoven with a sense of vulnerability. Grossman argues that, over time and centuries of conflict, human society has stripped itself of the evolutionary protections that propelled the species to the lofty heights of world domination. As a result, our levels of anxiety about confrontation can be traced to an acute sense of our own vulnerability in light of fewer "relief valves" and other options in what has been classically posited as the human "fight or flight" response. Both arguments share a notion that the advance of civilization cannot be perceived as uncritically good in all areas. Both point to the ways in which increased levels of civilization can reveal their own failures and shortcomings, particularly as they attempt to provide safeguards for human life.

The experience of conflict—in the explicit space where one is actively engaged, using weapons, with another who is likewise engaged—is an experience of legal and moral anarchy. While combatants certainly bring to the conflict a wealth of enculturated ideas that represent their societal mores, and where authorities who enforce certain rules are not absent, combat takes place at a great distance from what we would consider a "civilized" order—and its particular ideals about acceptable and unacceptable forms of behavior. It is far removed from the place where people—in any other circumstance—build lives, become educated, pursue careers, make friends, marry and raise families, and live with neighbors in a community.[2] In the combat environment, the nature of

2. Certainly, for American troops, and most of those from allied nations in our most recent wars, this is both a conceptual "space" and a physical one. The homes and mundane situations in which they otherwise "live" apart from combat are thousands of miles away. This acknowledges both the privilege of not having one's education, career pursuit, family, and life with neighbors impacted directly by war in one's home

conflict itself demands that we destroy others and, in modern warfare, do so swiftly and quite violently. In most peacetime societies, lives are spent building and attaining; in conflict, combatants survive by effectively and efficiently destroying and killing. In this sense, combat takes place in an extra-civilized environment where combatants encounter each other, not as their civilized selves, but as something made more feral and basic through the demands of violence.[3]

In *Origins of Totalitarianism*, Hannah Arendt's discussion of the encounter with "savage" humanity is compelling in its understanding of civilization itself, as is her articulation of the fear of the savage "other." Her argument is deeply informed by the expulsion of mass groups of nationals from newly revitalized European states that took place following the Treaty of Versailles. Arendt argues that the central bond that civil or "human" rights hinge on is not a common humanity but the agreement among those in political organizations to grant each other equality and access to human rights (290–302).[4] Therefore, she understands that the denaturalization of the minority groups within nation-states results in two distinct losses that in effect remove them from the community of human beings. First, the denaturalized peoples lose their homes and are removed from the very cultural fabric in which they live and find meaning. Following this physical and social displacement is the legal maneuvering that removes them from the rolls of citizens, not only of one particular country but of any country at all. This effectively entails

---

country and the fact that many around the world have to pursue all of these activities within the violent crucible of an active combat zone.

3. Hannah Arendt, *The Origins of Totalitarianism* (New York: Harcourt, 1968). (Hereafter, page references to this work appear in parentheses within the text.) Arendt, of course, argues that the encounter with "naked" humanity is something that civilization itself finds utterly repulsive and threatening because its very savageness threatens the civilized order. For her, the encounter often seems imagined as one between the civilized and the stateless, savage other. Here I focus on her critical insights through a very narrow lens—the environment of combat.

4. Clearly, Arendt is suspicious of either of these terms that attempt to describe the reality of the rights to which we try to assign a category, particularly "human rights" since the appearance of socially dislocated "naked humanity" often was the result of or resulted in the elimination of said rights. I use the terms here simply because no better alternatives present themselves for describing the reality of protections and freedoms that they attempt to identify. This section will track with Arendt's brilliant argument in *Origins of Totalitarianism* (290–302) regarding the precarious position of stateless peoples and the way their rights are essentially ended.

the loss of national citizenship and any access or right to appeal to a political community. The two losses function to remove the stateless person from any connection to civilization, and this effectively denies any persons or groups a way of asserting their rights. Once unmoored from any political community or any access to basic societal supports, the people are truly "expelled" from humanity. Lacking an identifying polity—and belonging to or participating in no governmental structure—the stateless person is reduced to the representation of humanity in the abstract: he or she is defined through no formal, organized connection to other human beings and thus represents what Arendt terms "naked humanity" (301).

The deeper revelation about humanity in its "savage" state involves a philosophical and psychological reflection on the revulsion toward this state of "naked" humanity. At the point of separation from a civilized society, we as individuals are left completely within our own interior life, with the aspects of our personality that can only be discerned within the private realm of inner consciousness. In our interior being, "each of us is made as he is—single, unique"; the "unchangeable" character of our own interior lives poses a deep threat to the highly organized society, which regards individuality as a "disturbing little miracle" due to its inability to be completely sublimated into the civil political system (301). Individuality and difference, which come into full view in the state of "naked" humanity, bring into sharp relief the boundaries and natural curbs on human potential to unite and construct a functioning and inclusive civilization. The very essence of our individuality is threatening, then, because it indicates clearly that there are areas of existence in which external human action is utterly inert. What stands out as truly disturbing in the state of "naked" humanity, then, is the individuality of human beings that cannot be completely equalized through a polity or civilization. "Civilized" humanity thus sees this irritating reminder as a great threat to its world-building, and seeks to destroy those who bear it.

A key aspect of this concept is that what is different and alien in this state of humanity is not simply threatening to collective civilization, but it is also terrifying to the civilized person. It reflects a deep fear that we are not ultimately in control, that, no matter how masterfully we construct our civilizations, there are wild elements of ourselves and our frightening neighbors that cannot be accounted for in any "civilized" calculus.[5]

5. In terms of the argument put forth by Milgram—that people accept a shift into

What is exhibited in the plight of the stateless peoples is the precipitous fall from participation in full, civilized humanity into a participation in humanity in a primitive and animalistic way. The fear of humanity in this "savage" state is that it will destroy civilization, much in the way "the wild elements of nature once threatened the existence of man-made cities and countrysides" (301). What is ultimately frightening here is that, instead of being comforted by the protection our civilization affords us, the encounter with the savagery of the "naked" human suggests that we are ultimately vulnerable—to each other, to the whims of the wild and the forces of chance—in the precariousness of the fight for survival.

Nowhere do the forces of chance, wildness, and human savagery intersect more directly than on the modern battlefield. While the experiences of daily life within a functioning society often provide a psychological shield from the encounter with vulnerability that Arendt describes, members of the military cannot derive comfort from this. They must be prepared to confront the enemy in an intimate physical and psychological capacity. In some ways, the training that the military offers "ups the ante" of the frontier mythology, intensifying the dehumanization of the enemy and providing mechanisms that carefully guard against any notion of human vulnerability that may prevent a soldier from acting effectively in combat situations. Yet the psychology of killing certainly differs from the psychology of remote apathy. The deaths of others that occur at a great physical and psychological distance from the American populace pose a minimal amount of stress on the daily moral framework of the average American civilian. Direct killing, on the other hand, imposes a significant stress on the psyche of the soldier and presents an urgent challenge to his or her moral conceptions. The psychology of military training thus uses different tools in preparing the mind of the soldier[6] for a violent encounter with the enemy "other."

---

the agentic state without significant resistance for the benefit of participation in a larger, differentiated society—Arendt essentially argues that this encounter reminds people in the agentic state of the threat posed by the unassimilated. Perhaps even drawing on the knowledge of their own internal, individual resistance (however minor and ineffective) to the larger agentic demands, it reminds them that it is not impossible for them, too, to become savage. The savage human is problematically alien and different but, perhaps more problematically, is also "like them."

6. A term that literally only refers to a member of the Army. Because it is too cumbersome to use the term "airmen" for members of the Air Force, "sailors" for members of the Navy, and "Marines" for members of the Marine Corps—and since

There are two different ways in which the US military trains its soldiers to "overcome" certain psychological factors that inhibit killing. In his understanding of presdisposition and conditioning in the psyche, Grossman finds two "default" positions of the human psyche that seem to underscore an inherent awareness of our own vulnerability. First, he shows how traditional psychology has held that when a member of a species (human or animal) is confronted with a threat, he has two responses: fight or flee. Grossman argues that, when confronted with a threat from another member of the same species, the standard set of "fight-or-flight" responses must be expanded to include "posturing and submission."[7] He argues that we view aggression far too simplistically if we understand its only expression in nature as a confrontation ending in a violent fight to the death. He argues that many confrontations end in varying displays of "very orchestrated, highly ritualized" posturing and aggression; but he draws a sharp distinction between this and a "fight" response that results in violence (6). He finds that very few incidents of intra-species confrontation in the natural world actually end in a truly violent response. Instead, the majority end with the submission of one of the (nearly always) males by "fawning and exposing some vulnerable portion of the anatomy to the victor, in the instinctive knowledge that the opponent will not kill or further harm one of its own kind once it has surrendered" (6). This common knowledge and understanding of the implicit rule of surrender reflects an inherent interest in "damage limitation" on behalf of both the "winner" and the "loser" that is in the interest of the species: that is, younger males are not killed off in early violent confrontations with stronger, more mature males—and thus they live to procreate later. The participants in the action seem acutely aware of their own vulnerability, and they are concerned not to risk undue damage to themselves or the species as a whole over small-scale intraspecies conflict.

The second default position builds on the first and essentially reflects Grossman's larger claim that a psychological injunction against killing is present in the overwhelming majority of men.[8] This injunction

no all-encompassing term exists—I will use the word "soldier" when referring to all members of the US armed forces.

7. Grossman, *On Killing*, 5. Hereafter, page references to this work appear in parentheses within the text.

8. Since the presence of women in direct combat situations in any significant number is a relatively new phenomenon—and all of the combatants he studied are

is closely related to the fundamental responses of flight, fight, posture, and submit, and it reflects again some notion of vulnerability inherent in the human psyche. Killing other human beings, it turns out, rends the fabric of this natural "agreement" in confrontation, and it runs counter to our biological evolution. This conclusion, in its own way, supports Arendt's suggestion that, in the encounter with the "other," we are particularly reminded of our own underlying human vulnerability in the "savage" world.

Considered in the context of these basic evolutionary adaptations, Grossman argues, the encounter with killing, death, and human vulnerability in combat is psychologically devastating, and he critiques the Veterans Affairs psychologists who attempt to treat PTSD as maladjustment. It is certainly an undeniable factor—and Grossman correctly assesses it—that "as a society, we seem unable to deal with moral pain or guilt" (96). The result of our "othering," and its continued appeal to American exceptionalism in the larger cultural context, is to provide us with a substantial opiate against any notion of moral pain or sense of extreme vulnerability. If our actions, no matter how violent and destructive, can be incorporated into the greater narrative of the good and noble American project, then we can justify the destruction of the "other" as one who stood in the way of the grand enterprise of American civilization-building. But we should note that, for the veteran who has experienced killing and has reaped the psychological consequences in acute PTSD, such illusions are profoundly unhelpful. The guilt and moral pain is a real and terrifying consequence of killing; yet it is perhaps not the only way to understand the psychological break that has occurred here.

To be sure, naming the issue of PTSD as a "problem in adjustment" is not totally inaccurate, because the veteran has come face to face with his own vulnerability, and it turns out that it is utterly unbearable. The veteran's reassimilation into a society that is in the grip of such a profound denial of the very vulnerability that he has experienced so devastatingly seems ludicrous. What this suggests is that a significant psychological balance has been dismantled: we have rent asunder the psychological fabric and evolutionary biology that allows us to live au-

---

male—the study possesses the limitation of focusing exclusively on men and the male psyche. Significant insight might develop from a study of the ways the female psyche works similarly or in contrast to the male in these areas.

thentically with the occasional confrontation with another member of our species. The illusions constructed in military training were exercises in disrupting—or, more accurately, short-circuiting—a psychological revulsion toward killing. Grossman at least suggests that our inbuilt injunction against killing allows us to live with a comfortable and healthy understanding of this vulnerability, knowing that the "other" is like us and therefore unlikely to harm us, even when disagreement leads to confrontation.

Worlds Polarized by Vulnerability: Retreat and Isolation

One primary effect of the wanton killing evidenced in conflicts (American and otherwise) around the globe is thus to eliminate the psychological hope of escape from confrontation without killing, being killed, or suffering considerable harm. With these possibilities removed from any confrontation, the psychological vulnerability experienced is absolute—the understanding that "posturing and submitting" are acceptable forms of navigating a confrontation has deteriorated in modern thought. The options are to run, kill, or be killed; and given these choices, confrontation becomes utterly terrifying, since we are at risk continually. This is a weight of vulnerability that is difficult for the psyche to process and that the psyche was probably never designed to handle. Its safeguards have been violated, so that a sense of equilibrium cannot be achieved either through the illusions that distract others or through incorporation into a greater frame of meaning (i.e., the "noble" cause). Vulnerability can no longer be experienced as anything less than extreme and total, and this gives it an unbearable weight that leads to our creation of abstractions simply to shield ourselves from the psychic pain of realization.

In my view, the forces of dehumanization and "irrational hatred" that Grossman describes not only speak to personal experiences, but they also fundamentally shape the landscape of the current conflicts. The experience of personal hatred toward one's enemy has become extreme in the conflicts in Afghanistan and Iraq; yet it is diffused through new forms of media, in which it is documented and easily accessible. In the dynamics that dominate the current conflicts between the United States and Al-Qaeda affiliates throughout the world, each side views its enemy as an existential threat—a threat to its very survival as a political entity. In some ways, this is a legacy of the "total war" strategy adopted in World Wars I and II, but it has taken on a particular virulence in the Global War on Terror. In the recent conflicts in Afghanistan and Iraq, modern technology and the resultant rapid dissemination of information have made the "irrational hatred" of the enemy much closer to each combatant.[9] Graphic images and videos in recent years have become ubiquitous and have carried the message of hate to a wide audience around the world. The American capacity for hatred and denial of humanity is clearly evidenced in the brutal and degrading treatment that American women and men administered to prisoners at the Abu Ghraib prison in Iraq, as well as in the persistent use of torture methods, such as "waterboarding," at the Guantanamo Bay detention camp. Likewise, the groups affiliated with Al-Qaeda have demonstrated their capacity for hatred and denial of humanity through numerous displays of torture and killing designed to exhibit their brutality and disregard for the lives of their enemies.[10] Images that display this intense hatred have reached nearly every corner of the globe, thanks to the internet and the twenty four hour news cycle. These images reach a large and significant number of participants on both sides of the conflict, and they are often used as "shock-value" propaganda to reinforce the savagery of the enemy on the psyche of the combatant, further dehumanizing the enemy. While most of those who view these graphic images of hatred do not expect to confront the enemies depicted, the combatants do, and this reality can channel a sense of revulsion that would be common to any viewer—what Grossman describes as "dread." The message transmitted is received as one of deep hatred: not only is the cause so noble that it justifies killing the other, but it demands the *elimination* of the other.

Further, the strategic necessity to wipe out the enemy creates a particularly unforgiving set of rules of engagement that severely restrict

9. I must acknowledge that this in some way contradicts Grossman's overall point: to experience the dread he describes is to experience the hatred of an enemy embodied physically by the personal encounter with the human being set upon killing. However, my point is that the images of hatred and slaughter that can now be viewed online by combatants on either side of the conflict inculcate a sense of real and deep horror in the mind of the combatant. In other words, they are psychologically affected by the hatred on display.

10. Exemplified in the videos posted online, which showed in horrific detail, e.g., the beheadings of Nick Berg and Daniel Pearl.

the agency and imagination of the combatants, creating continued stress on their psyches. As the current conflicts in Afghanistan and Iraq quickly became insurgencies (a particular variety of asymmetrical conflict), both the American and insurgent forces sought to inflict maximum casualties whenever the battles were joined, since direct confrontations were not especially common.[11] In other words, because there are few opportunities to kill each other openly, when the opportunity presents itself, the combatants must seize it. If either participant attempts to retreat while engaged with the other, the retreating group will generally be attacked until the attacking side is no longer physically able to inflict damage, or is somehow prevented from doing so. While the classic options of "posture" and "submit" that are commonly available in intraspecies conflict cannot be said to be entirely nonexistent in this environment, there is no signal that will cease hostilities and allow both parties to walk away unscathed.[12] To expose oneself as a combatant to the other is to be faced with a version of irrational hatred that continues off the battlefield as well, so that surrendering is potentially submitting oneself to torture, a life sentence in a military prison (or an indefinite period of detention without a hearing), or even execution. Both sides have demonstrated a clear capacity for accomplishing any of these options. From the standpoint of an American combatant, the net effect of these realities is the internalization of the message that the status of the others as enemy is essential, not contingent or tem-

11. An insurgency is a conflict in which one side's military advantage is significantly greater than another's. The term is frequently associated with insurgencies of nonstate actors fighting a developed and mature state power. To me, its importance here is to suggest that perhaps the nature of this conflict increases the need for the lesser-equipped side to maximize casualties in the battles it chooses to fight, further increasing the experience of "irrational hatred" of the soldiers fighting the insurgency and the sense of dread among the soldiers of the greater-equipped side. Likewise, the greater-equipped side seeks to "root out" the insurgents from among the local populace—an arduous and delicate task. When direct conflict occurs, the greater-equipped side understands this as a rare opportunity to decimate the enemy numbers.

12. The option to retreat in light of a disadvantageous situation remains viable, as would a demonstrable show of military might that would serve to deter an enemy attack rather than eliminating the enemy entirely. Yet the crucial point is that there is virtually no situation in either the war in Afghanistan or the war in Iraq in which one could effectively submit without severe and perhaps violent consequence. Given the existential threat associated with either side by the other in the "Global War on Terror," there is effectively no option to surrender with the understanding that hostilities toward one would cease.

porary.[13] To encounter this world is to experience a highly polarized reality that psychologically reifies the boundaries between others and in which violence and death govern these relationships. One cannot exist here with anything other than an extreme experience of one's own vulnerability, the sense that life can be—and often is—snuffed out at any given moment.

To experience this world is to internalize a distorted and broken relationality marked by a sense of mistrust of outsiders based on the profound vulnerability and hatred demonstrated in conflict. While this mistrust of those outside of one's own unit likely has a positive benefit in terms of survivability on the battlefield, it ultimately proves to be deeply distorting in other areas of life. What is formed by participation in (and thereby the willing of) this polarized reality of combat is a distinctive bond of trust between those who have proven to be "on your side" in the conflict. The distortion of relationality often is most visible when combatants return home and have difficulty adjusting to life, particularly with close loved ones who have not experienced combat with them, but with whom they are expected to resume intimate relationships that require trust. Yet it also manifests itself in a more concretized mistrust of those who are different, who are put in positions of "others" and whom the combatants, in light of their experience of hatred and violence, view as a significant threat.

The crushing sense of vulnerability that soldiers experience in combat zones lies at the root of one of the primary effects of this low-intensity traumatic event: the veterans' struggle to integrate the reality of combat within the American culture and daily life. There are two major ways in which veterans encounter deeply discordant realities on their return home, and both of these mechanisms threaten to suppress the traumatic event in veterans' psyches.

First, in deep contrast to the combat zone, it can be argued that a strong feature of contemporary American society is its denial of mortality. In *The Coming of God*, Jürgen Moltmann argues, for example, that we have pushed death to the margins of society: we move cemeteries to "the periphery of towns and cities"; we die in hospices and hospitals

13. It would be presumptuous to speak of the effect of these images on Al-Qaeda combatants, though it seems highly unlikely, given the tenor of most communications from Al-Qaeda leadership, that the psychological result would be categorically different.

away from the public view, with the result that we no longer encounter death in public.[14] Serene Jones similarly argues that even the concept of trauma as a psychic wound itself is difficult for our culture to accept, "because it exposes how vulnerable we are, deep inside, to the many forms of violence that surround us and that we ourselves enact."[15] Veterans are thus thrust into a world that continually distances itself from the sense of vulnerability that they cannot ignore and are deeply troubled by. There is no middle ground for veterans to move toward, a place where mortality is understood and accepted in a capacity that neither denies its reality nor grants it complete and violent hegemony over the mind. The juxtaposition of the two extremes creates a strain for veterans, who certainly do not want to accept the brutal reality of the combat zone as normative for all of human life, but cannot accept the denial of mortality once death has been exhibited in the extreme form associated with contemporary military combat.

Second, while most combatants who have encountered the enemy at close range have difficulty fully denying the enemy's humanity, a powerful force in our culture is set on implicitly denying this in order to uncritically affirm the righteousness of the American cause.[16] For the veteran who has witnessed the violence of the combat zone and is unable to deny an enemy's humanity, this creates another powerful dissonance. In the culture's denial of mortality, the uncritical praise of the veteran and the national cause crosses the boundary of "positive disposition" of social support that Grossman identified, and it comes to exacerbate trauma: it leaves no space for the veteran to explore the deep ambiguities of a traumatic encounter with the world of war, defined by violence and dehumanizing forces. The strain presents another abrasive collision of realities for the traumatized veteran and greatly inhibits his or her ability to process and make meaning out of the experience of conflict after the fact.

Both of these polarizing aspects of a veteran's return may function to suppress one of the major healing mechanisms of trauma: the op-

14. Jürgen Moltmann, *The Coming of God: Christian Eschatology*, trans. Margaret Kohl (Minneapolis: Fortress, 1996), 55.

15. Serene Jones, *Trauma and Grace: Theology in a Ruptured World* (Louisville: Westminster John Knox, 2009), 13.

16. While it is certain that the force of dehumanization powerfully conditions the willing and the psyche of the combatant, Grossman observes that combatants who have encountered and killed the enemy at close range are most traumatized by the realization that the enemy other is "just like them."

portunity for traumatized persons to witness to their experience and the opportunity for that witness to be heard. It is in this process, as Felman and Laub note in *Testimony*, that the unknown and unintegrated event of trauma begins to become known by both the witness and the hearer.[17] Felman and Laub also argue that there is a danger in hearing the testimony of the witness as well, that one risks experiencing the trauma and, in some smaller way, being traumatized by it. Jones argues that even in the best of circumstances people "often find it uncomfortable to be around trauma survivors," and the deep differences in understanding of mortality and the reification of military enterprise only exacerbate this.[18] Thus it appears to the veteran that the larger culture is particularly hostile to hearing this witness. Indeed, to hear it would be to risk destabilizing some of the formative principles of cultural identity, and so veterans rarely attempt to give that witness. For veterans, particularly those without extremely acute symptoms of trauma, such witness often remains beyond the realm of communication and comprehension—and thus ends up frequently invading the present.[19] Freud observed that this is one of the primary markers of trauma: the inability of the past to recede into memory, and its persistent and undesirable recurrence in the present.[20]

These profound differences in perceived reality can end up exacerbating a traumatized veteran's sense of isolation and contribute to a cycle that deepens the distrust of those most able to help. Jones names this profound sense of isolation as "the most insidious feature of PTSD," as the veteran's inability to trust effectively removes the veteran from communities of care "and affection" that provide avenues to healing.[21] The natural consequence of the encounter and prolonged exposure to a reality in which the injunction against killing is inoperative is a difficulty in building trust. Recall that this injunction often manifested itself in intraspecies conflict when a member submitted to the other, trusting that the confrontation would end and he would not

17. Shoshana Felman and Dori Laub, *Testimony: Crises of Witnessing in Literature, Psychoanalysis, and History* (New York: Routledge, 1992), 57.

18. Jones, *Trauma and Grace*, 18.

19. Who are thus less likely to be referred to psychatric therapy and thus less likely to have access to someone who will listen to their witness.

20. Shelly Rambo, *Spirit and Trauma: A Theology of Remaining* (Louisville: Westminster John Knox, 2010), 19.

21. Jones, *Trauma and Grace*, 18.

be harmed. In the conflict where this is absent, where vulnerability is apparent everywhere, trust proves to be a very difficult commodity. It is granted on the battlefield to one's friends and comrades, those who understand the way the reality of combat is shaped, those who have experienced and digested the traumatic reality, and those on whom the soldier depends for insulation from his own responsibility and guilt. The veteran who has experienced this naturally distrusts those who have not experienced these realities, and this distrust is exacerbated by the fact that the larger culture seems not simply to be oblivious to them, but to actively deny them.

The Loss of Blessedness: The Precariousness of Civilization

The precariousness of human life and a person's psychological hold on it is a primary feature of Augustine's concept of Adam's Fall and its consequences for humanity. His concept of the death of the soul, which occurs when God forsakes it, bears remarkable similarity to some contemporary descriptions of trauma, particularly what is suffered by those who have had a profound encounter with the physical death of those around them. The Augustinian concept of humanity's loss of the deep and intimate connection with God, as the power that underwrites human life and sustains its existence, holds a particular descriptive power in naming the inability of natural evolution and civilization itself to serve as guarantor of human existence. Crucially, Augustine affirms the vulnerability of humanity to death and the effects of this vulnerability on the living, providing something of a "gaze into the abyss" of the human predicament that serves to illustrate the deep brokenness of the world and its inability to mend itself.

Augustine argues that as a result of Adam's turning from God, humanity has turned from the source of life and goodness and is thus subject to death.[22] God is not just the source of all being; God is also the one who exists in the fullness of being: God "supremely *is*," connoting that God's being is the very completion and fullness of being itself (12.2). In creating, God makes entities that exist; yet, in virtue of their mortal and

22. Augustine, *City of God* 13.2–3. Hereafter, citations of this work appear in parentheses within the text.

mutable natures, creatures possess existence less perfectly. The soul, the seat of the highest level of human being, draws life directly from God, the one whose being is supreme and whose existence sustains itself. Creatures are not created having the fullness of life and blessedness in themselves, but they are able to share in the enjoyment of the God who exists supremely. The most secure blessedness of life comes from "cleaving" to God, remaining in communion with that supreme source of life on which the soul draws.

In turning to themselves, fallen angels and humans break from this close communion, moving from dependence on God, who has being supremely, to dependence on themselves for their own sustenance and existence. In the case of human beings, this amounts to disconnecting from what gives the soul its life, vitality, and meaning—and "defecting" to ourselves for the soul's own satisfaction (12.7). For Augustine, this defection from God is the very point at which the angel or human begins to have an "evil will." Sinfulness comes into the cosmic equation here, and through Adam, into the life of all humanity. The soul as created by God has its own existence independent from its creator, but in its state of alienation from God, the source of its life and ground of its being, it draws no life from God. This "dead soul," which in its sinful state is alienated from God, still provides life to the body; but it retains none of its own life and vitality. In turning inward toward himself, Adam's "being became less complete than when he clung to the one who exists supremely. Thus, to forsake God and to exist in oneself—that is, to be pleased with oneself—is not immediately to lose all being, but is to come closer to nothingness" (14.13).

While Augustine certainly speaks of the retributive purpose of death as the "just punishment" of sin, there is also the sense in which it is a disconnection from what undergirds humanity's very existence. Without this connection, humanity faces a series of "deaths" that result from Adam's Fall: the first is the death of the soul, which is forsaken by God. The soul, being immortal by its very nature, has the capacity to confer life to the mortal body, even when the soul is forsaken by God and does not have any life of its own. Augustine attributes this dead-yet-living soul to the condition of ultimate eternal alienation from God in which one's soul is unable to experience blessedness in any capacity. Life in this state is "made neither sweet by pleasure nor wholesome by quietude," but faces the constant agony of despair (13.2). Following this death of the soul is the eventual death of the body, when it is left by the soul itself and no longer is able to draw life from it. But the final and most severe form of death is what Augustine (drawing from Revelation) terms the "second death" (13.2): it involves the reunification of the mortal body and immortal soul in eternal separation from God. The body and soul in this state cannot draw on anything that quickens life, pleasure, or goodness; they simply experience eternal pain. Existence in this state is more aptly and truly understood as death rather than life.

Implicit in this account of the Fall is the claim that humanity cannot sustain or guarantee its own existence apart from God. Humanity has inherited the state of alienation from the source of life and blessedness that enlivens the human soul. Afflicted by this inheritance, humanity attempts to serve as the guarantor of its own existence, depending on the "dead soul" for all of life and blessedness. Evoking the language of being and nonbeing, specifically the notion that we are deprived of our proper connection to God, Augustine asserts that we come "closer to nothingness" (14.13). He echoes the language Athanasius used a generation before him: the latter argued that the chief effect of sin was that it threatened to cause humanity to pass back into "non-existence."[23] The "dead soul" cannot sustain human life as it is meant to be in the fullness of participation in the divine life. As a result of the Fall, Augustine understands that humanity is facing the abyss of ultimate death and consumption by evil.

When we read their work through this particular Augustinian lens, perhaps we could understand that Arendt and Grossman are describing structures that attempt to sustain human life and ultimately fail to do so. Arendt essentially points to a particularly ironic seam in what could be interpreted as civilization's attempt to sustain blessedness for those within it. Through the cultivation of particular cultures and attempts to safeguard the homes, civic identity, life, and future of certain peoples through the re-formation of European nations along ethno-national lines, millions of people suddenly were placed outside the bounds of "civilization." The encounter with the savage and naked human occurs when one who is inside civilization meets one who has been expelled from it. The particular irony is that it is not that these savage and stateless people exist because the world possesses an insufficient degree of

23. Athanasius, *On the Incarnation* 30. Augustine, of course, does not actually believe this to be possible, owing to the immortality of the soul. There is a sense in which Augustine's whole purpose in naming existence in hell as "existence" is simply to preserve the full horror of eternal punishment, in which one retains full sensory capability but experiences only negative stimulus: bodily pain and agony.

civilization, but rather that their expulsion from civilization and existence as "naked" humans is the result of a kind of hypercivilization that occurs when nations attempt to secure the blessedness of their people in an intense and ultimate way. The encounter with the savage human, Arendt argues, ultimately reveals that basic human rights to land, identity, life, and future are not inalienable, but are granted and guaranteed by governments. The encounter with the "savage" and "naked" human strikes a somewhat paradoxical fear in the civilized human: they fear the loss of their own place within civilization, and perhaps even civilization itself; yet they also experience the realization that civilization is itself precarious and even fickle. The encounter with those who have been made "savage" and "naked" via their loss of civilization's protections for themselves evinces civilization's inability to effectively guarantee life, identity, and future for any of its inhabitants.

American combatants may have experiences that reveal the underbelly of American civilization and the costs of our relative serenity.[24] The exposure to human vulnerability in the extreme—and to the randomness of wartime violence—can reveal the precarious blessing of security in America. In my own experience as a veteran of the conflicts in Afghanistan and Iraq, the violent realities of daily life experienced by civilians in these extremely war-torn areas are not easily forgotten, even as one returns to the more quotidian and secure family life of an average American. My most recurring nightmares feature my own children as victims of the wartime violence that I've experienced. In those nightmares, violent people often enter my home and threaten my young family; or my wife and children find themselves in the minefields of Afghanistan and in the crosshairs of mortar-firing insurgents in Iraq. In either case, they seem to evoke my own deep fear that our security is an illusion, that its illusory nature depends primarily on the randomness through which it is granted. My family lives in America only by the chance of our births, and those unlucky enough to have been born elsewhere experience my nightmares as their daily realities.

The injunction against killing that Grossman describes can be understood as an evolutionary protection, both to the individual human

24. The power of the term "relative" in this sentence cannot be emphasized enough. It is certainly true that many groups within the borders of our nation enjoy lesser status than others do, and what exactly it is that entails identity as a full "American citizen," with all its concomitant privileges and rights, is not universally agreed on.

psyche and to the species as a whole. It is a mechanism that ensures that intraspecies conflict does not end up decimating the species itself. As I have argued, however, the human history of warfare has unraveled these mutually assured protections.[25] Militaries have found ways to train and condition soldiers to overcome the injunction against killing, and the strategic necessities of modern combat and the influence of ideological radicalism have eliminated many of the basic allowances for retreat, surrender, and safe quarter on the battlefield. The trauma of veterans, particularly in its severest forms of PTSD, testifies to the totality of the failure of these evolutionary psychological mechanisms to sustain life, particularly in terms of any sense of peace or pleasure. The failure of the injunction has something of a cascading domino effect, since its breaking unleashes effects that condition even those who would consciously choose not to kill. If we use Nash's concept of "damage to one's core beliefs," a critical cause of psychic injury is the loss of the necessary belief that one is not going to be killed at any moment.[26] Whether one chooses to kill or not, the loss of this sense of safety is deeply debilitating, and this very safety has been threatened by one willing to break the injunction.

These injunctions function to allow the psyche to bear the natural vulnerabilities that come with human life in community. In the absence of these safeguards, it would appear that the human reaction to this vulnerability has become extremely polarized and dichotomous in ways that further alienate the community from the fullness of human life. Veterans who have experienced vulnerability firsthand in an intense and profound way struggle to recover and rebuild their core sense of safety and security in the world. American society as a whole attempts to ignore human vulnerability and pushes thoughts of death and mortality to the fringes of society and cultural memory. The dichotomy serves to isolate each group from the other in a way that increases veteran trauma and hardens tribal boundaries within the larger national community. Both are reflections of the sense that naked human vulnerability is such a terrifying reality, particularly in our current environment, that facing it is to be avoided at all costs—lest we become deeply traumatized.

The loss of the core belief of one's own safety and relative security is not necessarily a permanent one. As Nash argues, broken and shattered

25. Drawing on Grossman, *On Killing* (chap. 3).

26. Nash, "Combat/Operational Stress Adaptations and Injuries," 53.

senses of goodness and confidence in life "are not beyond repair," but they must be rebuilt in a way that takes seriously the reality of human vulnerability without "sacrificing everything that is positive about human existence."[27] Yet there is a sense that in the human psyche, the experience of intense and extreme vulnerability is not one that can be easily incorporated into a new belief system. To use a legal phrase, it is a bell that cannot be unrung: the "death imprint," psychologist R. J. Lifton argues, is extremely difficult to "assimilate and detoxify."[28] In other words, the cultural reaction that takes the form of attempting to resist and repress this notion is perhaps simply a highly cultivated outgrowth of a necessary psychological defense mechanism.

The model of original sin that I have described does little to make this somewhat bleak aspect of the human situation any less so. In fact, what Augustine argues is essentially that this understanding of human vulnerability is an accurate assessment of humanity's plight and the severity of the problem of sin. Disconnected from God, the source of life and goodness, there is nothing that can sustain human life or effectively shield us from looking into the abyss and experiencing terror at our fate. Combatants who experience this reality firsthand in an acute battlefield situation essentially have encounters with death in the ways that Augustine describes them. Often, they have encounters with physical death—whether that of comrades, enemies, or civilians—that leave lasting impressions. Army medics often experience this particular sense acutely, because they witness large numbers of mortal injuries and they deal not simply with the dead body of a fallen soldier, but with the agonizing final moments of terrified soldiers dying in great pain.[29]

Augustine's understanding of the ways in which death threatens postlapsarian humanity resonates with the ways in which contemporary trauma theorists understand the psychological effect of being overwhelmed by an experience of physical death. Those struggling to assim-

27. Nash, "Combat/Operational Stress Adaptations and Injuries," 54.

28. R. J. Lifton, "Understanding the Traumatized Self: Imagery, Symbolization, and Transformation," in *Human Adaptation to Extreme Stress*, ed. J. P. Wilson, Z. Harel, and B. Kahana (New York: Plenum, 1988), 18.

29. John Keegan and Richard Holmes, *Soldiers: A History of Men in Battle* (London: Hamilton, 1985), 154. Keegan and Holmes recount the firsthand narratives of soldiers dealing with the screams of the dying and, in their traumatic pain, their reversion to childhood sources of comfort: many soldiers with grievous wounds cry out in their last moments for their mothers.

ilate the "death imprint" may describe their professed "joyless" state of being and may testify to their incapacity to experience enjoyment in any activity—a resonance with what Augustine describes as a "dead soul." In one of the formative texts in trauma theory, Cathy Caruth names trauma as an event of death that lingers into life, focusing on the "endless impact" that it makes on the one who survives.[30] Caruth describes the impact of the experience as a certain kind of struggle between two compelling poles, "the oscillation between a crisis of death and the correlative crisis of life." For Caruth, trauma at its core involves the psychological attempt to return to equilibrium that has been disrupted by the "unbearable" brush with death in a stressful experience—and the "unbearable nature of its survival." Similarly, Serene Jones differentiates a traumatic event from one that is simply an instance of extreme stress by noting that in a traumatic event, one "experiences the threat of annihilation."[31] It is precisely in the brush with one's own vulnerability and the vulnerability of others that one becomes traumatized. Jones argues that this experience of being overwhelmed by the prospect of annihilation can result in a paralyzing feeling of passivity in the world and a loss of agency. In other words, those traumatized by this annihilating force may also experience a failure of memory and a diminishment of language use, a deep sense of dissociation from their own experiences, a loss of hope, and an "emotional and cognitive deadness."[32] The experience of human vulnerability penetrates deep into the psyche, and its effects appear to numb the mind's capacity for positive emotion.

As one attempts to rebuild from an experience of deep vulnerability, the concept of original sin holds that, in humanity's postlapsarian state, there is no absolutely secure foundation on which to begin. It is important to note that this does not suggest that all efforts at reconstructing a sense of what Nash describes as "core beliefs" that are necessary to function are doomed to failure. Certainly, Shay, Tick, and many other psychologists, religious leaders, trauma theorists, medical professionals, theologians—and, most importantly, those who live with and care for traumatized veterans—all of these are making huge strides in developing positive and beneficial avenues of healing built on the power

30. Cathy Caruth, *Unclaimed Experience: Trauma, Narrative, and History* (Baltimore: Johns Hopkins University Press, 1996), 7.

31. Jones, *Trauma and Grace*, 15.

32. Jones, *Trauma and Grace*, 17.

of truthtelling and supportive community. But this concept of sin does serve to define all of those avenues as temporal and penultimate. The difficulty in healing from trauma testifies to the power of the "annihilating force" to disrupt the functioning of the human mind. Perhaps the traumatic memory itself is so difficult to assimilate because of its power to name the unbearable state of vulnerability in which we all exist, yet cannot bring ourselves to truly confront.

At its heart, the Augustinian concept of postlapsarian human life in the power of death provides a way to name the brokenness and extreme vulnerability that combatants experience. Civilization and our own evolutionary developments cannot sustain our existence or our psychological health in the midst of death and destruction, particularly in the extreme forms in which it is experienced on the battlefield. In a dark way, this concept of original sin validates the authenticity of this human experience in all its horror as a profound and very basic description of the world's wrongness. The forces of sin have so distorted the fabric of human existence that we exist in a state of extreme vulnerability of both body and soul. The doctrine of original sin upholds an experience of the fragility and precariousness of human life as disconnected from the divine source, which can alone uphold and sustain life in all its fullness. In many ways, this is a statement of the gospel understanding of sin in its rawest form. Rowan Williams argues that a key aspect of witness to Christ is to authentically name and witness to the darkness of the world, to be unafraid of "looking with honesty at that chaos."[33] The naming of human fragility as a profound consequence of the world's sinfulness and brokenness does precisely that.

33. Rowan Williams, *Being Christian: Baptism, Bible, Eucharist, Prayer* (Grand Rapids: Eerdmans, 2014), 5.

CHAPTER 5

The Enslavement of Agency and Betrayal of Identity

> For I delight in the law of God in my inmost self, but I see in my members another law at war with the law of my mind, making me captive to the law of sin that dwells in my members. Wretched man that I am! Who will rescue me from this body of death?
>
> —ROMANS 7:22–24

I argued in chapter 2 that there are external forces that profoundly restrict and delimit the boundaries of a combatant's willing. In this chapter I will return to that theme in order to more closely examine the ways in which McFadyen's notion that victims of abuse "may feel trapped in the trajectory" of their own willing—as a result of the external distortions they have deeply internalized—may profoundly describe the situation in which many veterans find themselves.[1] Resonant with Paul's description of the captivity and misery of sin in Romans 7, many veterans experience war as a force that radically consumes and enslaves their very selves and greatly distorts their capacities to act in the world. The trauma of veterans is deeply connected to the disfiguring of combatants' sense of good; as a result, their agency is profoundly abused and betrayed by a power that combatants trust to uphold moral and social order. When the experience of war demonstrates a totalizing disregard for either moral or social norms and instead promotes a singular

1. This line of argument certainly begins to blur the boundaries of the abuser and the victim—or, more accurately, continues to blur the lines that McFadyen began to blur in the trajectory of his thought. This is a crucial issue that bears a great deal of comment, and I will return to it for a thorough treatment in this book's final chapter.

desire for domination, the combatants' identity and their very character suffer at the hands of the cause to which they have committed their "lives, fortunes and sacred honor."[2]

A critical element that differentiates veteran trauma from more classical presentations of PTSD is the substantial difference in the character of the agency that veterans exercise. Many victims of assault, rape, or other violent crimes describe a debilitating sense of powerlessness or passivity in the face of an annihilating force during the traumatic event. Combatants, as one would expect, describe their own agency in more active terms, even during events of extreme stress. In many ways, their trauma is a direct product of their active agency and its constriction through the powerful forces that impact their willing in combat. These differences are crucial in understanding how the experiences of veteran trauma exhibit the character of "perpetrator" violence, and have many similar psychological byproducts in terms of guilt, pain and remorse. What I will argue in this chapter is that, despite these crucial differences in agency, the concept of original sin is deeply resonant with the agential distortions that combatants experience and is descriptive of their broken relationality in a way that calls into question simplistic and rigid definitions of moral identity that easily separate individuals into the categories of perpetrator and victim.

In arguing this larger point, I will examine the ways in which veteran "perpetrator" trauma differs from many instantiations of more passive "victim" trauma; I will posit that a different understanding of the forces involved illuminates the distinctions well. I will then draw on the insights of Stanley Milgram and trauma researchers to argue that the unique way that agency functions in combat deeply distorts the character and identity of veterans in a way that inhibits their ability to navigate their moral and social worlds. Finally, I will turn to Augustine and McFadyen once again, drawing on the conceptual vocabulary of the universality and radicality of sin to argue that the power of sin to bind the will is so great in combat that it becomes difficult to distinguish between victim and perpetrator as radically opposed positions on an axiological spectrum.

2. US Declaration of Independence, 1776.

Shattered Agency and the Threat of Being Devoured

Serene Jones argues that one of the key markers in the psychological makeup of one who has been traumatized is the experience of an "unraveling of agency." She traces the problems traumatized individuals have in viewing their actions as meaningful and effective in the world to the extreme sense of powerlessness they experienced in the traumatic event itself. She argues that this "loss of will" coincides ultimately with a "loss of hope" for the future.[3] While military veterans suffer many of the same depressive symptoms, their initial experience of trauma cannot, it seems, be described in terms of complete powerlessness. If Jones is speaking about a victim of rape, for example, the powerlessness she or he feels cannot correspond directly to that of a combatant wielding a weapon of war. If Grossman is correct, many combatants were, in fact, traumatized by their own willed actions. Thus it is crucial—if these experiences of trauma ultimately yield similar psychological conclusions about effective agency—to identify the ways in which the differential in agency during the traumatic event may affect the way in which the traumatized person exhibits this sense of resignation.

Jonathan Shay subtly shifts the tone of the trauma narrative, particularly as it pertains to agency, in describing the generally distrustful posture of combat veterans toward authority structures. While Jones notes that the force encountered by many trauma survivors is one that threatens "to annihilate,"[4] Shay describes the metaphorical encounter of the veteran as one with a force that seeks, not simply to annihilate, but to utterly consume. The distinction is a subtle one, but while an annihilating force seeks to render someone powerless and even lifeless, the consuming force seeks to capture, ingest, and devour, leaving no trace of individual being or personhood, but assimilating all it consumes into itself. Shay draws on Odysseus's encounter with the carnivorous Cyclops to describe veterans' feelings of powerlessness in their interaction with the government. Just as the vast power differential between the enormous Cyclops and Odysseus's men prevents them from realistically struggling against it, so do veterans often feel that, in interactions with the authoritative government, they are "liable to be

3. Jones, *Trauma and Grace*, 17–18.
4. Jones, *Trauma and Grace*, 13.

eaten alive."[5] Against a governmental force that consumes their very sense of identity, Shay notes that, like Odysseus, they may have to rely on their cunning in order to survive. Odysseus declares himself to be "Nobody" in order to escape the Cyclops; many veterans probably feel that they must embrace this same nonidentity in order to escape being consumed by something far larger and far-reaching than themselves.

While Shay does not develop the "consuming force" metaphor extensively, it is effective in providing a lens that accounts for the authoritarian power, not simply to destroy that which stands in its way, but to carefully bend the agency of individuals to serve its own ends. Those who have served in the hierarchy that Milgram describes—and have understood firsthand the way responsibility, decision-making, and agency itself are ceded to higher authorities—may well feel that they are in danger of being consumed by the force defining the terms of what is "good." The uniform, badges, insignia, ribbons, and awards constitute a highly developed system that forcefully depicts one's identity and how it has been defined within the strict confines of military service. Indeed, if (as I have argued in chapter 2) combatants find themselves in the midst of myriad and profound forces that have the power to constrict, limit, and condition their own agency and greatly impinge on their individuality, then veterans may fear being consumed and assimilated. The act of killing, however, reveals a separate, distinct way in which this metaphor works. Recall that Grossman argues that killing directly contradicts a deep-seated injunction against it; through training, one is conditioned to overcome this injunction in the service of a greater good. If this is the case, it is possible that what veterans relate to in this fear of consumption is that they have become monsters themselves, and that their agency has been devoured and compelled to perform deeds they see as monstrous. Shay notes that, in his work with Vietnam veterans, he has found that many isolate themselves from others due to the fear of inflicting their self-revulsion on someone else. He notes that they seem to feel as they do "because of the actual cruelty, violence, and coercion they have committed"—both in Vietnam and to those close to them after they have returned home (83).

As one's agency is intimately linked to an expression of selfhood, particularly in the modern conception—then against the forces that condition and shape willing in combat—a veteran's very sense of identity and

5. Shay, *Odysseus in America*, 47. Hereafter, page references to this work appear in parentheses within the text.

self may be in danger of being consumed. In arguing that PTSD should best be understood as an identity crisis, Edward Tick is essentially arguing that war fundamentally reshapes the interior drives and relationships that constitute the self, notably those of love, beauty, order, and form.[6] The dictates and demands of combat consume the combatants' sense of self and identity, and as their behaviors become more isolating, violent, and aggressive, they reflect how the forces of conflict consume their previous identity. Tick argues that what we understand least about war is precisely that it "changes its participants forever"; instead, we choose to "promote the idea . . . that vets and survivors can resume an ordinary civilian identity."[7] If conflict reduces one's self-prescribed identity to that of "nobody" as an adaptive survival mechanism, veterans may exhibit behavior that seeks to crucially preserve key parts of their own memory, particularly the memories of lost comrades. Shay notes that many veterans are deeply committed to "keeping faith" with those brothers and sisters in arms who were close to them. It is a sense of deep honor for most veterans who, as Odysseus promises to the fallen Elpenor in the underworld, refuse to "forget a thing" about the deaths of their friends (80). In my view, this is a stand against the forces of war that threaten to utterly consume the fallen comrades. It is a refusal to allow them to be lost to memory, to be consumed by the larger conflict, and to be remembered only in war memorials that present their goodness in terms of the degree to which their agency and individuality were sacrificed to the larger war effort.

Among those suffering from PTSD—even those who do not exhibit many of its more severe symptoms—researchers have noted dichotomous and polar behaviors, categorized on the one end by an extreme recklessness and on the other by an intense and all-consuming safeguarding of one's own responsibility and actions. While the precise causes of these behaviors involve complex series of chemical and psychological processes and cannot be easily ascertained, I will present them with the assumption that my argument in the previous section holds explanatory power: that the veterans have experienced an encounter with a threating force, notably one that threatens to utterly devour agency and individuality.

On one end of this spectrum of behavior is an attitude that appears to exhibit a complete recklessness, an extreme sense of adventure or "thrill-seeking" the combat veteran takes to an unhealthy level. Shay

6. Tick, *War and the Soul*, 122–24, 151–55.
7. Tick, *War and the Soul*, 155.

recounts veterans' narratives of behavior that seem to belie any level of concern for the self or cognizance of the consequences of one's action (44–60).[8] Veterans admit to, among other things, diving off roofs, driving motorcycles at extreme speeds on busy roads, and randomly punching an unsuspecting family member in the head as they pass by in the hallway of a home. These actions reflect a certain level of "boredom" with civilian life, whose monotony and daily grind they find utterly unbearable. When asked about their rationale for these somewhat wild and seemingly reckless actions, many veterans testify to an almost childlike sense of curiosity about pushing the bounds of behavior to simply find out how people will respond. This behavior can be understood as an "attraction to danger" that reflects an inability to live apart from the excitement and intensity of combat; Shay argues that it demonstrates a need to "live on the edge" and continually act in a way that demands a response from the cosmos (44). Like Odysseus's decision to remain in extreme danger in the cave of the Cyclops (rather than to flee) simply to see what gifts he might receive, the reckless impulses that veterans struggle to control reflect the sense that, no matter what, chances must be taken, fate tempted, and the cosmos questioned.

On the other end of the spectrum is the veteran who clings desperately to his own agency by becoming an obsessive, mission-focused workaholic. The veteran's workplace attitude may become an extreme determination, in certain cases even fanatical. Evidence suggests that financial considerations have little or nothing to do with the work habits of combat veterans. Instead, their primary motivation in immersing themselves in job-oriented tasks is the distraction it provides from virtually everything else that might occupy their minds. Shay notes that many veterans who operate this way tend to rely solely on themselves, to avoid interaction and even contact with other employees, to trust only themselves, and often to have difficulty cooperating with co-workers. Those who are successful seem to perform jobs that allow them to work in relative isolation and, like Odysseus, to attempt to do everything by themselves. Shay notes that combat veterans in civilian jobs, even those in positions that permit them to work unimpeded by others, would often arrive earlier and leave later than their co-workers, thus minimizing interactions with them.

8. Recounted by Shay in *Odysseus in America*. My next section builds on the idea Shay develops from Odysseus's adventure in the cave of the Cyclops—and the subsequent veteran attitudes that develop from it.

The unfortunate irony of the situation is often that, in their efforts to reclaim some control of their own agency, they end up devastating other parts of their lives. While these employees often achieve accolades for their dedication, their family lives suffer greatly. Shay recalls that one veteran in his treatment program worked a relatively low-wage job on the docks at Boston harbor, but worked so much overtime that he was able to purchase a large home in an upscale Boston suburb for his wife and children. But his family testified that he was never at home with them, and the marriage ended in divorce. In a particularly telling turn of phrase, Shay declares that many veterans "never brought themselves home with their paychecks" (59). The perfectionism that works well in the closed circuit of an individual project at a job does not translate well into a stable family life. Shay reports that many veterans that he would describe as "workaholics" are in fact detached physically and emotionally, are easily provoked to anger, and hold themselves and family members to unreachable standards (29). Many of these marriages end in divorce.

Without taking anything away from Shay's analysis, I would observe that these behaviors can be interpreted as a response to an encounter with the force that devours identity, reflecting a deeply distorted view of individual agency.[9] In terms of the extreme recklessness demonstrated in the first set of behaviors, veterans appear to exhibit an almost paradoxical view of their own agency and ability to affect events. On the one hand, those behaviors—notably the more dangerous and extreme ones—exhibit a considerable amount of disregard that veterans have for their own safety and well-being, which in turn would seem to reflect a level of having resigned themselves to the fact that their actions are not effectual in the world (since, otherwise, they would more highly value their own well-being, on which those effectual actions depend). On the other hand, the randomness of the actions does seem to reflect a desire on the veterans' part to provoke a response to what they have done, whether it be a response from the cosmos in actions that only endanger themselves or a response from others in seemingly random outbursts of violence. This would suggest that veterans do not view their agency

9. It would be too easy to argue that the danger-seeking actions taken by veterans exhibit a nihilism or a sense that the world is utterly meaninglessness. Shay's analysis and Tick's discussion of self-destructive behaviors (*War and the Soul*, 122–30) compellingly suggest that these actions exhibit far more nuanced and complex psychological injuries and conditionings.

as completely ineffectual, but that they are somewhat agnostic as to the ultimate effects of their own actions and seek continually to test them. Following an encounter with a force that devours agency and identity, veterans perhaps understand their actions to be ultimately ineffectual in the macroscale. They are unable to change the world, stem the tide of global violence, or stand up to the government, and they may even be unable to control the outcome of their own lives or have an effect on major aspects of their lives. Yet, in response to a force that threatens to utterly devour them, they seek to remind the "cosmos" that they are there, pushing boundaries in order to provoke a divine response.

Those veterans who exhibit a certain level of workaholism at their jobs in the ways I have described can also be acting in response to a force that has profound power to persuasively devour agency. In recognition of this power, veterans essentially shut out all human interaction that might influence their own agency and impede them from accomplishing what they can control. Aware of the awesome power of forces to utterly consume and compromise their individual agency and even moral beliefs, veterans effectively attempt to distance themselves from any outside force that might demand their attention and focus. Thus they seize on the aspect of life they can most control—their performance at work. Shay is certainly insightful in arguing that working continuously and compulsively is a way for veterans to contain internal distress and disorder, ensuring that their minds do not dwell on traumatic memories. But there also appears to be a strong element of control involved: veterans may avoid contact not simply because others will negatively affect outcomes that they could fully control, but also because other influences will dilute their own sense of agency and mission focus.[10] Collaboration with others at work can feel like a compromise of con-

10. Shay uses the tale of Odysseus's interaction with Aeolus, the King of the Winds, to illuminate the veteran's relationship with habitual and obsessive work habits. In this passage, Odysseus is given a wind that will direct his ships straight home. Aeolus then captures all of the winds that could blow the flotilla off course and puts them in a bag to be stowed on Odysseus's ship. Odysseus mans the sail for nine days without sleep, never trusting his men to do it, nor trusting them with the knowledge of what is in the bag on his ship. When he at last succumbs to sleep, his men, curious as to what treasure lies within the bag, open it and thus unleash the winds that blow the flotilla off course and extend their perilous journey. Shay likens veterans' behavior both to Odysseus's behavior in refusing to trust his crew with critical information and to the "lesson" Odysseus seems to take from their "mutinous" actions: If you want something done right, you have to do it yourself.

trol in service to a larger "good." As opposed to the demands of a job (particularly one that involves skilled labor and often involves relatively straightforward problems and solutions), family life is difficult because personal relationships require certain amounts of compromise. Most people who have raised children will testify to the difficulty—if not outright impossibility—of exerting simple "control" over them: their reactions seem random and unpredictable. The "good" of the family can consume veterans' actions and can perhaps cause them to feel as though their own individuality is becoming lost within this dynamic.

Constricted Agency and the Distortion of Character

While the behaviors discussed above certainly can be understood to distort character, the moral tension experienced by combatants can disfigure it in ways that are even more profound. Grossman argues that, while people can be conditioned to overcome the injunction against killing other humans, when they do so they will often respond to their own action with disgust and guilt. After the fact, the tension, guilt, and revulsion occupy such a significant portion of the psyche that combat veterans must eventually undergo an attempt to rationalize and accept their actions. Grossman notes that it is often a lifelong process that in many cases is still unresolved at the veteran's death. Shay, Tick, and other psychologists make the same claim in differing ways. Forces can powerfully and effectively cause a subject to act in a certain way, but not without significant stress reactions. This stress, or psychological tension, constitutes the grounds for trauma and, more to the point, for psychiatric and moral injury.

While the primary focus of Stanley Milgram's famous experiments was on the ability of an authority figure to evoke obedience in test subjects, a significant and often-overlooked finding of the study is that many subjects experienced significant stress, even as they followed the instructions of the experimenter (to shock another person) to the conclusion of the experiment.[11] He even called the presence of this pro-

11. Here I am interacting with Milgram's analysis in two primary sections of *Obedience to Authority*: the discussion of what he terms "Unexpected Behavior" (40–43) and his more detailed analysis of "Strain and Disobedience" (chap. 12, pp. 153–64), in which he articulates the pressures of the agential state vs. the moral repugnance many felt at continuing the experiment.

found stress the "second unanticipated effect" of the experiment as a whole—second only to the alarming rate of obedience. He argued that the cause of this stress was the fact that there was a profound differential between what their "conscience" dictated was acceptable, and perhaps "right," and what the experimenter was asking them to do. While very few continued to follow the experimenter's instructions to the end with no apparent discomfort, the strain experienced by those who did obey the experimenter to the end was generally greater than that of those who eventually disobeyed. In other words, it seems likely that the decision to disobey resolves the tension felt by the subject, while the tension continues to increase and is unresolved in the majority of those who obeyed until the end. Obedience, Milgram argues, must be a force of such a magnitude that it essentially prevents disobedience, even in cases of extreme tension. The sheer magnitude of the desire or compulsion to obey, he argues further, is so strong that the presence of stress or tension is a poor predictor of disobedience. Even in states of extreme distress and significant moral ambiguity, most of the subjects were unable to do the thing that would resolve the tension—that is, refuse to participate further. Instead, a subject would tolerate extreme amounts of tension, remaining in what Milgram termed an "aversive state": a situation in which the dictates of his or her own moral disposition were in profound conflict with the tasks he or she was performing.

This particular claim about the sources of the tension and stress, as well as the methods of resolving it, has profound implications. The desire to obey, Milgram found, is essentially the sum product of the forces that act on the willing of the subject. All those forces that condition the shift into the agential state (antecedent conditions) and hold the subject there (binding factors) result in the person's acting as the recognized authority directs him or her. While the power of both the antecedent conditions and binding factors effectively colonize the person's actions, there are several sources of observed strain, including the visceral aversion to the victim's protests and cries, the violation of internalized beliefs, the competing demands of the victim ("stop!") and the experimenter ("you must continue"), and, perhaps most critically, the fact that the administration of pain "is incompatible with the self-image of many subjects."[12] Stress arises as each of these—particularly the subject's internalized beliefs and self-image—come into direct conflict with the demands of authority.

12. Milgram, *Obedience to Authority*, 156.

While disobedience would most fully eliminate this tension and stress, this action does not appear to be universally available, and, in the absence of the ability to disobey, the psyche resorts to other options to reduce the stress. The subject may attempt to avoid the victim's protests, a goal achieved often in the Milgram experiments by the subject's reading of the questions the victim was to answer loudly and over his cries. The subject may also resort to outright denial, reducing moral strain by rejecting empirical data supporting an unwelcome conclusion in order to interpret the events in a way that is more palatable to the actor's conscience. In the course of the experiment, the subject may actively and passively deny that he or she is harming the victim by the shocks and may reject the notion that the victim is suffering at all.[13] The subject may also resort to subterfuges designed to minimize his or her part in the experiment or to subvert its more draconian aspects. Milgram found that some subjects, for example, would attempt to pass the correct answers to victims through vocal variation in order to avoid having to shock them for providing incorrect answers. Whether the subterfuge was effective or not, it allowed the subject to believe that he was resisting the experimenter in some way, and it helped "preserve his self-image as a benign man."[14]

This analysis reveals two critical aspects of the psyche of Milgram's subjects. First, even though the majority obeyed the experimenter to the end of the experiment, their interior self-image and sense of morality were not entirely brought into alignment with the demands of the experiment. Second, even though they were not able to disobey the experimenter, they took actions to distance their own psyches from the actions they were taking and to mitigate what they felt were the immoral aspects of the experiment. In short, the experiment suggests that the psyche seeks to preserve its own self-image and moral ideals within the crucible of a situation that demands the pursuit of the "good" of obedience to the higher authority. The subjects, in other words, are aware of the distance between their own ideals and what they are being asked to do, even as they perform the action in obedience to the experimenter.

13. Ironically, the victim in Milgram's study was, in fact, not suffering at all. The fact that an accurate perception of what is actually happening would be understood as denial, even when all empirical evidence available to the subject would indicate that the victim is indeed suffering, points to the limitations of the artificial situation created by the experiment. I will address this in more detail later in the chapter.

14. Milgram, *Obedience to Authority*, 160.

The tension between one's self-image and one's actions in the agential state is resolved in the psyche of the subject most fully through the assurance and reassurance that the responsibility for the subject's actions does not rest with him or her, but with the experimenter.[15] The fact that subjects sought these subterfuges and assurances of ultimate responsibility suggests that they were aware of the constriction of their willing, and were taking small, perhaps even meager, actions to preserve their own ideas about their identity, even as they could not refuse to do what they were asked to do.

The nature of the relationship between one's self-image and one's personal (though directed) actions is a critical aspect of human willing and identity that Milgram's study brings to the fore. A detailed analysis appears to lie outside the scope of Milgram's experiments and analysis for two crucial reasons. First, the experimental scenario is ultimately artificial: no victim is actually being shocked or killed. The tension and stress experienced by the subjects are certainly real, as they believe the victim to be in pain. Yet their obedience or disobedience has little tangible consequence, since the tension and stress is completely resolved when they discover that the "victim" is alive and was never in any pain—that is, it was all an act. Even if, on reflection, the subjects felt that they had acted horribly, the guilt or shame could be easily dismissed by the psyche as a learning experience, that there was no real consequence of their performance.[16] In other words, the self-image of the subject of the experiment is preserved because the subject has not *actually* had to harm anyone. The subject's psyche, while confronted for a brief period with that possibility, does not have to try to integrate the experience of harming or killing another human being into her or his self-image. Second, Milgram's study contained no reliable mechanism for measuring how the actions of the subjects impacted their view of themselves after

15. Milgram is able to conceptually keep the person's self-image and the actions of his or her agential state separate because, in his model of agency, an individual moves between an autonomous state and an agential one. In the autonomous state, one takes care of oneself and performs the daily tasks necessary for survival and enjoyment; an individual shifts into the agential state, essentially, to "do what he has to do" at the direction of properly recognized authority.

16. It could be envisioned, even by the most thoughtful and self-reflective subjects as a failure in a training environment, designed to allow the learner to experience situations and explore the best outcomes without any fear of consequence or negative outcome.

a substantial period of time. While Milgram did solicit feedback from participants several months after their participation in the study in order to gain insight into how they had reflected on what had occurred, the sporadic nature of the responses he received undercut any attempt to conduct a detailed or rigorous analysis.

Evidence suggests that the most psychologically difficult acts demanded of combatants do, indeed, affect their self-image. Grossman argues that after combatants kill in combat, the psyche attempts to continue to deny the humanity of the victim, working its way through a variety of denial-defense mechanisms. In the action of killing, one is at risk of being identified (primarily by oneself) as "a killer," and these defense mechanisms function to shield the psyche from this damaging identification. One of the more powerful defense mechanisms available to combatants, Grossman argues, is the diffusion of accountability into a group identity rather than an individual, personal one. Through the experience of stress and combat, individuals in military units—particularly those who have been together for lengthy periods of time with relatively few personnel changes—are bonded together in ways that are intimate and intense. Grossman notes that a great deal of research indicates that "the primary factor" in motivating a combatant to kill "is not the force of self-preservation but a powerful sense of accountability to his comrades on the battlefield."[17] The unit so bonded, which itself becomes a cohesive group rather than a collection of individuals, thus takes on a certain amount of internal logic and character. When members of such a unit kill in furtherance of the unit's mission and in protection of its members, the unit itself is accountable. The individual, in other words, does not have to hoist the identity of "a killer" upon himself, but can hoist it upon the unit. In this way, the group identity serves to absolve the actions of the individuals in it and shields them from the power of individual guilt and shame associated with having killed another person, who is fundamentally and unalterably "like me."[18]

17. Grossman, *On Killing*, 149.

18. Grossman, *On Killing*, 152. Drawing from Milgram, Grossman argues that group absolution and the diffusion of responsibility within a group to which one is tightly bonded (a much lower bar than what Milgram assumed was a legitimate authority to which one would cede responsibility) is what allows groups to do things that the individuals within them would likely not do on their own. This power enables the group to more easily kill those different from them, whether it be a lynch mob killing a black person in the South or a military unit killing those in the uniform of

Implicit in this construction of group absolution is the notion that if individuals have killed, the realization that they have done so is accompanied by their self-identification as killers. When the mechanisms of group absolution and denial-defense fail, Grossman argues that combatants go through a set of reactions similar to Elisabeth Kubler-Ross's famous "stages in response to death and dying."[19] While these stages move from senses of euphoria from the act of killing to moments of profound regret, they end in a process that attempts to make sense of and provide a rationalization for the act. This final stage is essentially the struggle of combatants seeking to come to terms with their identity as killers in a way that allows them to still preserve their image of themselves as "good" persons. In other words, it is a struggle to justify their actions and killing within a larger framework of meaning that can sustain the weight of the combatants' identity as killers. When this process "fails"—when the killing cannot be justified, or cannot be seen as morally just or justified, and the combatants view themselves as simply murderers—the result is PTSD. Yet, even when the "lifelong" process of rationalization results in some positive justification, one who has killed still has great difficulty leaving behind feelings of regret and guilt. Whether one's own killing was justified or not, one cannot deny one's identity as a killer. The presence of guilt and shame, and the veteran's grappling with her or his own identity as a killer, particularly over the course of a lifetime, can fundamentally distort the veteran's self-image.[20]

another military. Grossman notes that police are regularly trained to call individuals in a violent or dangerous group by name in order to remind them of their individual accountability and to attempt to de-escalate violent situations.

19. Here I am paraphrasing Grossman's detailed argument about denial-defense and the rationalization of killing (*On Killing*, 231–40).

20. It is worth noting that in this case the limits of the label "PTSD," particularly as used by Grossman in 1995, become apparent. It is certainly true that the distortion of self-image that occurs as a result of killing and the grappling with a long process of internal justification transcends the clinical diagnosis of PTSD. Many who are haunted by these actions are able to function highly and exhibit few of the behaviors that Shay describes: they are not reckless or driven compulsively to devote themselves to their jobs; they have loving relationships with their families and meaningful friendships with others. Yet this does not mean that they are free of distortion or that they do not often feel that their worldview is narrowed to the point that their own willing is "trapped in the trajectory" of their own self-image and the self-identity that results from their combat experiences. Their identities may still revolve around their image of themselves as killers and the subsequent guilt and shame can restrict their actions and thought patterns.

It is important to note that the self-imaging of combatants is not simply a matter of interior identity either; but in an Augustinian sense, it also has profound implications for further willing. The very attempt to assimilate the category of "killer" into one's own identity is, as Tick argues, the very forging of a "new personal identity" that accounts for the loss of innocence and the savage world the combatant has encountered.[21] As such, the combatant goes into the enterprise of combat with the self-image of a mythic warrior and departs it (if at all) with a much darker and more negative self-image that has been reshaped by the dictates of war. The forces acting on combatants in training and the combat environment, according to Tick, radically shift and shape their identity by redefining the relationships between concepts such as love, beauty, and order within the innermost beings of those combatants. Since combatants are unable to fulfill the "mythic warrior" identity, their interior relationships are deformed in such a fundamental way by combat that lust, desire, killing, and survival mechanisms become intermingled and confused.[22] Caught in between the unfulfilled ideals and identity of the mythic warrior, on the one hand, and the deforming nature of combat, on the other, the distortions of the combatants' self-image often result in self-destructive and desperate behaviors. After repeated encounters with death and killing, some veterans exhibit this "death imprint" via an insatiable sexual appetite, and they engage in high-risk and even anonymous encounters in order to "feel the touch of life again."[23] Many destroy their families and their relationships with spouses in response to this need, which stems from their perceived identity as one who brings death. Others, Shay notes, may accept their self-understanding as violent people and slide into criminal careers. He argues that "a criminal career allows a veteran to remain in combat mode, use his hard-earned skills, and even to relive aspects of his experience."[24] Either from the guilt and shame of understanding themselves to be killers, or from the need to forget experiences that threaten their self-image, many veterans become alcohol- and/or drug-dependent. And they do so at a rate significantly higher than that in the general population.[25]

21. Tick, *War and the Soul*, 170.
22. Tick, *War and the Soul*, 184.
23. Tick, *War and the Soul*, 124.
24. Shay, *Odysseus in America*, 31.
25. Shay, *Odysseus in America*, 36. Shay notes that 45.6 percent of Vietnam veter-

A primary source of psychological tension and distorted willing in many veterans is the distance between the heroic self-image often foisted upon them and the ambiguous and perhaps even monstrous self-image they often have as a result of fighting the nation's wars. This contrast can be debilitating, as demonstrated by one account from a veteran of World War II who had become reclusive after retiring from the Army. The man had been awarded the Distinguished Service Cross, given for actions of "extraordinary heroism"; these actions must by definition involve "risk to life so extraordinary as to set the individual apart from his or her comrades."[26] Yet the man was suffering from PTSD, and his self-withdrawal from the world appeared to be rooted in the fact that, as Grossman puts it, "he is obsessed with the idea that he is a coward."[27] The dichotomy between what his award noted about his character and what he felt it to be resulted in a debilitating paralysis of his own willing. During the Vietnam War era, the rejection—and at worst, outright demonization—of veterans by vocal groups in America contributed to a significant gap between the veterans' conceptions of a hero and their own self-images. Shay recounts a similar tale of a Vietnam veteran who described how the war, rather than producing heroes, "strips you of all your beliefs, your religion, takes your dignity away." He later said that it makes you an "animal in the sense of being evil," and he recounted that when he returned home, he often acted in animalistic rage, attacking his own family members in inexplicable acts of anger.[28]

The differential in character between the recruiting-poster self-image of American warriors, filled with implicit exaltations of honor and glory, and the self-image many veterans have after their experiences in conflict, involves a sense of *social betrayal*. For Milgram, one of the crucial antecedent conditions that would move subjects into the agential state was their perception of the legitimacy of the authority to which they were ceding their own sense of responsibility and personal agency. The

---

ans abused or became dependent on alcohol (according to the American Psychiatric Association's criteria for abuse and dependence), which contrasts with a 26 percent rate among their civilian peers. In terms of drug abuse, the rate for Vietnam veterans was 8.4 percent vs. 3.4 percent in their civilian counterparts.

26. Decorations, Medals, Ribbons, and Similar Devices, *Code of Federal Regulations*, title 32, pt. 578.10.

27. Grossman, *On Killing*, 281.

28. Shay, *Odysseus in America*, 33.

legitimacy of the authority, he argues further, was based on the power of a justifying ideology to which the subjects had already acceded on a basic level. If the subjects, then, understood the authority as acting in accord with this basic societal ideology, they tended to view the authority and its demands as tacitly necessary. This is a crucial step, since, as Milgram later notes, subjects ceded nearly all sense of morality and responsibility to this authority, and their own moral horizon narrowed to questions of obedience to the duties the authority required of them. Implicit in his analysis is the notion that some level of axiological agreement concerning the moral values within which the authority will operate is necessary for the subject to willingly enter into the agential state. Shay similarly argues that actors, most notably combatants, trust that legitimate power will be wielded in a way that is consistent with the communal understanding of what is right. Shay notes that the breaking of this trust is catastrophic and results in what he terms "complex PTSD"—a betrayal of the shared values and moral commitments that undergird social order.[29]

Those who join the military implicitly trust that their participation in the just and right exercise of power will positively contribute to their character formation, since, in joining, they are committing themselves to a cause that they know may demand their very lives.[30] Essentially, they are "buying" what is sold to them by the recruiter (at least on some level): that honor and heroism are to be found and crafted through their participation in the noble enterprise of national defense. Enlistment and commissioning ceremonies are profound and sacred rituals that emphasize duty, honor, and commitment. When, in the actual experience of conflict, they experience moral injury and the subversion and destruction of what Tick refers to as the "mythic warrior" identity, they experience a sense of betrayal. The damage done to identity and character in these cases of breached social trust is so profound in part because of the power of the agential state to compel human willing. As the results of Milgram's experiments most directly attest, it is extremely difficult to extricate ourselves from the agential state once we have en-

29. Shay, *Odysseus in America*, 151.

30. This is not to assume that all who enter the military carry such a relatively exuberant view of their own commitment to the enterprise. Certainly, many who enlist or enter commissioning programs do not have this degree of optimism about their service; they may be doing so for a variety of perfectly valid financial and personal reasons. Even so, it is unlikely that they enter fully aware of the damage that may occur to their own character, psyche, and moral grounding in the process.

tered it, even when we understand the command given to be morally objectionable. One of the largest "binding factors" that keeps people in the obedient, agential state is their own willing commitment to the enterprise. The refusal to abandon a commitment one has made is such a powerful psychological force that it essentially binds combatants to the enterprise, and even holds them there while they endure significant moral injury and de-forming of character.

This commitment bond and the other demands that the situation of conflict places on the will of the combatants constitutes a system of inescapable psychological bondage that severely damages their character. Shay describes the struggle for the will of the combatants as a contest between their own "side" and the enemy: their own military must prepare them to kill the enemy and withstand the fear of them, and the enemy attempts to "dominate the soldier's will" through fear. Shay argues that, because of the physical terrors of war and the psychological "barriers to escape," the modern conflict is a "condition of captivity and enslavement as harsh as any political prison or labor camp."[31] The conflict is all about power, and each side equally attempts to psychologically dominate its own troops as well as its enemy. This struggle for power places willing combatants at the mercy of a force that, at least in terms of its participation in warfare, not only does not seek to uphold any notions of moral order (Shay uses the Greek word *themis* to connote moral order, a sense of "what's right") but also disregards—and thus distorts and ruptures—this order in its quest to dominate. The system of enslavement and nearly inevitable betrayal of *themis* in the mind of the soldier who is committed to a cause to which he or she assigned some degree of nobility causes a trauma that "destroys virtue" and "undoes good character."[32]

The encounter with the enslaving, consuming, dominating force does not simply destroy one's faith in a particular institution or ideology, but damages one's overall psychological capacity for trust and

31. Shay, *Odysseus in America*, 36. Shay provides macabre examples of this, as units on both sides of the war in Vietnam would "mark" their kills with what amounted to calling cards to instill a fear of the lethality of a particular unit. He notes that an American unit would place an ace of spades card in the mouth of all the enemies they killed. This section further develops the ideas he understands as the betrayal of *themis* in *Achilles in Vietnam* (36–38) and the more developed understanding of moral injury that he expresses in *Odysseus in America* (149–63).

32. Shay, *Odysseus in America*, 36–37.

for moral commitment. Shay argues that the breach of trust granted by military members to the government they serve is akin to the rape of a child by a relative. That image both describes the power differential and the level of trust the combatant grants to his "superiors"; but it also underscores the level of psychological damage that results from it. Shay speaks most frequently of the injury as one of damaged character, or *thumos*, the Greek term that connotes the influence of the communal and ethical realms in which one resides. The injury suffered by those whose social trust is damaged is one that severely restricts, if not utterly devastates, their ability to navigate their social and moral worlds. Bound up with anger, guilt, and pain, these veterans manifest psychiatric symptoms that range from apathy to suffering, anhedonia, self-loathing, rage, social withdrawal, irrational suggestibility, hypochondria, extreme belligerence, rage at the slightest disappointment, coercive attempts to establish power dominance, destructive fantasies and behavior and apocalyptic ecstasy. These symptoms and behaviors all reflect a damaged relationship to authority and contribute to a great difficulty in developing and maintaining healthy relationships with family members, employers, friends, and the larger social and cultural world.

Synthesis: Distorted Relationality and the Problem of Guilt

A practicing psychiatrist, Jonathan Shay writes in *Odysseus in America* that he tells his (mostly Roman Catholic) veteran patients that the Catholic Church's ideas about sin, if they "are about anything, they're about the real stuff. What the Church offers is about cruelty, violence, murder—not just the sins you confessed in parochial school."[33] I have argued in this study that sin holds explanatory power in situations of pathological harm because of its nuanced description of the interplay between external forces that deeply affect human willing and our very own individual capacities to act. Sin speaks both to the power of the force itself that constitutes the situation and condition from which we act as human beings, our sinful actions within that situation, and the continuing disfiguring of our character and identity that results from our sinful willing. If sin is a fundamental distortion in our very relation-

33. Shay, *Odysseus in America*, 153.

ality as human agents to ourselves, each other, then attention to the radicality of sin provides a conceptual framework that can in some ways help to illuminate the encounters with the consuming, enslaving, and traumatic forces that bind the willing of combatants, and distinctively warp the centers of their own selves. The very notion of universal and radical sinfulness is expressed in these distortions and, at least in this situation, raises questions about how neatly we are able to conceive of the distinction between "perpetrator" and "victim."

One aspect of sin's radicality that is experienced by veterans in a unique way is its breakdown of moral categories. Recall that McFadyen contends that, rather than occurring episodically or occasionally, sin's radicality is evident in that it constitutes the very situation of human willing and action.[34] It endures, he argues, as a fundamental and even primal element of brokenness in our very ways of existing in community, and it fundamentally conditions our most basic patterns of interaction and relationality. These distortions, he argues, work themselves out through the narrowing of horizons, or the instrumentalizing of the willing of, for example, those in the Nazi killing units. Because they were not authorized to make the larger decisions about Nazi policy regarding the Jews or, on a smaller scale, about whether they were to kill those they were ordered to kill, their horizons of choice became narrowed to simply the effective execution of their task. Moral notions are similarly wound around this same axis as "right" and "wrong" become terms to describe one's effectiveness in executing the orders of higher authorities. What McFadyen here essentially argues theologically, Milgram argues psychologically: humanity in a differentiated society requires its members to shift into an agential state at various times and places in order to function coherently as a whole. Milgram's experiments demonstrated the power of the agential state to compel willing, even in cases where the participant experienced great moral stress and tension in doing so, as well as subjects' capacity to shift responsibility to those in higher positions of authority.

The move from a homogeneous and egalitarian society to a hierarchical and differentiated one was evolutionarily advantageous. Yet if sin is, as McFadyen argues, a poisoning of human relationality at its most fundamental level, then the experience of veterans whose wills are enslaved by the forces of war illuminates the distortions present

34. McFadyen, *Bound to Sin*, 17.

in the structure of differentiated society itself as a means of human civilization. Having people dedicated to varying tasks and duties certainly provides innumerable benefits to a society as it advances nearly all areas of technology and culture. Almost inarguably, the greatest early advantages of having differentiated professions in the development of human civilization, however, were military ones. It allowed for the creation of a responsive, professional army that was united under the leadership of a single commander, made up of soldiers who were dedicated to their craft, the profession of arms. Historically, these armies have annihilated those made up of less organized, agrarian societies; the latter armies were populated by conscripts whose "day jobs" consisted of a multitude of things not centered in combat. It is noteworthy that, through the evolution of combat, the most crippling effects of this way of being and relating to each other become apparent.

As the studies, observations, and analyses of Milgram, Grossman, and Shay suggest, the move into the agential state, particularly in situations involving violence and conflict, creates a struggle for the will of the actor. Each of these researchers presents a picture of human willing that suggests that, in certain situations, the combatants' capacity to will is extremely narrowed: they are at the mercy of the force that seeks to dominate (Shay), are held in the agential state by the conditioning and binding forces from which they have a great difficulty escaping (Milgram), and have been conditioned to overcome their own senses of morality in service to the greater national good (Grossman). From a theological standpoint, the radicality of sin in the system of a differentiated society threatens to utterly devastate one's sense of reason and personhood precisely because one's personal willing remains active even as one navigates the dictates of higher authorities. McFadyen argues that "will, in these situations, is co-opted into a more potent and more highly energized dynamic," and yet nonetheless "remains personal."[35] This is true because the exercise of the will that underlies every action is what makes us who we are: our ability to will is what "marks us out as personal agents."[36] To be sure, the antecedent factors, conditioning, and binding forces may truly create a situation that is enslaving to the will, in that it so colonizes the combatants' sense of good that it narrows the horizon of choices available to the psyche to a very few, and

35. McFadyen, *Bound to Sin*, 133.
36. McFarland, *In Adam's Fall*, 63.

thus enjoys a certain degree of hegemony in terms of compelling actors to act. However, even in situations such as these, a personal sense of responsibility, character, and identity—perhaps terms that McFadyen would sum up using the phrase "life-intentionality"—are all involved and subject to distortion as a result of these actions.[37] This is because they remain ineluctably the agent's actions, something she or he *did*. The close tie between agency and identity is evident in the ways combatants suffer distortions in self-perception, experience guilt, and undergo significant stress as a result of their actions.

Within the conceptual universe of original sin (as McFadyen interprets it), the distortion present in the sinful situation and condition from which we act is internalized and distorted as we add our personal energy toward it and intensify this distortion within ourselves. The stress that Milgram's subjects felt and the subterfuges to which they resorted reflect both their personal inability to escape from the situation and their desire to uphold their own personal sense of morality within the confines of their narrowed horizon of choice.[38] Similar stresses were felt and subterfuges were sought in the wars Americans fought until the Vietnam War, when military training began to condition combatants to act reflexively and to shape their internal senses of "good" more deeply around military endeavor. In the period since then, combatants have increasingly felt the distortion that results in their participation in combat, such that their very life-intentionality is powerfully reoriented as they struggle to assimilate their identities as "killer" and "monster" into a coherent and moral sense of self. The encounter with this threatens to utterly consume agency and identity, to infect and distort until the actor has no agency left that is untarnished by the demands of the consuming force. In theological terms, this can be interpreted as an encounter with an Augustinian notion of sin in its profound radicality: that is, a force that utterly twists and binds the willing of human agents, deforming them and their life-intentionalities in the process.

Combat is often discussed in terms of a moral duty, invoking the goods of safety and security; yet the radicality of sin distorts and disfigures this enterprise at a communal, social level. As Shay and Tick both argue in explicit terms, war as a force itself tends to annihilate all sense

37. McFadyen, *Bound to Sin*, 127.

38. This is the case, at least, for the majority of his test subjects who did not disobey the orders of the experimenter and carried out the experiment to its conclusion.

of value and claim on morality and to redefine it in strict terms of duty to the "side" to which actors have committed themselves. But, as McFadyen argues, the Augustinian tradition views sin as a precondition of our own action and intentionality. In the case of combat, this happens by undermining notions of morality that are not inherently evil by creating illusory moral "goods" under which the utilitarian demands and true moral order of war operate. Shay notes that the differential between these two moral orders experienced by combatants constitutes a betrayal of "social trust" that not only damages them but "destroys the capacity" for that trust itself, replacing it with a sense of hyperparanoia and extreme anxiety in the most severely traumatized veterans.[39] McFadyen argues that sin is, at its very core, a relational problem, expressed in terms of one's relationship to God and to each other. Its primary distortion is the impairment of our abilites and capacities to relate to God, ourselves, and each other. What Shay articulates is the ability of conflict to distort (if not destroy outright) our very capacity for relationality with other human beings. Combatants experience this in an extreme way, propagating this distortion through extreme aggression in their behavior toward others on the battlefield and in their unpredictable and volatile behavior at home. Their very ability to relate to themselves and each other is damaged via the profound distortion of their ability to organize themselves at a social level.

The resulting damage to the combatants' willing that results from their experience with the consuming force of combat resonates greatly with McFadyen's description of willing in situations of child abuse. While there would seem to be a clear prima facie power differential between children, whose developmental, intellectual, emotional, and social capacities have not fully matured, and adult combatants who have been trained to carry a weapon and make combat decisions under intense pressure, the magnitude of the forces at work on the psyche of the combatant completely dwarfs his or her own "personal power" to resist, and lends veracity to the analogy.[40] Shay argues that the specific relationship between "child and parent is a metaphor for the relation-

39. Shay, *Odysseus in America*, 151.

40. I use the term "personal power" here for lack of a better alternative to describe how one could theoretically actualize one's potential for agency against constricting forces. As McFadyen argues in *Bound to Sin* (131–40), the term itself is problematic in that it tends to be seen as an enduring personal characteristic rather than a transient one, whose potential for activation occurs "only at the point of agency in a particular case."

ship between a soldier and his army," particularly when it comes to the cultivation of character through the concepts of "trustworthiness, reliability . . . self-control, self-esteem" and social behaviors.[41] The power differential of psychological forces is similar, based on a certain capacity in combatants to trust, in that individual soldiers in Shay's metaphor rely on the army (notably the culture as represented by their peers and those in higher positions of authority in the hierarchical military structure) for the development of ideals, including "prosocial rather than antisocial activity," as well as a "reliable capacity to distinguish reality from fantasy."[42] Shay argues further that the breaching of this trust results in character distortions that lean toward antisocial behaviors, paranoia, difficulties in self-control, and an inability to trust. This betrayal of trust and power results in a distorted sense of relationality and bends combatants' life-intentionalities in directions that are often destructive.

There is a critical connection between McFadyen's notion of consent and distorted willing in cases of child abuse and the experience of combatants who have committed themselves to the national cause. Abusers of children, McFadyen argues, are able to exploit the child's own active willing to create a dynamic of "entrapment and isolation."[43] At the heart of that distorted dynamic is the child's notion of consent, since an abuser will often offer rewards to a child in order to confuse the child's desire for the reward with the desire for the abuse itself. The result is the confusion of desires and consents within the child's psyche, to the degree that the child may come to believe that he or she has consented to (and therefore actively willed) the abusive acts and the overall abusive dynamic. Similarly, the combatants' commitment to the nation, demonstrated by their oath to "obey the orders of the President of the United States and the orders of the officers appointed over me," constitutes a similar trusting form of consent that a more powerful entity will not abuse their develop-

41. Shay, *Achilles in Vietnam*, 32.

42. Shay, *Achilles in Vietnam*, 32. A similar argument based on Milgram's concept of the differentiated society and the move to the agential state would be that in recognizing the *legitimacy* of an authority, the individual agent places some degree of trust in the authority's values. When there is a dissimilarity in the moral values of the authority and those of the agent, even if the agent is bound in the agential state and obeys the authority's commands, he or she usually does so under a significant degree of strain, resulting in subterfuges in an attempt to protect the agent's own self-image.

43. McFadyen, *Bound to Sin*, 73.

ment and agency.[44] It is also precisely this commitment that binds combatants to particular situations of willing and nonresistance to orders. Combatants are often faced with cascading moral demands on their character that stem from this central consent: since they have committed to joining the US military, they have consented to the (morally distorting and even abusive) situations in which they find themselves as a part of military life and culture. Recruits may have joined the military seeking the fulfillment of what Tick describes as the "mythic warrior ideal"; but when they encounter a more morally ambiguous path, the external pressure from both authority figures and their peers often plays on a sense of duty.

More importantly, however, combatants have internalized the idea that, even if they were "duped" in the recruiting station, the situation they find themselves in is one that they "signed up for." In other words, recruits consent to join for the promise of moral fulfillment (reward), and this consent is twisted by the forces involved into their consent to perform actions that do not conform to the initial ideal of moral fulfillment. Yet, since this committal bond is so powerful within the psyche to hold them within the agential state, the combatants, despite the fact that they might have willed otherwise in the absence of the authority, begin to equate their own consent in joining the military as consent to perform morally damaging actions. This is added to a pattern of apparent consent to morally difficult actions—such as killing—that tend to make disobedience a less accessible option as it opposes the profound commitment that one has made to what the national cause and higher authority demands.

The ways the combatants internalize the dynamics of war and attempt to resolve their understanding of their own agency and consent in these

44. The following line of this oath is "according to regulations and the Uniform Code of Military Justice," which is almost universally understood to qualify the clauses in front of it such that it is the duty of the service member to obey the *lawful* orders of those appointed over them. This means that a service member has an equal duty to obey lawful orders and refuse orders that are "illegal or immoral." With the looser classifications of combatants and noncombatants post-9/11, and in view of the George W. Bush administration's sanction of "enhanced interrogation" techniques, these lines become blurred, and situations of immoral and illegal orders become more difficult to recognize, particularly in a combat environment. In addition, the considerable psychological weight of obedience, of course, makes disobedience in a moment of moral consciousness a much greater theoretical than actual possibility.

situations bears remarkable similarity to those of children in situations of abuse, as described by McFadyen. At its base, the abuser "bends the child's willing for nonabusive objects to abusive purposes by eliding the difference between them, so that the child's willing and intentionality is incorporated into those of the abuser."[45] Similarly, the combatant's desire for honor and the "mythic warrior" identity is bent in pursuit of the more utilitarian concerns of the conflict as directed by those in positions of authority. The willing of the combatant, particularly given the power of the legitimate authority to move the combatant into an agential state, is incorporated into that of the authority: of the larger aims of the government or military force. Combatants—similar to abused children—often develop a negative self-image that is bound up with their own participation in the larger dynamic. Due to the constriction of shame and guilt over their own perceived complicity, they view themselves as "monstrous" and "evil," just as children in situations of abuse view themselves as "dirty" or "unclean." In both cases the distance between one's image of what is good, proper, and heroic and one's self-image drives them to a certain degree of isolation. McFadyen argues that the crucial point is that the psychological scarring and the enduring of long-term trauma are the direct result of the abuse of "the child's active willing and intentionality" by the abuser.[46] The resonance with Shay's description of social betrayal is striking, primarily because, just as in the situation of child abuse, the damaging aspect is its distortion of intentionality, its distortion of character in the destruction of the capacity for social trust.

The confluence of these two situations suggests that the very abuse of active willing is what causes one to feel "trapped in the trajectory of one's own willing."[47] McFadyen's term "life-intentionality" is relevant here in describing the distortion of character and identity, the crucial parts of the self that have great influence on our future trajectories of action. As the behavior of veterans suffering from PTSD appears to indicate, the changes to character and identity that take place in combat have the capacity to radically reorient life-intentionality. As McFadyen argues, the healing of this reorientation is difficult partly because the distortion at the core of one's identity, which is born of the abuse of one's agency, cannot be eliminated, forgotten, or ignored—even when

45. McFadyen, *Bound to Sin*, 124.
46. McFadyen, *Bound to Sin*, 124.
47. McFadyen, *Bound to Sin*, 124.

forging new identities. He notes that the active agency of abused children during the abuse enables survival through the development of a new identity; yet he notes that any new identity is constructed on the reality of the abuse. They recover by establishing an identity as a survivor of the horrendous situation of abuse, and this identity, however more positively oriented than within the closed orbit of the abuse itself, is in some ways bound to it and distorted by it. Their intentionalities and horizons and future possibilities for willing are all narrowed by it. Similarly, Tick describes the recovery of veterans suffering from PTSD as the fulfillment of the warrior identity that had been arrested through moral distortion. What this involves in practice is the honest reckoning with what war and violence actually are and serving, among other things, as a "truthteller" to a society that continually misunderstands this. This, too, is a "survivor" identity: while providing a positive framework of meaning within which to understand one's experience, it is still rooted in the reality of the abuse of agency that one has endured and the betrayal of social trust that one has suffered.

This discussion of active agency in pathological situations yields another valuable contribution to understanding extreme situations of harm: a framework of meaning in which to understand guilt and shame. According to the Augustinian doctrine of sin, we congenitally inherit an existential guilt by virtue of our own participation in a distorted human nature. What McFadyen interprets suggests that we experience guilt as we contribute our own personal energies to the distortions exerting pressure on our willing, and we intensify those distortions in our own lives. Given the power dynamic differential in intellectual, developmental, and emotional maturity between children and adults who would abuse them, it would seem improper to validate the sense of guilt and shame that abused children feel. If guilt and shame are connected immediately with "blameworthiness," then such ascription of blame is indeed an improper and morally repugnant position. Yet if the experience of guilt is a psychological reaction to the commitment of our personal energies to the dynamic of toxic and disfiguring brokenness that conditions human relationality, then it loses the sense of moral repugnance and can connect situations of "perpetrator" trauma and "victim" trauma as experiences of and contact with sin in a direct and terrible way. One can simultaneously affirm that the shame felt by the soldier who kills is a valid reaction to his level of responsibility as agent in an active encounter with the distorting sinfulness that deeply breaks and disfigures human relationality, and that it is also true of the shame felt by the victim of child abuse as the result of an active encounter with that same force. Certainly, adult soldiers possess a far greater degree of understanding than a child does, and they are responsible for their actions in a way that a child is not. The distinction between one who commits an act of violation and the one violated by it cannot be eliminated; yet the process by which the willing of both participants is distorted and their relational capacities disfigured is similar.

If guilt is the way we understand our active participation in this universal distortion, then we certainly experience and participate in it in an interconnected, relational way. McFadyen argues that pathological dynamics cannot be centered on particular instances of human action; rather, they appear "as a supra-individual network of interrelations and interactions extended through time." He also says that this network "habituates the whole life-intentionality of victims, perpetrators, and bystanders into disorientation."[48] For McFadyen, this distinction is directly related to addressing the moral problem inherent in many descriptions of pathological situations that presume that the "perpetrator" in any given scenario has access to avenues of choice to not commit a particular act against another person. Yet, with sin understood as a universal, radical, and deeply distorting force, the key differentiation of the perpetrator, victim, and bystander simply becomes the space they occupy at a given moment in their interaction with others at a particular time on that extended timeline of distorted relationships. Certainly, this is not to contend that many occupy one end of the spectrum a far greater amount of the time than others, with significant consequences for themselves and those around them. The universality of sin and the experience of combatants, however, suggests that there are not enduring differences in these categories when projected over time, as though any individual were inherently, solely, and irreversibly "victim" or "perpetrator." Rather, there are variations—albeit variations of extraordinary significance existentially in the lives of those who are impacted by them—in the degree of distortion that a given individual experiences within any given temporal space that she or he occupies on the extended timeline.

The demonstrable power of sin to distort one's life-intentionality—particularly shown through an examination of the forces that act on

48. McFadyen, *Bound to Sin*, 195.

the psyche of the combatant in situations of conflict—questions the fixity of demonstrable moral categories of "victim" and "perpetrator." As Shay argues, there is little "personal power" that combatants are able to muster in order to resist the forces that constrict their willing; it becomes a condition of psychological enslavement that is inescapable. Both "victim trauma" and "perpetrator trauma" (as demonstrated here in the combatant) involve a similar experience of constricted choices that manifests itself through a feeling of powerlessness against vastly superior forces. What the particular notion of sin draws our attention to is the magnitude of the distorting force itself and the ways that both those who commit violence in conflict and those who are victimized by it are overwhelmed by a force larger than themselves, a force to which they cannot effectively muster a resistance—either physical or psychological. In other words, the distinction between the victims and perpetrators of violence in any situation is at least partly a function of circumstance: whether they experience the distortion in a way that completely colonizes and enslaves their willing and agency or whether they are overwhelmed by that force in a physical way.

This is not to suggest that the category of blame is rendered ineffectual under the distorting power of sin, but that its connection to responsibility is not straightforward or simple. The framework of meaning I am proposing can be used to critique acts of violence unequivocally: they are blameworthy *acts*. Yet the power of the conditioning force and the near inescapability of the distorting power suggest that blame should be reoriented primarily toward the forces that distort willing in addition to the acts themselves. The forces of hatred, violence, and the goods we inordinately love (nationalism, security, tribal identity, etc.), which distort our actions and identities, are blameworthy and are products of the larger force of sin. To be sure, adult combatants who commit acts of violence cannot escape responsibility and some degree of blame for them, nor should they. "Perpetrators," even if occupying that identity impermanently, do occupy that space in a given moment. But the person who is closest to committing a violent act in a combat setting may be the person with the least available agency to resist the larger distorting force. The frontline soldiers who are trained and conditioned to engage in combat and to immediately obey orders certainly have the least capacity to actively resist killing and the excesses of violence on the battlefield. Further up the hierarchy are those in positions of authority who have the capacity to shape policy, who formulate the rules of engagement, and who give standing orders in a way that can either mitigate some of the more deleterious effects of violence or intensify its destructive and disfiguring power. These higher-ranking individuals possess a greater degree of agency, and thus the exercise of their agency exposes them to a greater degree of blame when they act badly. Even so, it should be noted that, even at the highest level of authority, there cannot be an unequivocal relationship between agency and blame. The President of the United States is deeply affected by the distorting force of nationalism and consumer culture, and her or his decisions are shaped by the weight of the myriad influential forces that attempt to sway her or his position. The President and all policy-makers and high-level officials are ensnared in the condition of sin and are unable to escape the political, economic, and strategic realities that often present them with few good options.

CHAPTER 6

Sin as Poisoned Memory and Hopeless Future

> When Judas, his betrayer, saw that Jesus was condemned, he repented and brought back the thirty pieces of silver to the chief priests and the elders. He said, "I have sinned by betraying innocent blood." But they said, "What is that to us? See to it yourself." Throwing down the pieces of silver in the temple, he departed; and he went and hanged himself.
>
> —MATTHEW 27:3–5

The exhibition of veteran trauma is often centered on an experience of guilt that involves betrayal and even collusion that is born of the act of killing or an encounter with death. Like Judas, many come to see their own actions as a deep compromise of their own moral principles through the very act of "betraying innocent blood." It is a tragic fact that many take a path similar to the one Judas chose, in Matthew's account, in the aftermath of his remorseful confession: as many as twenty-two American veterans take their own lives every day. They often cannot contend with their own memories, and their experiences have damaged their capacity to envision a worthwhile future. My argument throughout this work has been that a recovered understanding of original sin holds explanatory power in naming the wrongness of the world—experienced intensely and acutely by combatants in wartime—and by providing a framework that enables a fuller and richer accounting of morality through the forces that actively distort character and disrupt moral order. Part of the explanatory power of the concept of sin is, of course, its ability to corrupt and compel human willing and its immense capacity to distort life-intentionalities in destructive ways. But it also enables us to converse in moral terms that lie somewhat beyond the bounds of most psychological analysis by virtue of its vocabulary of sin and guilt, repentance and restoration, forgiveness and hope. Using these deep constructs, we may be able to provide a moral framework that frees individuals from absolutizing their own guilt and sense of moral injury and opens up avenues for self-understanding that are not essentialized and can perhaps lead to experiences of healing.

Consequently, I argue here that the enduring effects experienced by veterans with PTSD are a poisoned memory that prevents them from being able to properly construct an identity for themselves in the aftermath of the traumatic events, and from being able to envision a hopeful future that is pregnant with possibilities for their healing and flourishing. In this examination I argue that sin, particularly in its radicality, universality, and inescapability is—as suggested by Augustine and McFadyen—valuable in describing the ongoing condition of wrongness to which both of these situations testify. Like the ancient symbol of the *uroborous*, which depicts a snake eating its own tail, both writers present ways in which the power of sin has the effect of both binding our orientations in a cyclical pattern and conditioning us to consume ourselves. Here I essentially offer a contemporary interpretation of Augustine's concept of humanity's broken and damaged nature through the lens of the combat veteran. In arguing the first point—that the distorted willing and intentionality (as well as the exposure to a combat world) produce a poisoned memory in veterans—I examine the critical role that memory plays in psychological trauma, particularly as described by Pierre Janet. Then I turn to Marjorie Suchocki's understanding of sin as the failure to transcend the self, particularly as that relates to our relationship with our own past as it is preserved within our memory. The poisoned memory often leads to a sense of hopelessness, and I then draw on Jürgen Moltmann's concept of sin as despair to argue that this hopelessness has a profound theological dimension. In the final part of this chapter, I examine the ways that the radicality and universality of sinfulness in the modified Augustinian framework I have used illuminate profound areas of human brokenness in terms of combat violence and the human psyche, but I also explore unexpected avenues toward healing and hope.

Poisoned Memory and Moral Injury

As human beings, we process the world and our own experiences of it through the medium of our own memory. Bessel A. van der Kolk and Onno van der Hart show how the early trauma theorist Pierre Janet describes the memory system "as the central organizing apparatus of the mind, which categorizes all aspects of experience and automatically integrates them into ever-enlarging and flexible meaning schemes."[1] This system of meaning-making can be stressed and profoundly disrupted by traumatic events, which may resist any form of categorization and organization or may simply stretch the credulity of the scheme of meaning to the breaking point.

Many researchers understand the human capacity to remember as determinative for shaping the ways we interact with the world in the present and the ways we develop the characteristics that make us unique as individual people. Van der Kolk and van der Hart note that Janet actually developed the term "subconscious" to denote "the collection of automatically stored memories that form the map that guides subsequent interaction with the environment" (159). In other words, this mapping of our own experience is the baseline from which we interpret and attempt to categorize new experiences. Janet theorized that there are essentially two capacities by which this is realized: through "automatic synthesis or habit memory" and through "narrative memory" (160). *Habit* memory, which is a capacity we share with all animal life, is the way our minds integrate quotidian events that require little conscious processing or attention. The capacity for *narrative* memory, which is unique to human beings, represents the ways we assign meaning to our experiences. Narrative memory categorizes experiences together in ways that make up a worldview by which a person can process events and give positive meaning to them.

It is interesting to note that the degree to which we remember the specific details of events is inversely proportional to how easy they are to integrate into our cognitive systems of meaning. The experiences that occur that fit with our existing mental structures and systems of

1. Bessel A. van der Kolk and Onno van der Hart, "The Intrusive Past: The Flexibility of Memory and the Engraving of Trauma," in *Trauma: Explorations in Memory*, ed. Cathy Caruth (Baltimore: Johns Hopkins University Press, 1995), 158. (Hereafter, page references to this essay appear in parentheses within the text.) I will draw on this essay and its evocative suggestions about trauma and memory in this section.

meaning are integrated almost seamlessly into our memory systems, and in the process of organization they are often subtly altered in order to fit the existing cognitive construction. Van der Kolk and van der Hart argue that the process of remembering allows for the continual revisiting of memories as one's framework of meaning shifts. The content of the memory, then, tends to be pliant and ductile as it is adapted and readapted through a continual process of re-forming and recontextualizing. However, Janet theorized that when experiences occur that lie farther outside the accepted cognitive system of meaning—those that are particularly frightful or occur under conditions of extreme stress—they may "be remembered with particular vividness or may totally resist integration" (160). More modern researchers have demonstrated the utility of Janet's theory in many ways, as they have found that traumatic memories that resist contextualization and cannot be integrated within the cognitive system that assigns meaning tend to become "fixed" in the memory with an incredible amount of precision and detail. Many who experience the return of these memories experience them repeatedly in exact and consistent detail.

While these memories remain vivid and clear somewhere in an uncategorized aspect of the memory, they must be placed in a meaningful context in order to acquire meaning themselves. Traumatic memories are essentially experiences that cannot be categorized because they cannot be translated into any of the ways that the central nervous system encodes information. In other words, traumatic experiences resist integration into a linguistic framework consisting of words or symbols; instead, they become concretized in the memory on a more basic level as sensory experiences and dreams. Therefore, the memory is often triggered by neural stimuli that in some way recall the approximate conditions present during the traumatic event and trigger the memory encoded in visceral and somatosensory forms. This often signals the *locus coeruleus* (or "alarm bell") of the central nervous system, which in turn triggers the body's physiological response to danger and initiates the "fight or flight" system (173). For healing to occur, the memory must be translated into narrative terms, and thereby assimilated into cognitive schemes of meaning-making, and thus contextualized in order for it to be integrated. Van der Kolk and van der Hart describe this as a bridging between two aspects of life that are temporal and yet to be integrated: "the traumatic past," which the person experiences as unknown, inaccessible, and terrifying; and the "bleached present," which is contemporary existence that cannot be processed because of the disconnected, unintegrated state of the past (173). The distance between these two states and the disconnect between them form a certain dissociation from the traumatic event itself.

As we integrate traumatic memory, it is crucial that it lose its fixed sharpness and that it become flexible, so that it may attain the degree of malleability necessary for it to be continually recategorized and recontextualized. It is apparent that once memories become pliant and malleable, the hold that a traumatic experience over the present moment begins to wane. The cognitive meaning schemes must be able to hold the traumatic past and the present experiences together in a way that gives meaning to both. Many in extreme stress tend to have a bifurcated system of cognitive patterns: one is inaccessible—in the internal world in which the traumatic event resides—and another, known to the consciousness, is the one in which all other experience resides. In order to bridge these interior worlds, the traumatized individual will often have to overcome an extreme phobia of the traumatic memory, which tends to harden its edges and maintain its unnarrated rigidity. When a person is healed and integrated, she or he no longer experiences the sudden, visceral, and imminent return of traumatic memories that can be seen as invasions from the frightening and inaccessible inner world that exists separate from the world known to the consciousness.

The bridging of these two worlds is, of course, a difficult endeavor; indeed, it may even be impossible for many who have experienced severe trauma and suffer from severe PTSD. Van der Kolk and van der Hart note that a tension can develop over time that makes the integration of these worlds particularly difficult. The traumatic memory is essentially frozen in a timeless sense: it has no contextual narrative or story that it belongs to, but simply exists in the memory as an event outside of time. One's "normal" interior world has a guiding personal narrative that develops and evolves as one grows, yet the traumatic memory is ossified outside that temporal developmental context. In the more extreme cases of trauma, the psychic break between the traumatic experience and its subsequent existence in the mind, and the narrative memory that constitutes a person's "ordinary" lived existence, can become a "permanent duality, not exactly a split or a doubling but a parallel existence" that the traumatized individual experiences continually as a simultaneous reality (177). The ossified and fixed traumatic existence ceases all development, and, after some time, as the quotidian portion of one's psyche has continued to develop, these two separate worlds cannot be bridged.

A difficulty that arises from the attempt to integrate the traumatic and quotidian interior worlds is the moral aspect of meaning that one must construct to bridge the two worlds. When a person is consciously cognizant of traumatic memories, even after that person has translated them into narrative memory, the integrated framework of meaning draws heavily from the traumatic experience. In other words, in developing a self-image and identity from these traumatic experiences, a person constructs a worldview in which actions and events (notably one's own) take on a measure of moral value. Van der Kolk and van der Hart argue that, particularly in the case of "incest victims and combat veterans," though subjects are able to narrate their experiences, "their current life is characterized by doubt and humiliation, by feelings of guilt and shame: past meaning schemes determine the interpretation of the present" (178). When the past trauma is remembered and translated into narrative memory—and yet engenders these moral responses—van der Kolk and van der Hart describe the remaining work to be done as that of "reconciling" the traumatic past with the present (178). Yet the authors do note that, for many, even these accessible memories prove to be intractably irreconcilable with the identity formed through the individual's nontraumatic memory.

The avenue of healing that the authors suggest in most cases of ossified traumatic memories consists of encouraging the traumatized individual to remember the events or images in a way that more easily integrates with a hopeful and meaningful worldview. Put another way, the flexibility necessary for integration is somewhat artificially introduced as the psychotherapist may suggest to the traumatized person "an alternative, less negative or even positive scenario" (178). For example, in treating a patient suffering from the memory of the sight of "horrendous nude corpses of victims of a cholera epidemic," Janet eventually suggested to the person that perhaps one of the corpses got up and walked away (178). However, each example of this type of treatment, van der Kolk and van der Hart note in their discussion, involves what may be described as "victim trauma," or "passive trauma"—an event that one has witnessed or experienced with a negligible commitment of personal energy (178). By contrast, the moral element involved with "perpetrator" trauma seems particularly resistant to externally prompted flexibility: the feelings of guilt and shame cannot be ameliorated without fundamentally changing the memory; and even if they could, the possibility of doing so would raise serious ethical issues.[2] The simple moral framework used by most of society, which is based on an absolutized sense of personal autonomy, compounds the issue for many veterans suffering from PTSD, since it influences their inability to renarrate their own memories within a framework that would allow for some degree of moral flexibility and for incorporation into a different schema of meaning.

Theologian Marjorie Suchocki argues that our ability to form and transcend our selves takes place at the most fundamental level in our relationship to our own memories. But in order to fully appreciate the connection between this concept of self-transcendence and the psychological studies of memory and trauma just surveyed, we must first examine Suchocki's understanding of creation and the role of original sin with regard to human nature. While understanding the value of the concept of original sin in articulating the brokenness and wrongness that permeate human instantiations of violence, Suchocki argues that "pride" and "rebellion against God" cannot be understood as the root metaphors for sinfulness, since they are inadequate to describe the full scope and intensity of our violence and, in fact, often contribute to it.[3] Suchocki wants to redefine the base structure of sin so that it is not understood first and foremost as an action, posture, or way of being that is directed against God; but, she argues, it should be conceived primarily as a violence done to creation and secondarily as opposition to God as creator and sustainer of that creation. In critiquing the traditional understanding of sin as directed primarily against God, she argues that this view, by providing "one umbrella" of rebellion against God under

2. It would seem highly morally suspect, for example, to attempt to ameliorate a convicted murderer's feelings of guilt and shame by attempting to introduce flexibility into his own memory of his crime in ways that would suggest that he did not, in fact, commit it. Later in this chapter I will discuss a possible resonance with the framework I have proposed, in which we can perhaps suggest to the perpetrator (at least in the context of combatant trauma) the way in which his or her own agency is connected to the hierarchy and sequestered within certain horizons of choice.

3. Marjorie Hewitt Suchocki, *The Fall to Violence: Original Sin in Relational Theology* (New York: Continuum Publishing, 1994), 17. (Hereafter, page references to this work appear in parentheses within the text.) In this section I will draw on the way Suchocki seeks to conceive of sin in a way that emphasizes the victims of sins as well as its perpetrators (notably on p. 48), her focus on violence and creation (notably on p. 28), and her section on sin and memory (pp. 30–38).

which to hide "the enormity of political torture, massive wars, cruel oppressions, child abuse," together with more mundane and less damaging personal sins, effectively annihilates any distinction between sins (18). Insulting someone during a heated argument becomes axiologically equivalent to torturing him or her to death. Similarly, she argues that the traditional view focuses on the perpetrators of sin and subsequently ignores the real suffering of sin's victims, allowing one to spiritualize the consequences of one's actions and ask forgiveness from God rather than from the one most directly and tangibly harmed. Perhaps most compellingly, Suchocki argues that, rather than illuminating the nature of wrongness and sin, the traditional view propagates a sinful problem itself in artificially removing individuals from their context as one part of the created cosmos. Humanity becomes elevated to such a powerful role over and above creation—rather than an intimately connected part of it—that this concept, Suchocki argues, upholds the very prideful elevation of self that it ostensibly decries. Granting humanity a special status over the rest of creation actually encourages us to sin against it by implicitly sanctioning forms of abuse of creation that appear to further human interests.

Suchocki thus proposes a definition of sin that revolves around violence to creation itself, formally defining it as "the unnecessary violation of the well-being of any aspect of creation," and defining the act of sin directly as "unnecessary violence" (48). Direct violence becomes, not simply the larger, second-order effect of sin in this conception of it—but its cause as well. She then provides a variation on the Augustinian concept of the transmission of original sin by arguing that violence is propagated and transmitted through both a received disposition and societal conditioning. She argues forcefully that all of creation is fundamentally relational, and that original sin and its effects are perhaps best understood as a violation and distortion of those relationships (which is similar to McFadyen's point).[4] These distortions are manifest in our social institutions, in our relationships with our environment and the living things within it, and in our relationship to ourselves and to each

4. Suchocki and McFadyen have a similar view on this specific point: that creation is best understood relationally, and sin and its effects are perhaps best understood by way of distorted relationality. Their underlying theologies are strikingly different: Suchocki argues from a "process theology" posture, whereas McFadyen is more committed to a classically Reformed, or Augustinian, viewpoint. There are obviously plenty of profound differences that result from these divergent starting points.

other. Also, these distortions can all be traced back to a broken relationship with God, albeit in a secondary way, since violence done to the well-being of creation is, by direct corollary, violence and offense done to God as the creator and sustainer of life and creation.

Suchocki's conception of violence as the root and effect of sin is particularly relevant to this study, since she develops it in terms of the human failure to transcend ourselves for the sake of creation. Building on Niebuhr's conception of the "natural" and "spiritual" aspects of humanity, Suchocki argues that they are not polar opposites within human experience, but that spirituality is found within nature. She argues that nature, despite its particular finiteness, is not a stranger to infinity; instead, through its vast and infinite variety, through its varying transience and permanence, and through its actual and potentially infinite number of forms, its finitude exhibits infinity. Though the lives of individual beings begin and end, Suchocki argues, we cannot know that life itself is not infinite, and therefore that by virtue of participation in that infinite life, "finitude is a form of infinity" (35).[5] This is crucial because she makes the case—again based on Niebuhr's understanding of transcendence as reaching for infinity—that self-transcendence can be achieved through nature, "horizontally" through nature rather than "vertically" by stretching upward toward God. Transcendence that stretches outward for the divine in this way does so from a perspective that affirms its ground within creation, as opposed to an Archimedian point that is external to the world. If, in fact, we transcend ourselves through a certain awareness of our interrelatedness within creation—through which we are able to respect each member as a valuable other—then it is the failure to do so that conditions violence and provides a creation-centric understanding of sin itself. If we conceive of ourselves as "over and above" creation, we are demonstrating a tendency to dominate, control, and do violence to those lesser aspects of creation (as well as humanity) that further cement our position at the top of the created hierarchy.

To transcend the self is, finally, a process of achieving authentic "selfhood" within an egalitarian creation that "is in itself finite and

5. In this section I make use of the framework and vocabulary of the argument Suchocki uses in the second chapter of *Fall to Violence* (31–46), notably her argument about the presence of the infinite within the finite world and the integration of this concept with Niebuhr's understanding of transcendence.

infinite" (36). Suchocki argues that this transcendence is established as the self and is constructed in three distinct modes: "in relation to one's own past through memory; in relation to others in the present through empathy; and in relation to the future through imagination" (36). Each correlates with a distinct propensity for the perpetuation of violence against creation: the failure to transcend the self with respect to memory presents the violence of perpetuating the past; the failure to empathize with others in the present correlates to violence against the solidarity of the human race as is; and our inability to transcend ourselves has consequences for the future in terms of our capacity to imagine and live into that future. Most fundamental, however, is the relationship of the self to the past as present in memory. Through our ability to understand and incorporate the remembered past (both our immediate past and the historical "fullness of one's whole past") into an understanding of our own identity and being in the present, we form a self that relates and is able to relate not only to itself but to others (36). In Suchocki's conception, the self is not simply the historical past itself nor what transcends it in the present but rather the event of the relationship of the two. The self that understands and has incorporated its own past into itself "emerges" from that past as it is able to "respond" to it (37).

Through this construction, Suchocki provides a way of naming sin as that which prevents the proper formation of self, of a wrongness at the heart of our very being that continues to malform us by leaving parts of our historical past unreconciled. She argues that when one is able to transcend one's own memories and become a "historically constructed self," the benefit is that one is not tied to that past, since the construction of the self is inherently fluid and necessarily includes the potential to shift and recontextualize its memories of the past into new categories (37). In other words, it involves the ability to reinterpret one's past in light of new experiences of the present: to continue to construct the self and build new levels of relationality with events in the present and with other people and elements of creation. Trauma, Suchocki notes, is to be trapped in one pattern that dominates the conditioning of the present. Trauma can thus be said to be the demonstrating of one's own inability to form a self at the most fundamental level. As such, it is a mark of the brokenness of the world and of human nature. It shows the sin at the heart of the human experience that damages or destroys our ability to form authentic selves and to achieve the self-transcendence that Suchocki implies is necessary for a harmonious existence within creation. The unrelated and unincorporated past (which, given the nature of trauma is almost always associated with a form of violence) is dangerous because it produces a malformed self that exhibits a distorted pattern of relationship to the present.

While the resonance between Suchocki's concept of sin as the failed transcendence of past memory and the discussion of intractable traumatic memory is readily apparent, it also evokes the Augustinian notion of sin's radicality in infecting and disfiguring human nature itself. It suggests that the effects of sin—in terms of poisoned memory—are less like a significant, disfiguring, or debilitating injury and more like a mutated gene within our DNA. Our bodies work to heal injuries, and even though profound and catastrophic injuries can produce lasting effects, the word "injury" itself implies that it is something that can be healed or repaired in a relatively straightforward way. If we break an arm, we have the broken bone set, after which it is left to the body's own healing processes to repair in the proper orientation. If we sustain a deep cut, we have it sewn, and the body eventually generates a blood clot as it produces new skin and tissue to repair the damage. A mutated gene, however, produces continually malforming and deleterious effects. Medical researchers working with myeloproliferative blood cancers, for example, have isolated a particular gene whose mutation causes nodes within the bone marrow to produce a dangerously high quantity of deformed platelets in the person's blood. The patient often suffers a variety of debilitating symptoms, ranging from clotting disorders to migraines to a general degeneration into acute leukemia—all due to the continued malformation of the platelet, a natural part of the circulatory system. The body cannot simply heal this problem, because its natural processes have been distorted; indeed, as many of its natural balancing mechanisms can shift into "overdrive" in an attempt to correct for its effects, the result is the emergence of still other deleterious conditions.

Both in its power to create traumatic memory and in its presence as traumatic memory, sin produces malignant effects on our identity and its formation that are similar to those of the mutated gene described above, particularly in terms of our relationship with others. The poisoned, traumatic memory is not simply one that is unpleasant or embarrassing to recall; it is one that continues to deform our worldview in the present. The effects are not simply profound and damaging; rather, because our very identity (self) is constructed via our experiences of the past and how we relate to the world, traumatic memories continue to distort and malform all the subsequent constructions of our relationships with others. Writing about the malformation of identity in victims of child abuse, McFadyen notes that the distortions in the victim's formation of self, even long afterwards, cannot be predicted. They range from "adopting patterns of revictimization and abuse [of others]," to "the whole gamut of imbalances in personal identity and relationship, from domination to 'loss of self.'"[6] These distortions place the victims in varying degrees of dangerous relationships with others. At a point of congruence with Suchoki, McFadyen locates the distortion in terms of wildly varying degrees of empathy for others.[7] The result is the distortion of one's "network of social relationships and meanings," and the propagation of this distortion in terms of future control of willing in regard to others, a distorted respect of the natural boundaries of self and other and "the handling of intimacy and of affection."[8]

Veterans experience similar social distortions that result from the inability to construct an identity that transcends the poisoned and traumatic memories of the past, often manifest in behaviors that reflect the same issues McFadyen names. Many of the behaviors I have described in chapter 4 fit under this rubric as well. Concerning self-worth, recall that the experiences of veterans run McFadyen's gamut of distortions, from those who pursue absolute control in their jobs—with the seeming connotation that anyone else will do the job poorly—to those who exhibit self-loathing and almost callous disregard for their own well-being (e.g., taking motorcycle rides at extremely high speeds in unsafe conditions). Many propagate violence by objectifying those around them as merely instruments from which they gain data about their own agency. Recall the story Jonathan Shay tells of the veteran who randomly punched a relative walking down a hallway in his home just "to see what would happen."[9] The number of ways that the traumatic memories of veterans suffering from PTSD and moral injury can poison relationships and propagate psychological damage within families is almost incalculable. While wives, husbands, sons, and daughters suffer greatly in these situations, they are almost always secondary effects

6. McFadyen, *Bound to Sin*, 76.

7. The original victim of abuse may later find himself or herself in a dangerous relationship either as an abuser or as one without an appropriate understanding of the boundaries of self, one who is at risk of being continually taken advantage of by others.

8. McFadyen, *Bound to Sin*, 77.

9. Shay, *Odysseus in America*, 44.

from loved ones whose experience has greatly distorted their understanding of intimacy and their capacity to show affection.

The metastatic agent in both of these cases of malformed identity is the guilt and shame that the traumatic memory fuels in the psyche. In terms of the concept of original sin, the experience of guilt and shame is intimately bound up with the commitment of one's active agency in pursuit of distorted, false, and illusory "goods." Recall that McFadyen, in discussing the pathological event of child abuse, argues that the abuser will often intentionally offer the child some inducements and desired rewards in exchange for either "allowing" the abuse itself or keeping it a secret. This effectively confuses children's sense of willing in such a way that they come to understand that they have willed the abuse itself, and they may experience a paralyzing sense of guilt and shame about their involvement in it—even long after the abuse has ended. The memory of the violence in which the veteran has participated has a similar character: conceptions of commitment and honor have been invoked in the service of direct killing, and this engenders a distinct sense of guilt and shame. Van der Kolk and van der Hart lend a great deal of credence to the comparison of these two pathological events in terms of the formation of traumatic memory and its relationship to guilt and shame. They argue that, of those who are aware of their own traumatic memories, their present worldview is characterized by "doubt and humiliation, by feelings of guilt and shame." They mention two groups of people who are particularly haunted by these feelings: "incest victims and combat veterans suffering from PTSD" (178).

A contemporary way of describing the experience of this poisoned and metastasizing memory is with the term "moral injury." Jonathan Shay coined the term in 2010 in *Odysseus in America* to describe the betrayal of one's internal moral values by one in a position of authority, as well as to differentiate the physiological aspects of PTSD from its axiological component. A group of psychologists led by Brett Litz proposed a more generalized definition in arguing that it is "perpetrating, failing to prevent, bearing witness to, or learning about acts that transgress deeply held moral values."[10] Both Shay and Litz have noted that those struggling with moral injury tend to struggle far more severely with guilt and shame than those who experience the physiological ef-

10. Brett T. Litz et al., "Moral Injury and Moral Repair in War Veterans: A Preliminary Model and Intervention Strategy," *Clinical Psychology Review* 29 (2009): 695.

fects of what Shay calls "simple" physiological PTSD. The move from Shay's early definition to the one proposed by the Litz group reflects a different understanding of the agency of the one suffering from moral injury. While Shay focused his definition on the betrayal of one's values by another in authority, the Litz definition focuses more intently on the deliberate actions and perceptions of the one experiencing moral injury. The explanatory power of the concept of original sin is that it suggests another definition that takes an even more nuanced view of human willing and the formation of identity into account. It is more than simply a betrayal or transgression of our most deeply held values. A more Augustinian view reflects the very malleability of our deepest internal understanding of what is "good" and "right." Moral injury, then, may be best understood as the commitment of one's active willing in service of a powerful and compelling moral orientation that is understood at some point to be false; this is most evident in the fact that it does not engender psychiatric well-being. In their connection with a memory that continues to poison a person's sense of boundaries and relationality, feelings of guilt, shame, moral anguish, or ambiguity—all serve as markers of moral injury.

Sin as Hopeless Future: PTSD and "Guilty Willing"

In corrupting and distorting traumatized persons' capacities for relationality and clouding their sense of self-worth and efficacy, the experience of combat trauma often has a profound effect on their hope for the future. In terms of Suchocki's schema, the failure of veterans to transcend the self by relating to their past has profound consequences for their ability to transcend the present self and imagine a different and hopeful future. The astonishing rate of suicides by American veterans testifies to the sense of hopelessness that many of them feel, as do several recent studies that directly attempt to correlate PTSD and moral injury with a feeling of general hopelessness. While the correlation between hopelessness and moral injury and constricted willing is more ephemeral than that between traumatic memory and the commitment of personal energy, there is substantial evidence that they are related, and that the theological understanding of sin has the power to illuminate this area in a compelling way.

The most recent statistics on PTSD, suicide, and hopelessness among veterans of the most recent conflicts in Iraq and Afghanistan paint a sobering picture of the psychological effects of combat. A 2012 comprehensive Veterans Administration study concluded that between eighteen and twenty-two veterans take their lives each day, and that this rate has remained steady, with only minor fluctuations, since 1999.[11] While there is a significant debate about the precise causal relationship between PTSD and suicide among veterans of the Vietnam War and World War II (in part because of the myriad psychiatric stress classifications and illnesses suffered by those veterans and the difficulty in parsing out data that passes scientific muster), evidence from more recent studies suggests that PTSD is a strong predictor of suicidal ideation in veterans of the Iraq and Afghanistan campaigns.[12] One of the key factors in suicide is a feeling of hopelessness: a person cannot envision a future life trajectory that has worth or value.[13] A study of veterans being treated for varying ailments at a Seattle clinic found that, of those who met the criteria to be classified as experiencing "full" PTSD, 67 percent reported experiencing feelings of "hopelessness" and "suicidal ideation" (the two terms were used almost interchangeably in the study). Of those who met a slightly lower standard (i.e., "sub threshold" PTSD), 39 percent reported the same experiences.[14]

I have argued that guilt and shame are the primary metastatic agents of poisoned memory in the psyche; psychiatric studies also suggest that guilt and shame are primary predictors of suicide in veterans suffering from PTSD. One study of Vietnam veterans found that, even among patients who met all the characteristics for a diagnosis of PTSD, the primary predictor for suicidal ideation and completed suicide attempts was the presence of guilt related to combat actions.[15] The study

11. US Department of Veterans Affairs, "2012 Suicide Data Report," http://www.va.gov/opa/docs/Response-and-ExecSum-Suicide-Data-Report-2012-final.pdf.

12. Matthew Jakupcak, Jessica Cook, Zac Imel, Alan Fontana, Robert Rosenheck, and Miles McFall, "PTSD as a Risk Factor for Suicidal Ideation in Iraq and Afghanistan War Veterans," *Journal of Traumatic Stress* 22 (2009): 303.

13. The connection between hopelessness and suicide is so direct that most studies simply imply the connection.

14. Matthew Jakupcak, Katherine D. Hoerster, Alethea Varra, Steven Vannoy, Bradford Felker, and Stephen Hunt, "Hopelessness and Suicidal Ideation in Iraq and Afghanistan War Veterans Reporting Subthreshold and Threshold Posttraumatic Stress Disorder," *Journal of Nervous and Mental Disease* 199, no. 4 (2011): 272–75.

15. Herbert Hendon and Ann Pollinger Haas, "Suicide and Guilt as Manifestations of PTSD in Vietnam Combat Veterans," *American Journal of Psychiatry* 148, no. 5 (1991): 589.

further differentiated the effectiveness of guilt in inducing an "out-of-control" state and the crushing weight of guilt that often accompanied the actions taken while in that state. It found that those who committed killing actions while feeling "out of control" felt substantially and demonstrably higher levels of guilt and and more intense suicidal tendencies than did those who had committed those same actions in an affective state in which they felt more controlled.

These studies demonstrate the relevance of attention to moral issues apart from the simpler association of hopelessness and PTSD. My argument is that the modified Augustinian understanding of original sin that I have articulated throughout this study holds a unique capacity to illuminate these moral issues by offering a conceptual vocabulary that is resonant with the situation of veteran trauma. As I argued in chapter 4, the concept of distorted and malleable willing, based on the capacity of sin to subtly shape and distort the "goods" toward which our desires are oriented, holds a particularly powerful explanatory power in terms of the willing of combatants in wartime situations. I also argued that there is a distinct difference between the agentic deformation of a person who experiences a traumatic event passively (i.e., as a victim of external forces or actions) and one who is traumatized by his or her own actions as an active "perpetrator."[16] More passive trauma victims may experience an unraveling of agency in which they view their actions as completely ineffective and unimportant in the world, having faced a force that threatened to annihilate them. Those who experience a more active agency in the traumatic event—as more direct "perpetrators"—experience the ineffectiveness of their agency amidst a powerful force that threatens to consume their very individuality and self into its larger purpose. Whereas in some more diffuse cases of active trauma, traumatized persons may experience a loss of meaningful agency as such, in more acute cases, traumatized persons may come to understand their own willing as hopelessly corrupted and damaging.

The moral vocabulary of distorted willing and original sin has particular import here both in narrating the agentic issues and in naming

16. I use the terms "passive" and "perpetrator" here to contrast the two, while I freely acknowledge that both connote an essentialized idea of "innocence" and "blame," which I am expressly seeking to undermine. There is, unfortunately, no better linguistic way to make the categorical distinction I'm attempting to make in a way that is readable. In reality, these fall on a spectrum of active agency in sinful situations, the "passive" trauma victim toward one end and the "active" trauma victim toward the other.

the ways in which external forces create them. In my view in this regard, one's awareness of the distortion of one's willing—and its metastasizing effects on one's future willing—is central to one's experience of guilt, cynicism, and hopelessness for the future. As McFadyen argues, external forces distort our willing, and in acting on these distortions, we internalize them, propagating and adding to them in connection to our network of relationships, and our own life-intentionality becomes bent in its disfigured direction. Apart from divine grace, we cannot escape these sinful and destructive orientations. Veterans experience this in a particular way. Relating the veteran experience of guilt and hopelessness about their own situation to the experience of Odysseus upon finally returning home, Shay argues that they understand that they bring difficulty upon others through their actions. He notes that what is crucial is not that this is true, but that veterans believe that they indeed "spoil everything they touch."[17] The basis of this belief lies in their own experience, and it has epistemological and noetic roots. Shay writes that veterans "see themselves as toxic because they expect to harm others with their knowledge of the hideousness of war."[18] This belief in their own toxicity is often tied to guilt, not only about their past deeds in war, but also due to the real and substantive harm they have committed since returning home from the war. Veterans' isolation, he posits, is intensely tied to their own awareness of their destructive capacity, describing how many of his patients feel a deep sense of guilt and regret for the ways that their own families have experienced distortion and misery as a result of the moral and psychological wounds they bear. As he notes also, veterans are distinctly cognizant of the phenomenon of secondary traumatization in their immediate relationships, and that further damages their view of the future. In my view—and in line with the conceptual view of original sin—the "toxicity" that veterans internalize about their own character reflects an intense awareness of their disfigured willing and the continued metastatic effects of their combat experiences on their capacities to will rightly with regard to their own families and social networks.

A closer examination of the connections between combat experiences and guilt suggests that it is tied to an awareness of the power of external forces to distort willing and of their "yielding" to their corruptive

17. Shay, *Odysseus in America*, 83.
18. Shay, *Odysseus in America*, 83.

influence. Recall that the 1991 study by Hendon and Haas found that the guilt experienced by Vietnam combat veterans who were diagnosed with PTSD was most pronounced among those who understood themselves to be "out of control" at the time of their actions. The authors note that the "affective state" of such combatants often is one of either "fear" or "terror," and that a combatant's entry into it involves a vicious circle of circumstance. Often a buddy in the unit is killed, launching the combatant into a "berserk" state, in which he commits acts he later deeply regrets, and for which he later experiences guilt. In a slightly different chain of events, some veterans recount their "berserk" episode as the near-immediate onset of revulsion and guilt, and the way those emotions were crystallized through the death of a comrade who had not engaged in such behavior and was thus "worthier" than they, the guilty survivors. Either way, the fact that veterans are able to understand their guilt with respect to their affective state and the power of the forces of war to produce it in them suggests an acceptance of the premise that outside forces can deeply affect willing and can compel profoundly violent actions. These veterans, who experienced the forces of war in the most direct, primal, emotive, and visceral ways, also experience guilt and hopelessness in an extreme and almost absolute way, exhibiting both high numbers of suicide attempts and what the authors call "suicidal preoccupation" (the predominance of suicide in their thoughts). It seems safe to say that hopelessness is manifest most intensely in these acute and raw situations.

Other veterans, who exhibited slightly lower rates of suicide and suicidal preoccupation, engaged in killing and even committing atrocities indistinguishable from the first group's engagements, but came later to reflect on the wisdom, judgment, and "rightness" of their orders to do so. While these veterans had lower numbers of instances of the measures of hopelessness, it is significant to note that they still suffered from psychologically debilitating senses of guilt and shame, even though they understood their own actions through an additional lens of rationality. This lens may simply be psychologically unavailable to those who experience the most intense and acute sense of guilt and shame as a result of their out-of-control actions. The experience of these veterans appears to point to their acceptance of the conditioning force of authority (in a way very reminiscent of Milgram's analysis) and its questionable "goodness," even while they did not resist—and likely acquiesced willingly to—the orders.[19] These cases represent a slightly more nuanced view of the conditioning force to alter veterans' very sense of "good." Veterans in this situation, for example, may feel that their actions were horrible and reprehensible, but not entirely avoidable; they may understand that they had little recourse at the time to act otherwise, given the constraints of the situation. Those who committed actions in out-of-control states, however, seem to have a greater sense that they could have acted otherwise: they could have simply maintained control.

In either case, both groups experienced significant degrees of guilt centered in the fact that their life-intentionalities and identities were deeply distorted by their experiences. Not only did they report that they experienced a deep sense of guilt at having been "made into a murderer," but that this distorted identity threatened them and those around them in the present.[20] "Significant motivating factors" in suicide attempts were the fear of losing control again and killing others around them, and the feeling that they deserved to be punished for their lingering feelings of aggression and rage. In the most acute cases, it seems safe to argue that they understood their own life-intentionalities to be hopelessly disfigured in a way that made a redemptive or meaningful future impossible to envision.[21] In addition, the secondary traumatization of loved ones when the veterans returned home, and the self-isolation that many veterans impose in order to protect others from them, compound what Shay describes as "irretrievable losses."[22] The broken familial relationships are added to the deaths of comrades for which veterans feel responsible, guilty, and shameful, and this psychological weight binds their willing in a self-destructive trajectory.

While these are the most intense cases of hopelessness and acute guilt and shame, there are certainly more diffuse cases that one can illuminate by using the Augustinian definition of moral injury that I have proposed. As the realization dawns on veterans that the moral orientation, to which they commit or have committed their willing, is aligned

19. Grossman's analysis of the shift in military training between World War II and Vietnam and the resulting marked increase in firing rates among soldiers ordered to do so supports this conclusion. As the enemy is dehumanized, the capacity for the combatant to accept an order even to commit an atrocity—to kill an entire village of civilians—becomes more palatable.

20. Hendon and Haas, "Suicide and Guilt," 590.

21. Hendon and Haas, "Suicide and Guilt," 590.

22. Hendon and Haas, "Suicide and Guilt," 590.

toward a "good" that is false, they may come to reflect in a more cynical way about the future itself. Attempting to live into the identity that Tick proposes, that of a "truth-teller" and elder of the community whose experience of war is valuable and worthy of communication to society at large, the veteran may find it a hard sell. Psychologist James Hillman argues that PTSD as experienced en masse by scores of American veterans is, in fact, a distinctly American problem tied to "the endemic numbing of the American homeland and its addiction to security."[23] As a result of this addiction, our society upholds the "good" of military conquest and war both overtly and subtly in myriad ways. Tick notes (and I have argued similarly in chapter 3) that "our entertainment-driven consumer society markets empty icons of the war experience. We turn camouflage into a clothing style and sell toy replicas of advanced weaponry."[24] The larger force of "consumer patriotism" deeply affects the culture's moral values, and those who speak against the conditioning power of this force certainly will face resistance and risk judgment about their own moral character. While veterans suffering from a lower-intensity form of moral injury than those who killed in a "berserk" rage may not contend with the crushing guilt and suicidal ideation that show a deep hopelessness, the encounter with the intractable and ubiquitous force of "consumer patriotism" and its profound influence on axiological orientations in contemporary America may certainly damage their capacity to imagine a hopeful future in which violence does not dominate the cultural consciousness.

Jürgen Moltmann, the renowned German theologian who narrowly survived the Allied firebombing of Dresden as a German army auxiliary, argues that an aspect of the original sin passed to humanity from Adam is an attitude and orientation of despair. While many follow Augustine in naming "pride" as the original form of sin in human action, Moltmann argues that "the other side of such pride is hopelessness, resignation, inertia, and melancholy."[25] For Moltmann, the promise of God through the resurrection lies in its radical hope, which contradicts the seemingly inescapable realities of the present situation, which we experience intensely in death, suffering, and misery. In fact, he argues,

23. James Hillman, *A Terrible Love of War* (New York: Penguin, 2004), 31.

24. Tick, *War and the Soul*, 244.

25. Jürgen Moltmann, *Theology of Hope: On the Ground and the Implications of a Christian Eschatology*, trans. Margaret Kohl (Minneapolis: Fortress, 1991), 22.

hope means nothing at all if it does not first deal with the reality of death and the extreme violence and brokenness of humanity. Echoing Augustine, Moltmann conceives of resurrection hope as exactly the inbreaking divine action that enables us to reorient our lives toward what is truly good; it is what is able to pierce the impenetrable condition of brokenness under which humanity labors, spanning "the horizons which then open over a closed existence."[26] For Moltmann, the resurrection means that the forces that seemingly "close the book" on lives, movements, and hopes for the future do not, in fact, do so. In light of the Christ who overcame death, death's capacity to close off the meaning and purpose of a life is negated, and its capacity to render actions and purposes meaningless is annulled.

In light of this one true hope and God's eschatological promise of life beyond death that we glimpse in the resurrection, to despair is to refuse to believe and thus to sin. Moltmann presents a picture of hopelessness as an active refusal to embrace the hope offered and therefore to act as if the powers that condition human existence in the present have ultimate authority and exercise total and enduring control over human destiny. Yet he also presents existential despair at the condition in which humanity finds itself in the present, quoting John Calvin's claim that "we are surrounded by decay" and "oppressed by ineffable misery"; our experiences in this world are of death, real guilt, and deep human suffering—"to which there is no ready-made answer."[27] Hopelessness is not an irrational or absurd response to our situation; it is one that reflects an honest engagement with the realities of the world, of our orientations and trajectories apart from the grace of God. To interpret Moltmann through McFadyen's schema, when we apply our personal energies to this condition of hopelessness, we begin to despair and to act and to become oriented in ways that reflect a grim view that habitually limits our view of the future of our human condition.

Moltmann articulates an almost dichotomous view of sin and hope, of a world of death and guilt on the one hand and of life and renewal on the other, which resonates with the condition of those who have suffered trauma. Shelly Rambo says that those who have been forcefully impacted by death enter a psychological liminal space, between the experience of "a radical ending past in which it is difficult, if not im-

26. Moltmann, *Theology of Hope*, 20.
27. Moltmann, *Theology of Hope*, 19.

possible, to conceive of life" and future living.[28] Those studying combat trauma in particular would refer to this as the "death imprint"—the close encounter with death—that Rambo notes is "always here," present in the psyche for those who have experienced it; they are trapped in a situation from which they cannot derive further meaning.[29] For those experiencing moral injury, who have committed their active energies to the enterprise of warfare and understand it to be a false good, their guilty identity is also "always here." For those who have direct experiences of combat and find themselves "made into murderers," that identity is always present and serves as a major impediment toward envisioning a hopeful future, as any guilt-free future would involve altering this guilty identity. For those who have experienced a lower-intensity version of moral injury, hopelessness may still be found in the distorted, guilty identity that they have participated in, and this guilt damages their capacity to envision a guilt-free future.

Moltmann's profound personal experience of guilt certainly informed his articulation of human brokenness; as such, his conception of the boundary between hope and despair holds descriptive power for those who experience moral injury and distorted identity. He was drafted from the air force auxiliary into the regular German army in 1944 and sent to the front, where he was present at the German surrender in 1945 to British troops. He was held in Allied rehabilitation camps until 1948, and in those camps he was forced to confront the realities of the "final solution." In his autobiography, he reports that he was utterly stricken with guilt and horror when he and his fellow German prisoners were made to view pictures of the concentration camps at Belsen and Buchenwald. He notes that, while some struggled to accept the veracity of the images, "slowly and inexorably the truth seeped into our consciousness, and we saw ourselves through the eyes of the Nazi victims."[30] He connects a sense of personal and communal despair with deep guilt in conveying his sense that "depression over the wartime destruction and a captivity with no end in sight was compounded by a feeling of profound shame at having to share in shouldering the disgrace of one's own people."[31]

28. Rambo, *Spirit and Trauma*, 4.

29. Rambo, *Spirit and Trauma*, 4.

30. Jürgen Moltmann, *A Broad Place: An Autobiography*, trans. Margaret Kohl (Minneapolis: Fortress, 2008), 8.

31. Moltmann, *A Broad Place*, 8.

In *A Theology of Hope*, which he wrote more than two decades later, Moltmann notes that despair is a feeling that is predicated on some vision of what life looks like. In his words, despair "presupposes hope," and he quotes Augustine's dictum that "what we do not long for, can be the object neither of our hope nor of our despair."[32] In other words, despair is possible only if one can envision what a proper life would be like. The guilty memory of the one who has experienced moral injury breeds a particular kind of despair, namely, that there is indeed a life that can be glimpsed; but the morally injured believe that they (and perhaps even the whole world) are too broken for it to apply in any way to *their* future. Moltmann embraced Christianity in the Allied detention camp, and in his view this provided the vision of hope in the Christ who forgave his own abusers and deserters. Conversely, however, his view of the reality of human life apart from the hope of the gospel and the resurrection is one of utter hopelessness and brokenness, so much so that, given the human experience of brokenness that he and other veterans of war have experienced, it follows from his conception of hope that the only authentic reaction to the encounter with extreme human brokenness is to lose hope and to absolutely despair for the human condition. Their guilt and the malformation of their identity is haunting and gut-wrenching precisely because it does not occur against the imaginative backdrop of complete moral greyness, but because so many veterans believe that they *should* be other than they are. As Tick argues, soldiers enter service with a vision of a mythic warrior; then they utterly fail to fulfill that identity, incurring an increasing sense of guilt and shame as their malformed identities become less and less like the ideal they envision as ultimately "good." An ideal is there, perhaps even notions of justice and hope; yet, as Moltmann argues, the problem is that it in "no way opens up towards its fulfillment."[33]

Sin, Blame, and the Universality of Guilt

In this chapter I have argued that sin has the capacity to powerfully name the brokenness at the heart of the experience of combat trauma in terms of traumatic memory and the general expression of hopelessness

32. Moltmann, *Theology of Hope*, 23.
33. Moltmann, *Theology of Hope*, 23.

for the future. Yet the themes of guilt and blame feature prominently in the discussion of both of these pathologies, and they deserve further attention. If the doctrine of original sin that I have proposed is to hold explanatory value, then perhaps its greatest contribution to an understanding of trauma and wartime violence is its nuanced valuation of guilt, blame, and responsibility. I have woven these threads through previous chapters, but now I will attempt to clarify the relationship between guilt and the ability to will otherwise; the importance of the universality of guilt as it relates to the experience of brokenness; and, finally, the ways in which a more nuanced understanding of the forces of guilt and blame may provide a way of healing traumatic memory.

While the radical power of the force of sin to direct willing provides a framework for understanding the limited options available to those bound in pathological situations, perhaps the most prominent parallel of an Augustinian view of sin and willing to this study is its relationship to morality in terms of guilt. As I argued in the introduction to this book, a major problem present in the guiding ideologies of our society is the essentializing of legal categories of "innocence" and "guilt" in order to avoid the crushing psychological burden of blameworthiness. This burden, as I have argued in this chapter, is borne in a particularly acute way by many of our nation's veterans. The intense experience of guilt and shame is linked directly to many veterans' understanding that they deserve blame and hence punishment for the actions they have committed.[34] The profound feeling of guilt as blameworthiness conditions both the traumatic experience that cannot be categorized into the mind's system of memory and meaning-making, as well as the hopelessness that is borne by those who cannot envision a future devoid of blame and punishment.

A great deal of this experience of guilt involves the fact that combatants operate with the implicit understanding that individuals are morally autonomous. This understanding resonates with an essentially Pelagian understanding of the freedom of the will. More precisely, it involves the belief—primarily on the part of combatants or veterans—that they could always have chosen otherwise when faced with the actions they took. For Pelagius, it was crucial that we are capable of willing

34. Hendon and Haas, "Suicide and Guilt," 590. This study connotes exactly this: along with feelings of hopelessness and guilt, many suicidal veterans also believed that they deserved to be punished.

rightly and doing good at all times, because only then could our failures be counted against us as guilt. Even when there are crucial factors that may influence our willing, we are always able, according to Pelagius, to transcend those factors—that is, the "good" choice is always available to us. The US military ethos is predicated on the highest notions of personal responsibility, individual bravery, and honor. The Code of Conduct, which can be seen as a concise ethical guide to military behavior in combat, concludes with the reminder that every combatant is responsible for her or his own actions. That ethical guide and the training ethos create the powerful idea that there is always an honorable choice available, and military members are explicitly instructed to refuse orders that they understand to be "illegal or immoral" based on the US Code of Military Justice and the Geneva Conventions. The clear implication in this instruction is that the soldier is always able to understand an order to be illegal or immoral, and that she or he always has the ability to exercise an option to resist.

It follows that, against that backdrop, the guilt of veterans is connected with their belief that they could have acted differently than they did in crucial moments. As I have already noted, Hendon and Haas's study on guilt and killing notes that those who were out of control when they killed experienced demonstrably higher rates of suicide than those who did it while responding more rationally or simply following orders. This could be interpreted to suggest that those who felt "out of control" when they killed others feel more guilt because they feel that they should have been able to control themselves. This seems akin to a lower-impact situation in which a person says something in anger that she regrets and then feels guilty about because she should have been able to control her temper—precisely because she does exercise control over her temper and emotions the majority of the time. Edward Tick argues that a large part of the identity crisis of guilt and shame that veterans encounter is due to their failure to live up to the warrior ideal they envision. It is not crucial that the ideal is unrealistic, but that veterans themselves believe it to be attainable and measure their own actions against it, as though there were honorable and heroic choices available that they simply didn't have the courage to make. Grossman himself, even while recognizing and detailing the forces that constrain willing and make dissent nearly impossible in situations in which one is ordered to kill noncombatants, hails the "remarkable moral fiber" of those who are able to refuse to participate in that act.[35] This tacitly reflects the Pelagian view that, while these individuals experienced and felt the social and hierarchical pressures on their willing, they were capable of transcending them and accessing a "good" moral choice. When it is framed in this way, those who are unable to do so, despite whatever impossible situation they are placed in, necessarily must understand themselves to be guilty of not making that choice.

Multiple figures—from Milgram to Shay to Grossman himself—provide a great deal of psychological evidence that morally "good" choices are rarely available on the battlefield, for varying reasons. While some situations may exist in which one has a chance to consider the order before following it, many times one has to react instantly in a particular situation to a more general set of instructions. Here the reflexive conditioning that Grossman describes becomes crucial: the ingrained capacity to "shoot first" when viscerally assessing a level of enemy threat bypasses the entire decision-making system of the brain. The choice to "not fire" is in this case quite literally not available to the consciousness. Yet more generally, the forces of war so distort the combatants' sense of "good" that a truly "good" moral choice may seem to be a moral ill; moral realities are confused. For example, one could argue that even those who have gone into a "berserk" state do so out of a sense of moral righteousness or indignation: a soldier's friend has been unjustly killed, and justice must be done on that person's behalf. Quoting an interview with a participant in the infamous My Lai massacre in Vietnam, Milgram notes this very sense of moral justice. When asked why he killed men, women, and children, the participant responded that not only had he been ordered to, but "at the time I felt like I was doing the right thing, because . . . I lost buddies."[36] In McFadyen's terms, the horizons of choice have certainly been narrowed, since outright resistance and dissent may not be available. This does not mean that there are not choices that incur greater and lesser degrees of guilt. These minor choices certainly exist, but they must be understood to exist in the primary capacity of subterfuge: that is, the capacity of combatants doing their best to minimize the impact of their aggressive actions even as they commit them.[37]

35. Grossman, *On Killing*, 224.

36. Milgram, *Obedience to Authority*, 185.

37. It is worth mentioning that a more consequentialist view of morality would

Given the dichotomy between the internalized belief in moral autonomy and the actual experiences of veterans amid the forces of war, a Pelagian morality based on human autonomy not only fails to accurately describe the complexities of psychology in combat, it also becomes a pathogenic force itself within the psyche. One of Augustine's primary complaints against Pelagius's concept of human willing was that it created an untenable moralism, absolutizing blame for human actions and attributing responsibility to humanity for its own righteousness. Regarding the situation of combat willing, the Pelagian system suffers from the same problem: its ubiquity in modern society and its acceptance by combatants makes it harmful in its absolutizing of moral guilt. It is false precisely because it cannot account for the factors that have been shown by psychologists to affect human willing, and it assumes incorrectly that "good" moral choices are available in any situation to anyone. It is pathogenic because it engenders absolute feelings of guilt and shame for acts that have complex essential causes, and it attributes blame in toto to individuals who are caught in a profoundly complex web of responsibility, agency, and culpability without any attention to the interconnections that define those individuals.

Perhaps the primary benefit of the modified Augustinian conception of original sin that I have proposed is that it offers a more complex moral system, which holds individuals accountable for moral action without absolutizing their responsibility. It argues that because we share a human nature that is congenitally damaged, and the force of sin conditions our very sense of what is "good," all humanity is bound in a condition of universal sinfulness. It is impossible for any individual to escape this condition, and all humanity is disfigured and corrupted by the collective commitments of personal energies to the pursuit of distorted goods. As such, any individual human action is not merely influenced but actually constricted by the situation in which an individual

---

also make the seemingly simple "moral heroes" Grossman describes considerably less so. Grossman valorizes those who in one situation stepped out of their formation and refused their commander's order to kill civilians. These resisters were summarily executed on the commander's orders moments later, and the other members of the unit carried out the original order. It is possible that the less morally corrosive choice would actually be to engage in some form of subterfuge, such as shooting civilians in non-life-threatening parts of the body in order to actually give them the greatest chance of survival. Striving to be morally exemplary is again problematic as the forces of war also prey on those very desires.

finds him- or herself amid the forces of human nature and civilization. A critical point, then, is that our willing is not individually self-contained, but is influenced by our collective broken and damaged nature. This influence, as I have argued throughout this study, primarily coalesces into forces that fundamentally distort our conception of what is "good," such that our moral options are never decisions of "good" or "bad" but within a range of greater and less "bad" options.

The malleability of our very notion of "good" presents a concept of guilt that is categorically different from the absolutized guilt present in any system that assumes complete human autonomy as the ground of human willing. The problem is not only that a truly "good" choice is not truly available, but also that our sense of "good" is so distorted that, in claiming a false and distorted "good" as absolute, we are capable of truly believing that we are "doing good" in pursuing it. This is precisely the power of the force of sin: as McFadyen argues, it confuses our sense of morality and effectively orients it in corrupted directions; it is predicated on the fact that, as moral agents, we act in pursuit of desire for what we believe to be good; therefore, it is not as though soldiers are necessarily making choices they know to be morally wrong, but rather their very desire to do good, to be honorable, is sequestered into a limited horizon of greater and lesser wrongs. The crucial point is that this understanding complicates the determination of moral value for any action taken by an individual person. A deontological ethical system, for example, would argue that it is primarily a person's intent that matters when determining whether she or he has acted "rightly" or "wrongly" in any given situation. Yet, within the understanding of original sin and distorted willing, it is entirely possible to examine a hideous act of wartime violence and answer that someone acted with intent to pursue what he or she understood to be truly "good." In what way, then, is the person who committed this act guilty and therefore blameworthy?

The concept of original sin offers a different path: it contends that individuals are congenitally guilty by inheriting this damaged human nature and the concomitant forces of civilization that so distort human willing—and by the commitment of their own personal energies in pursuit of a distorted good. This dual aspect of human guilt is crucial, since it affirms that an individual retains responsibility for his or her own actions; yet responsibility does not rest *solely* on that individual. It recognizes the complex web of human relationality and the ways in which social and psychological pressures create the situations and environments within which individual actions occur. These situations and environments constitute our human nature and are thus inescapable. Naming "sin" as the nature and situation in which we find ourselves helps us recognize the wrongness and brokenness of the world and refuses to allow us to call it "good." Yet it also recognizes that our inescapable participation in it as human beings prevents us from being called "good" either. Both our constitutive existence within this broken nature and our actions that inevitably arise from it make us guilty. While the universality of sin so described raises immediate questions about the relationship between guilt and blame, it certainly does argue that individual actions cannot be judged as "guilty" apart from the context from which they arise.

This holds particular explanatory power in terms of the situation of veteran guilt in that it contextualizes their guilt in a particular way without dismissing it. The phrase "it's not your fault" is often spoken by therapists to those who have suffered significant trauma and whose life-intentionality has been consequently distorted. Ishmael Beah, recounting his conscription into the Sierra Leone civil war as a child soldier after the killing of his parents and of the majority of the members of his local village, notes that when he heard this phrase spoken to him by the UN workers when he finally arrived at a rehabilitation facility, he despised it. It did not reflect the reality of his own sense of personal accountability and identity—or his inner sense of guilt concerning the violence he had committed.[38] It seems unlikely that veterans of America's wars who suffer from PTSD and moral injury would react in a better way to being told "it's not your fault"; it would likely chafe against them for the same reasons. No veterans experiencing intense guilt for the act of killing or participating in killing other humans would relate to that phrase, for to do so would suggest that they had no active agency. Such an implication would ring untrue to them and would also be contrary to the moral logic of the modified concept of original sin that I am proposing. This concept does not hold that it is not one's fault that one committed individually sinful and violent actions; indeed, when one commits one's action toward a distorted good, one commits sin. It does hold, however, that it is not *entirely* the individual's fault. This perhaps provides a small yet significant amount of "breathing room" that recognizes the veteran's

38. Ishmael Beah, *A Long Way Gone: Memoirs of a Boy Soldier* (New York: Farrar, Strauss and Giroux, 2007).

complicity in a terrible action while simultaneously recognizing the power of the forces that conditioned it. It can also trace the path of the distortion in the combatant's willing and the way his or her own continually functioning sense of honor is abused and sequestered.

For veterans on the edge of despair and totalizing hopelessness, the ability to speak of their situation in an honest and sober way—while suggesting that they are not entirely responsible for their behavior—may be the difference between suicide and the beginnings of constructing a future that is worth living. The way original sin informs the understanding of moral injury as a category of human experience allows for both the recognition of guilt and the specific naming of the forces that shape and constrain willing in combat situations.[39] The very ability to name these forces as "sinful" and among those that deepen human brokenness in the world identifies a potential purpose for veterans: to struggle against these forces and to name them in the public arena.[40] In this way, veterans can potentially live into the role of the "truth-teller" that Tick describes and find purpose in passing on experience and wisdom to society at large. But it is important to note that this may involve rejecting the idea of the "mythic warrior" altogether and recognizing that that construction is precisely one that distorts our sense of the good. Less than living into or realizing some identity involved in it, the veteran who is able to name those forces warns about the very notion of the "mythic warrior," the force of obedience to sequester one's willing, the capacity of the predominant mythology of American exceptionalism to dehumanize those deemed to be dangerous, and the many other battlefield pressures that condition one to accept killing and violence as not simply necessary but morally "good." These ideas certainly do not constitute a therapeutic "magic bullet"—the clear and unequivocal cerebral answer to moral pain and trauma. But perhaps they may serve as a conceptual tool to help therapists, researchers, and veterans

39. The term "moral injury" is certainly not exclusive to combat trauma and the forces that shape moral choices there, though it was originally used to describe the axiological component of PTSD resulting from the combat environment. It is particularly apt in describing varying kinds of perpetrator trauma, and varying researchers are currently working out its application in wider arenas of experience.

40. In *Soul Repair: Recovering from Moral Injury after War* (Boston: Beacon, 2012), Rita Brock and Gabriella Lettini narrate the stories of several veterans who have experienced a similar sense of renewed life and purpose in speaking out against the way we conduct war based on their own experiences.

realistically envision a meaningful future where some seed of hope may germinate.

The more complex moral framework may also provide a way in which guilty traumatic memories may be contextualized and reimagined in a way that is faithful both to the rights of the victim and to the recovery of the combatant. Van der Kolk and van der Hart suggest that traumatic memories involving guilt and shame are the most intractable and that they most strongly resist flexibility and incorporation into the mind's normal system of meaning-making. Yet the treatment that they suggest for other patients, the suggestion of "a less negative or even a positive scenario," is fraught with ethical issues, particularly for veterans whose trauma involves their own actions of violence against others.[41] Is it morally proper to alter the memory of a violent act in order to lessen perpetrators' guilt and ease their moral culpability? This would seem to ameliorate the guilt of the perpetrator at the expense of the victim—and at the expense of the truth. But perhaps the more complex notion of morality found in Augustine's concept of willing is able to provide a different solution. It is certainly less problematic to think that the "guilty" memory of a combat veteran could be ameliorated in a way that focused on the factors limiting his or her agency, and thus sharing the responsibility for his or her actions. This neither changes the truth of the event nor makes a claim that actors have not committed their energies toward violent action; nor does it gloss over the suffering of victims. It simply declares to veterans that the totality of guilt does not rest solely on their shoulders. Contextualized in this way, the memory may be incorporated into a new schema of meaning wherein the veteran is able to recognize the power of those forces in shaping willing and perhaps is even able to understand the role of resistance to them as a moral duty.

If this conception of sin is valuable in providing both a way of naming human brokenness that cuts through the essentialized moral conception of innocence we've created, and yet also corrects that absolutized notion of guilt that veterans experience, then questions still linger about the relationship between guilt and blame. From the Augustinian perspective, we incur guilt congenitally through our inheritance of a damaged human nature. In this study, I have attempted to examine the myriad ways in which our human nature is damaged, and to identify the powerful forces within our evolutionary biology, our civilization, and

41. Van der Kolk and van der Hart, "The Intrusive Past," 178.

our society that propagate the damage and distort our nature further. Yet it has also been my declared intention to reclaim the language of "sin" in a way that is meaningful and defines what is truly wrong and broken. This, almost of necessity, means that there is some proper place for blame as it relates to the guilt associated with agents' participation in that brokenness.

Certainly, in seeking to rehabilitate the ability of the term "sin" to name the brokenness at the center of the human experience, this study has placed emphasis on the *force* of sin as blameworthy and lessened the emphasis on the sinful actions and inactions of individuals that thereby make them blameworthy as active "sinners." This is a necessary corrective for a society that has built a great deal of its moral foundation on a false conception of human autonomy and hence has placed too much blame on individuals for the particular actions they have taken. These forces condition a great deal of the way we think about ourselves, others, and the relative values of all aspects of creation. Consequently, they form the very center of our concept of moral order. In the context of warfare and violence, it is certainly the case that these forces make the killing of other human beings desirable in order to achieve a particular end. Here a distinct tension emerges within an Augustinian concept of individual guilt and willing: to associate blame entirely with the force of sin and not at all with the individual bound within it is to do violence to the conception of the will as a manifestation of the individual's status as a moral agent. In other words, it would be to hold that the individual has lost all identity as subject and is rendered pure object by the totalizing force. To hold the individual guilty but only the larger corrupting force as blameworthy appears to dissolve the tension between sin as *both* force and individual act entirely at the expense of the latter. It would also seem to entirely absolve the blame of those who commit heinous violence: it would be a version of "the devil made me do it," which denies their agency entirely.

On the other hand, the prevalence and power of the external conditioning forces to affect the will make it difficult to establish criteria by which we can easily apportion degrees of blame among the guilty. While guilt may be universal, it's true that military combatants experience the guilt and distortion of the shattered concept of "good" as that which benefits all humanity collectively in an acute way. They witness war and participate in war, which is the place where the fabric of humanity is rent beyond repair, and they bear this brokenness in the guilt and shame that deeply distort their own selves and propagate it to others via secondary traumatization and violent behavior. They are undeniably complicit in participating in great violence and visiting it on others, and they bear the guilt of the greater societal forces in a particular and unique way. They kill and are the instruments of a dehumanizing force that is propagated by all of humanity in general and more particularly by our American society. But is their "acute" guilt categorically different from that of civilians who enjoy, patronize, and thus support war films that extol American exceptionalism, who buy camouflage clothing for their children, and who support war efforts with the power of their vote? If the driving factor is the conditioning force of sin that distorts all actors—from voters to politicians to military leaders to filmmakers to advertisers to corporations—then it seems untenable to hold one member of this society more blameworthy than another simply because of the role he or she may play, and the actions he or she is compelled to commit, in service to the overall societal "good."[42]

Placed within its proper theological context, however, the Augustinian revision of the doctrine of sin is less concerned with the attribution of individual blame than it is with illuminating the human condition, in which grace and salvation are urgently necessary. Augustine conceptualized the radical, inescapable universality of human sin with an eye toward salvation, not, as McFarland argues, with "a sadistic enthusiasm for belittling human beings."[43] Augustine was concerned that the system developed by Pelagius created a significant amount of stress on people, who then had to worry about whether they were worthy of God's grace based on their "individual merits."[44] By arguing that sin is radical and universal, Augustine calms this anxiety in a seemingly strange way,

42. In this discussion, which focuses primarily on those who perpetrate acts of violence, we must not lose sight of the victims of that violence. I should note that what I am proposing here is not in any way meant to excuse or condone violent actions or to ignore the pain and suffering of the victims of rape, murder, and all manner of war violence. On the contrary, it is meant to identify the root causes of the brokenness that threatens to propagate and further enable these violent acts so that they may not continue to happen.

43. McFarland, *In Adam's Fall*, 46. As McFarland argues further, however, Augustine does propose that the congenital guilt of humanity does mean that all human beings deserve to suffer. This is a conclusion from theodicy that McFarland and many other scholars (including me) find untenable and quite harmful in describing the world today.

44. McFarland, *In Adam's Fall*, 46.

articulating that all stand guilty before God and none merit God's grace in a contest of moral goodness. Grace can be understood only against this backdrop. As McFarland argues, the role of the doctrine of sin is not anthropocentric: its purpose "should not be to focus attention on ourselves as good or bad, but on God."[45] If this is so, then the doctrine of sin should make our focus on God's response to the situation of human brokenness and guilt. Indeed, Augustine's concept is centered on the gracious character of God, and his exhortations in the anti-Pelagian writings often frame the entire discussion of human willing and sinfulness in terms of a defense of the fullness of God's entirely unmerited grace and forgiveness, through Jesus Christ, as the healing response to the condition of human sinfulness.[46]

If one aspect of the explanatory power of the modified conception of original sin I have proposed here is that it provides a framework by which we can more authentically understand human brokenness, then another pivotal aspect is the pathway to veteran healing that it provides through a more graceful moral order. Given the forces that constrict the willing of combatants, this study strongly argues against simple moral condemnations, even condemnations of those combatants who have acted with extreme violence in combat. I have attempted here to elucidate the ways in which the doctrine of sin may provide small measures of grace that may have real importance in healing veterans suffering from severe guilt and shame. While some would contend that the conception of universal and congenital guilt dissolves the pillars that uphold moral order, it is my contention that it reorients the moral order and emphasizes grace and forgiveness over (though not excluding) blame. While blame cannot and should not be abandoned as an ascription we apply to acts that we judge to be morally wrong—the forces that produce them or even the people who commit them—the doctrine of original sin does suggest that we apply it with a significant measure of grace and a fuller understanding of the conditions from which those acts arise. Given the distortion of our own sense of good, which permeates our societal values, it encourages us to examine our collective axiological values and constructed systems of judgment with a great deal of suspicion rather than an uncritical reverence. It should encourage

45. McFarland, *In Adam's Fall*, 47.

46. Most notably in *On the Spirit and the Letter*, as he repeatedly extolls the totality of grace in the early sections (4, 5, 7, 10, 12, 13).

us to identify blameworthy forces, situations, and institutions—and to hold our allegiances to these lightly. In response to the God who, in spite of our sinfulness, guilt, and blameworthiness, "values human life so highly as to guarantee indefeasibly with God's own life as given in Jesus Christ," it makes the difficult demand that we approach our moral judgments—particularly regarding individual actors—with a posture of grace and an openness to the possibility of forgiveness.[47]

47. McFarland, *In Adam's Fall*, 46. As Miroslav Volf also notes, in *Exclusion and Embrace: A Theological Exploration of Identity, Otherness, and Reconciliation* (Nashville: Abingdon, 1996), this is not a simple process, and many conditions must be met on this side of the eschaton for forgiveness and reconciliation to be truly effected. Victims must name injustices and wrongs, and perpetrators must truly repent of them. Yet Volf argues that the posture toward—and genuine desire for—forgiveness and reconciliation is the call of the gospel, even in the most difficult of circumstances.

BIBLIOGRAPHY

Arendt, Hannah. *The Origins of Totalitarianism*. New York: Harcourt, 1968.

Athanasius. *On the Incarnation*. Edited and translated by a religious of C.S.M.V. Crestwood, NY: St. Vladimir's Seminary Press, 1996.

Augustine. *The City of God against the Pagans*, edited and translated by R. W. Dyson. New York: Cambridge University Press, 1998.

———. *On Nature and Grace*. In volume 5 of *Nicene and Post-Nicene Fathers*, first series, edited by Philip Schaff. Peabody, MA: Hendrickson, 2004.

———. *On the Merits and Forgiveness of Sins and the Baptism of Infants*. In volume 5 of *Nicene and Post-Nicene Fathers*, first series, edited by Philip Schaff. Peabody, MA: Hendrickson, 2004.

———. *On the Spirit and the Letter*. In volume 5 of *Nicene and Post-Nicene Fathers*, first series, edited by Philip Schaff. Peabody, MA: Hendrickson, 2004.

Beah, Ishmael. *A Long Way Gone: Memoirs of a Boy Soldier*. New York: Farrar, Straus and Giroux, 2007.

Bonhoeffer, Dietrich. *Ethics*. Edited by Clifford J. Green. Translated by Reinhard Krauss, Charles C. West, and Douglas W. Stott. Volume 6 of *Dietrich Bonhoeffer Works*, edited by Wayne Whitson Floyd Jr. Minneapolis: Fortress, 2009.

Brock, Rita, and Gabriella Lettini. *Soul Repair: Recovering from Moral Injury after War*. Boston: Beacon, 2012.

Caruth, Cathy. *Unclaimed Experience: Trauma, Narrative, and History*. Baltimore: Johns Hopkins University Press, 1996.

Dekel, Rachel, and Solomon Zahaya. "Secondary Traumatization among Wives of War Veterans with PTSD." In *Combat Stress Injury: Theory, Research and Management*, edited by Charles Figley and William Nash. New York: Routledge, 2007.

Farley, Wendy. *Tragic Vision and Divine Compassion: A Contemporary Theodicy*. Louisville: Westminster John Knox, 1990.

Felman, Shoshanna, and Dori Laub. *Testimony: Crises of Witnessing in Literature, Psychoanalysis, and History*. New York: Routledge, 1992.

Gabriel, Richard. *No More Heroes: Madness and Psychiatry in War.* New York: Hill and Wang, 1987.

Girard, René. *Violence and the Sacred.* Translated by Patrick Gregory. Baltimore: Johns Hopkins University Press, 1977.

Gregory of Nyssa. *On the Making of Man.* In volume 5 of *Nicene and Post-Nicene Fathers*, second series, edited by Philip Schaff and Henry Wace. Peabody, MA: Hendrickson, 2004.

Grossman, Dave. *On Killing: The Psychological Cost of Learning to Kill in War and Society.* New York: Back Bay Books, 1995.

Hauerwas, Stanley. *War and the American Difference: Theological Reflections on Violence and National Identity.* Grand Rapids: Baker Academic, 2011.

Hendon, Herbert, and Ann Pollinger Hass. "Suicide and Guilt as Manifestations of PTSD in Vietnam Combat Veterans." *American Journal of Psychiatry* 148, no. 5 (1991): 586–91.

Hillman, James. *A Terrible Love of War.* New York: Penguin, 2004.

Irenaeus. *Against Heresies.* In volume 1 of *Ante-Nicene Fathers*, edited by Alexander Roberts and James Donaldson. Peabody, MA: Hendrickson, 1994.

Jakupcak, Matthew, Jessica Cook, Zac Imel, Alan Fontana, Robert Rosenheck, and Miles McFall. "PTSD as a Risk Factor for Suicidal Ideation in Iraq and Afghanistan War Veterans." *Journal of Traumatic Stress* 22 (2009): 303–6.

Jones, Serene. *Trauma and Grace: Theology in a Ruptured World.* Louisville: Westminster John Knox, 2009.

Keegan, John, and Richard Holmes. *Soldiers: A History of Men in Battle.* London: Hamilton, 1985.

Lepore, Jill. *The Name of War: King Philip's War and the Origins of American Identity.* New York: Vintage Books, 1998.

Lifton, R. J. "Understanding the Traumatized Self: Imagery, Symbolization, and Transformation." In *Human Adaptation to Extreme Stress*, edited by J. P. Wilson, Z. Harel, and B. Kahana. New York: Plenum, 1988.

Litz, Brett T., Nathan Stein, Ellen Delaney, Leslie Lebowitz, William P. Nash, Caroline Silva, and Shira Maguen. "Moral Injury and Moral Repair in War Veterans: A Preliminary Model and Intervention Strategy." *Clinical Psychology Review* 29 (2009): 695–706.

Maslow, A. H. "A Theory of Human Motivation." *Psychological Review* 50, no. 4 (1943): 370–96.

McFadyen, Alistair. *Bound to Sin: Abuse, Holocaust, and the Christian Doctrine of Sin.* New York: Cambridge University Press, 2000.

McFarland, Ian A. *In Adam's Fall: A Meditation on the Christian Doctrine of Original Sin.* Malden, MA: Wiley-Blackwell, 2010.

Milgram, Stanley. *Obedience to Authority: An Experimental View.* New York: HarperCollins, 1974.

Moltmann, Jürgen. *A Broad Place: An Autobiography*. Translated by Margaret Kohl. Minneapolis: Fortress, 2008.

———. *The Coming of God: Christian Eschatology*. Translated by Margaret Kohl. Minneapolis: Fortress, 1996.

———. *Theology of Hope: On the Ground and the Implications of a Christian Eschatology*. Translated by Margaret Kohl. Minneapolis: Fortress, 1991.

Nash, William P. "Combat/Operational Stress Adaptations and Injuries." In *Combat Stress Injury: Theory, Research, and Management*, edited by Charles R. Figley and William P. Nash. New York: Routledge, 2007.

Northup, Solomon. *Twelve Years a Slave*. New York: Sterling, 2013.

Origen. *On First Principles*. In volume 4 of *Ante-Nicene Fathers*, edited by Alexander Roberts and James Donaldson. Peabody, MA: Hendrickson, 2004.

Park, Andrew Sung. *The Wounded Heart of God: The Asian Concept of Han and the Christian Doctrine of Sin*. Nashville: Abingdon, 1993.

Pelagius. *To Demetrias*. In *The Letters of Pelagius and His Followers*, edited and translated by B. R. Rees. Rochester, NY: Boydell, 1991.

Rambo, Shelly. *Spirit and Trauma: A Theology of Remaining*. Louisville: Westminster John Knox, 2010.

Shay, Jonathan. *Achilles in Vietnam: Combat Trauma and the Undoing of Character*. New York: Scribner's, 1994.

———. *Odysseus in America: Combat Trauma and the Trials of Homecoming*. New York: Scribner's, 2002.

Suchocki, Marjorie Hewett. *The Fall to Violence: Original Sin in Relational Theology*. New York: Continuum, 1994.

Tick, Edward. *War and the Soul: Healing Our Nation's Veterans from Post-Traumatic Stress Disorder*. Wheaton, IL: Quest Books, 2005.

Tirman, John. *The Deaths of Others: The Fate of Civilians in America's Wars*. New York: Oxford University Press, 2011.

Van der Kolk, Bessel, and Onno van der Hart. "The Intrusive Past: The Flexibility of Memory and the Engraving of Trauma." In *Trauma: Explorations in Memory*, edited by Cathy Caruth. Baltimore: Johns Hopkins University Press, 1995.

Volf, Miroslav. *Exclusion and Embrace: A Theological Exploration of Identity, Otherness, and Reconciliation*. Nashville: Abingdon, 1996.

Williams, Rowan. *Being Christian: Baptism, Bible, Eucharist, Prayer*. Grand Rapids: Eerdmans, 2014.

———. "Insubstantial Evil." In *Augustine and His Critics*, edited by Robert Dodaro and George Lawless. New York: Routledge, 2000.

———. *The Truce of God*. Grand Rapids: Eerdmans, 2005.

INDEX

agency: active, 37, 129, 137, 140–43, 156–57, 159, 172; character of combatants'/veterans', 76–78, 114, 115, 116–22, 138–39, 150n2, 174; compulsion of, 10, 27, 30, 47; distortion of, 32, 47, 101–2, 159; and human willing, 20–21, 27–29, 134–35

agential state: and ceding of moral responsibility, 123–25, 129–30; and compelled willing, 131, 133–35, 137n42; and military, 51–53, 138–39; shift to, 49–50, 96n5

American exceptionalism, 2, 3; and national innocence, 9, 80, 82–83; violence and the idea of, 59–68, 80, 82–83, 86–91, 99

Arendt, Hannah, 93, 94, 99; and "naked" humanity, 95–97, 108–9

Athanasius, 16, 108

Augustine: on consequences of Adam's fall, 93, 106–8, 111–13; constraints of human willing, 15, 20–21, 35, 53, 135, 174; and doctrine of original sin, 5, 6–8, 11–12, 19, 20, 26, 174, 176–77; and free will, 18–21, 22–26, 27–31, 170; and grace of God, 11–12, 25–26, 93; and sin as "inordinate love," 59, 83–85, 87–88

authority structures: and individual obedience, 49–50, 122–26, 129–30, 133; of military and obedience, 51–54, 130–32, 137–38, 161–62

blame, 7–8, 142, 166, 167–68, 170; relationship to guilt, 8, 10–12, 140, 166, 171, 172, 174–77

Caruth, Cathy, 112

civilization, 94, 95, 106–8; hierarchical or differentiated, 133–34; and "naked" humanity, 96–97, 106–7, 108–9

combatants: bound willing of, 4, 40, 51–54, 114, 115, 117, 131, 134–43, 169–70, 173, 177; conditioning of, 43–47, 52, 54, 56, 71, 97–98, 100, 110; sense of guilt and shame, 54–56, 79–80, 86, 87, 90–91, 167–68; and vulnerability to violence, 69–75, 103, 113. *See also* veterans

conflict: nature of, 3, 59, 81, 89–90, 94–95, 100–103, 136; place in American culture, 59–67; psychological effects of, 4, 15, 41, 42–43, 54–56, 68–76, 79–81, 87, 99, 100, 103–6, 109, 118, 126, 129–32, 135, 142, 158

dehumanization: of the enemy, 44–45, 56, 72, 97, 100, 104; of the "other," 64–67
denial-defense mechanism, 54, 55, 72, 126–27

enemy: dehumanization of, 44–45, 56, 72, 97, 100, 104; "irrational hatred" of, 100–101, 102

Fall (of humanity): conceptions of, 6, 17–19, 51, 84–85; consequences for humanity of, 19–21, 26, 93, 106–8, 111, 113; and fall of the angels, 83, 89, 90
fields of force: and binding of the will, 30–33, 39, 58, 133–34, 177; devouring agency/identity, 112, 115, 116–22, 135–38, 159; and military/combat environment, 40–41, 43–47, 56, 79–80, 90, 104, 114, 131–32, 141–42, 161, 168–69; obedience as a, 48–51, 53–54, 123, 173; sin as, 24, 142, 167, 170–71, 175–76
free will, 17–18; Augustine's view of, 18–21, 22–26, 27–31, 170; and autonomy of individual, 21, 26–27, 150, 170–71, 175; Pelagian view of, 21–22, 26, 167–68, 169, 170. *See also* human willing
frontier myth, 2–3, 64–68, 87, 97

Girard, René: theory of violence, 1, 3, 11, 15, 83
Gregory of Nyssa, 16–17, 21, 25
Grossman, Dave: and human vulnerability, 94, 98–100, 109–10; *On Killing*, 41–47, 52, 54, 67–68, 69–72, 89, 93, 126–27, 129, 134, 168–69; and psychological trauma of veterans, 2–3, 9, 70, 71, 72, 80, 89, 104, 116, 117, 122
guilt: and the act of killing, 144, 149–50, 156–57; and distorted willing, 159–63, 165, 167–71; in light of original sin, 85–86, 90–91, 140–43, 172–74; sense of, in veterans, 54–56, 68, 70–71, 74, 80, 87, 99, 122, 127–28, 158–59, 166; sense of, in victims of abuse, 37, 56, 140–41, 156; universal, 7–10, 175–78; universal, and alienation, 8, 25, 28–29; universal, and blameworthiness, 8, 140, 142, 167, 174–77

Hauerwas, Stanley, 51, 61–62, 63, 87
Holocaust: and human willing, 26–27, 33–36, 40, 46, 51n8
hope: despair and, in Moltmann, 145, 163–64, 165–66; loss of, 112, 116
hopelessness, 145, 157–67, 173
human vulnerability, 73, 93, 96–97, 109; psychological effects of, 94, 100, 103–4, 106, 110–13; and response to threat, 98–99
human willing: and the agential state, 20, 123, 129–35, 138–39; binding/constraining of, 15, 19–21, 34, 39, 41, 43, 45–48, 53–54, 117–18, 131, 133–36, 140, 142; compulsion of, 27, 28, 30–31, 34–35, 45–47, 130–31, 171; distortions of, 5, 20, 23–24, 25, 26, 27, 31–32, 39, 40, 56, 129, 137–38, 140–41, 159–63, 173; in pathological context of child abuse, 36–38, 56, 136–37, 138–41; in pathological context of Holocaust, 33–36, 46, 133. *See also* free will

identity (personal): distortion/malformation of, 125, 130–32, 135, 139–40, 154–56, 162, 165–66; effects of violence on, 74–75, 83, 115, 126–27; veterans' struggle for, 77, 80–81, 82, 117, 118, 120–21, 128, 145, 149, 168. *See also* self (sense of)
injunction against killing, 41–43, 45, 70–71, 98–99, 100, 105–6, 122; failure of, in combat, 109–10, 116

Irenaeus, 16, 17–18, 21, 25

Janet, Pierre, 145, 146–47, 149
Jones, Serene, 76–77, 104, 105, 112, 116

life-intentionality, 135, 139–40, 141–42, 160, 172
Litz, Brett, 156–57

McFadyen, Alistair: *Bound to Sin*, 4–5, 15–16, 26–38, 39, 53–54, 56, 133–36, 137, 139–41, 151, 155, 156; fields of force and sequestration of the will, 40, 45–47, 50, 114, 160, 171
memory: healing of traumatic, 148–50, 174; poisoned, 145, 154–57, 158, 166, 167; role of, 146–47
Milgram, Stanley, 115, 116; *Obedience to Authority*, 48–51, 53–54, 122–26, 129–31, 133, 134, 135, 161
Moltmann, Jürgen, 103–4, 165–66; and sin as despair, 145, 163–64, 166
moral injury: and combat veterans, 9–10, 56, 68, 70–74, 75, 97, 99–100, 114, 122, 126–27, 130–32, 135, 138–40, 145, 155, 162–63, 165–66, 172–73; definition of, 156–57; and obedience to authority, 122–26, 129–30
moral order: disruption of, 74, 75–82, 133, 136, 144; doctrine of sin and, 83–91; and human autonomy, 17–18, 22, 25, 26–27, 39, 149–50; and individual responsibility, 40, 49–50, 167–69, 170–71
mythic warrior, 88, 89–90, 128, 129, 130, 138–39, 166, 173

Nash, William, 73, 74, 75, 80, 92–93, 110–11

obedience: and Adam's fall, 18–19; as a force over human will, 48–50, 130, 173; and military authority structure, 50–54, 58, 126–27, 138; and struggle between conscience and authority, 122–26, 131, 161–62
Origen, 18, 21, 25
original sin: Augustine's doctrine of, 6–9, 19–20, 26, 157; as conceptual moral framework, 4–5, 15–16, 39, 59, 85–87, 90, 112, 113, 115, 144–45, 156, 159–60, 167–78; effects of, 163–64; McFadyen's development of, 26–31, 39, 135; modified Augustinian concept of, 11, 111, 167, 170–78

Pelagius, 21–22, 25–26, 29, 167–68, 169, 170, 176
post-traumatic stress disorder (PTSD): effects of, 75–76, 78–79, 105–6, 145, 155, 158; as identity disorder, 75, 77, 80–81, 117–22, 127; moral component of, 9–10, 74–75, 81, 82, 86–87, 88–89, 99, 130, 156–57, 163, 172; veterans and, 115, 129, 139, 140, 150; Vietnam veterans and, 71–72, 161
psyche: and awareness of vulnerability, 98–99, 103, 111, 112; combat damage to, 5, 16, 54–55, 56, 72, 89, 101–2, 122, 126; and combat stress, 41–43, 68–75; compelled willing and, 124–25, 136–37, 138, 142; effects of combat on, 41, 43, 69–75, 89, 93; and encounter with death, 72–73, 92–93, 97, 99–100, 110, 111–12, 164–65

Rambo, Shelly, 164–65
responsibility: distortion of, 34–35, 117, 133; of group/unit, 35, 56, 106, 126–27; of individual for actions, 10, 39–40, 48–50, 53, 55, 118, 125–26, 129–32, 135, 140–41, 142, 167–72, 174, 175

self (sense of): in combat veterans,

117–22, 126–32, 134–35, 139–40, 149; and conflict with authority, 123–26; distortions/malformations of, 127, 139–40, 154–56; transcendence of, 145, 152–53, 157. *See also* identity (personal)
Shay, Jonathan: and the agency of veterans, 116–17, 118–20, 121, 134, 142; and concept of moral injury, 75, 81, 86–87, 88, 89, 122, 131–32, 135–37, 139, 160; and PTSD in combat veterans, 71n22, 77–79, 82, 118, 127n20, 128, 129, 130
sin: and Augustinian idea of "inordinate loves," 83–85, 87–88; concepts of, 13–15, 24, 27–31, 150–54; distorting power of, 40, 45–46, 90, 113, 115, 144–45, 159, 167, 171; and distortion of relationality, 36–38, 136, 140–43; doctrine of in early church, 16–26; radicality and universality of, 32–33, 115, 132–35, 154–55, 170–71, 172, 176–77; violence a manifestation of, 11, 57–58
social trust (betrayal of), 81n40, 88n60, 89n62, 114–15, 116, 129–32, 136, 137–39, 140
Suchocki, Marjorie, 145, 150–54, 157
suicide, 3, 144, 157, 158–59, 161, 162, 168, 173

Tick, Edward: and concept of "mythic warrior" ideal, 88–90, 128, 130, 138, 166, 168; psyche and encounter with death, 72, 79; and PTSD as an identity disorder, 75, 77, 118, 140, 163; war and the moral order, 74, 80–81, 82, 135–36
Tirman, John, 2, 3, 8–9, 63–67, 87, 88
trauma: agency and, 115–17, 140–41; moral aspect of, 9, 79–81, 86, 88–89, 90–91, 114–15, 122, 131–32, 144; and pathology of violence, 58–59, 82–83, 167; psychological, of combat veterans, 3–5, 15, 54–56, 68–75, 77, 110, 159; and role of memory, 76, 105, 145–50, 154–55, 167, 174; theories of, 111–12, 153–54, 157, 165; and vulnerability, 93, 103–4

Van der Kolk, Bessel A., and Onno van der Hart, 146–49, 156, 174
veterans: difficulties of returning home, 55, 75–82, 103–5; distorted willing of, 129, 133–34; and enslavement of agency, 114–15, 116, 122; and feelings of guilt, shame, and blame, 54–56, 74, 79, 86–87, 90, 158–59, 160–62, 166–68, 172, 174, 177–78; and loss of hope, 5, 144–45, 157–58; and moral ambiguity/tension, 4, 9–10, 55–56, 75, 79–81, 86, 90, 122, 132, 133, 159–63; and traumatic memory, 5, 145–50, 155. *See also* trauma: psychological, of combat veterans
violence: in American cultural discourse, 2, 3–4, 5, 8–10, 58–59, 60–68, 82–83, 86; of conflict, 6, 68–70, 72–74, 81–82, 86, 88, 95, 174; destructive effects of, 58–59, 75–76, 78–79, 115, 118; distorting power of, 4, 39–40, 41; as manifestation of sin, 7, 11, 40, 57–58, 89, 90, 152; moral consequences of, 74–75, 79–80, 156, 171, 176; nature of, 1, 4–5, 11, 15, 59, 83

Williams, Rowan, 23–24, 62–63, 113